Law and violence

Manchester University Press

CRITICAL POWERS

Series Editors:
Bert van den Brink (University of Utrecht),
Antony Simon Laden (University of Illinois, Chicago),
Peter Niesen (University of Hamburg) and
David Owen (University of Southampton).

Critical Powers is dedicated to constructing dialogues around innovative and original work in social and political theory. The ambition of the series is to be pluralist in welcoming work from different philosophical traditions and theoretical orientations, ranging from abstract conceptual argument to concrete policy-relevant engagements, and encouraging dialogue across the diverse approaches that populate the field of social and political theory. All the volumes in the series are structured as dialogues in which a lead essay is greeted with a series of responses before a reply by the lead essayist. Such dialogues spark debate, foster understanding, encourage innovation and perform the drama of thought in a way that engages a wide audience of scholars and students.

Published by Bloomsbury

On Global Citizenship, James Tully
Justice, Democracy and the Right to Justification, Rainer Forst

Published by Manchester University Press

Cinema, democracy and perfectionism: Joshua Foa Dienstag in dialogue, Joshua Foa Dienstag (ed.)

Forthcoming from Manchester University Press

Rogue Theodicy – Politics and power in the shadow of justice, Glen Newey
Democratic Inclusion, Rainer Baubock
Autonomy Gaps, Joel Anderson
Toleration, Liberty and the Right to Justification, Rainer Forst

Law and violence

Christoph Menke in dialogue

Christoph Menke
with responses from:
Alessandro Ferrara
Andreas Fischer-Lescano
Alexander García Düttmann
Daniel Loick
Ben Morgan
María del Rosario Acosta López

Manchester University Press

Published by Manchester University Press
Altrincham Street, Manchester M1 7JA
www.manchesteruniversitypress.co.uk

British Library Cataloguing-in-Publication Data
A catalogue record for this book is available from the British Library

ISBN 978 1 526 10507 3 hardback
ISBN 978 1 526 10508 0 paperback

First published 2018

Typeset by Out of House Publishing

Contents

Contributors

Alexander García Düttmann teaches aesthetics and philosophy at the University of the Arts in Berlin. His latest publications include *What Does Art Know? For an Aesthetics of Resistance* (Konstanz 2015), *Against Self-Preservation* (Berlin 2016) and *What Is Contemporary Art? On Political Ideology* (Konstanz 2017).

Alessandro Ferrara is Professor of Political Philosophy at the University of Rome "Tor Vergata" and former President of the Italian Association for Political Philosophy. He has taught and lectured in various capacities at universities including Harvard University, Yale University, Columbia University, Rice University, Cardozo Law School, The New School for Social Research in New York, and the Universities of California at Berkeley. His most recent book is *The Democratic Horizon: Hyperpluralism and the Renewal of Political Liberalism* (New York 2014).

Andreas Fischer-Lescano (LL.M.) is Professor for Public Law, Public European Law, Public International Law and Legal Theory and Managing Director of the Center of European Law and Politics at the University of Bremen. He is also the director of the research project "Transnational Force of Law" that is funded by the European Research Council (2015–2020). Fischer-Lescano is co-editor of several journals, including *Kritische Justiz*. Recent publications include "Sociological Aesthetics of Law," *Law, Culture & Humanities*, 2016, pp. 1–26 and "Struggles for a global Internet constitution," *Global Constitutionalism*, vol. 5.2, 2016, pp. 145–72.

Daniel Loick is Visiting Professor for Critical Social Theory at Goethe University Frankfurt. He has been a junior faculty member of the Philosophy Department at Goethe University, Postdoctoral Fellow at

Harvard University, Visiting Professor at Humboldt University Berlin, and Theodor Heuss Lecturer at the New School for Social Research in New York. His main research interests are political, legal, and social philosophy, especially critical theory and poststructuralism. He is the author of four books: *Kritik der Souveränität* (Frankfurt 2012, English translation forthcoming as *A Critique of Sovereignty*), *Der Missbrauch des Eigentums* (Berlin 2016), *Anarchismus zur Einführung* (Hamburg 2017), and most recently *Juridismus. Konturen einer kritischen Theorie des Rechts* (Berlin 2017).

María del Rosario Acosta López is Associate Professor in Philosophy at DePaul University. She conducts research on romanticism and German idealism, aesthetics and philosophy of art, and contemporary political philosophy. She is the author of books on German romanticism (2006), Friedrich Schiller (2008), and contemporary narratives of community (forthcoming). She is currently working on a book on philosophical approaches to trauma and memory in the aftermath of political violence.

Christoph Menke is Professor of Practical Philosophy at Goethe Universität. He has previously taught at Freie Universität Berlin, the New School for Social Research and the University of Potsdam. His book publications in English include *The Sovereignty of Art: Aesthetic Negativity after Adorno and Derrida* (Cambridge 1998), *Reflections of Equality* (Stanford 2006), *Tragic Play: Tragedy, Irony and Theater from Sophocles to Beckett* (Columbia 2009), *Force: A Fundamental Concept of Aesthetic Anthropology* (Fordham 2012).

Ben Morgan is Associate Professor in German and Fellow of Worcester College, University of Oxford. His research interests are in German intellectual history, German film, and comparative literature. His current projects are an account of the manuscript transmission of the late medieval mystical text "The Sister Catherine Treatise" from the 1310s through to the early seventeenth century; and, under the working title

"Fiction and other minds," an investigation in collaboration with Naomi Rokotnitz (Tel Aviv University) of the way fiction models and nurtures a complex understanding of human social interaction. He is the author of *On Becoming God: Late Medieval Mysticism and the Modern Western Self* (New York 2013).

Series editor's foreword

Christoph Menke is one of the leading figures in the current generation of Frankfurt School critical theorists. His work on aesthetics in *The Sovereignty of Art* (1998), *Tragic Play* (2009), *Force: A Fundamental Concept of Aesthetic Anthropology* (2012) and *Die Kraft der Kunst* (2013) marks a fundamental philosophical renewal of critical theory's engagement with this area of enquiry, while he has also made important and distinctive contributions to moral, legal, and political philosophy in works such as *Tragödie im Sittlichen: Gerechtigkeit und Freiheit nach Hegel* (1996), *Reflections of Equality* (2006), and *Kritik der Rechte* (2015). The essay "Law and Violence" presented in this volume exemplifies the character of his engagement with central topics of legal and political philosophy, and in particular his use of the analysis of literary texts as a medium for illuminating philosophical problems. Menke's work stands within the tradition of thinkers such as Adorno and Cavell, for whom attention to artistic works (for example, in music or film or drama) provides a way of both widening and focusing reflection on philosophical predicaments that express constitutive features of our practical condition.

The essay "Law and Violence" can be seen as developing themes from Menke's earlier work in *Reflections of Equality* addressing the relationship between equality and individuality as one of perpetual strife, and in *Tragic Play* analyzing the ironic character of tragedy. In this work, however, the focus is on the paradoxical character of law and specifically concerns the structural violence of law as the political imposition of normative order onto a "lawless" condition. The paradox of law which grounds and motivates Menke's intervention is that law is both the opposite of violence (and the medium though which cycles of vengeance, of repaying violence with violence, is brought to a close) and, at the same time, a form of violence, not merely instrumentally as a mode of action that utilizes coercion, but structurally as the necessary imposition of a normative order which integrates spatial, temporal, material and subjective boundaries concerning who can or cannot do what, where, when and how.

The essay develops its engagement with the paradox of law in two stages. The first part – "The Fate of Law" – shows why, and in what precise sense, the law is irreducibly characterized by structural violence. The second part – "The Relief [*Entsetzung*] of Law" – explores the possibility of law becoming self-reflectively aware of its own violence and, hence, of the form of a self-critique of law in view of its own violence. In both parts, the essay's philosophical claims are developed through analyses of works of drama: two classical tragedies in the first part (Aeschylus' *Oresteia* and Sophocles' *King Oedipus*), and two modern dramas in the second part (Heinrich von Kleist's *The Broken Jug* and Heiner Müller's *Volokolamsk Highway I*). The essay thus attempts to illuminate the paradoxical nature of law by way of a philosophical interpretation of literature. It does so on the grounds that whereas philosophical discourses on law are typically *either* discourses of legitimization *or* of critique of law, in that such discourses are almost ineluctably drawn to take up a stand towards law on the question of its violence, literary texts need take no such stand and hence are able to be much more sensitive to the internal duplicity of law, to dwell on rather than to attempt to deny or overcome its paradoxical character. By taking this literary route in his philosophical analysis, Menke aims to draw out the possibility and form of a relation of law to itself that acknowledges its structural violence and hence opens itself to the question of whether and when the enforcement of law is required; that is, rather than taking its enforcement to be necessary, it resituates enforcement as open to judgment.

Menke's essay is both rich and deep, and the responses from interlocutors as well as his reply to these responses draw out and develop the dimensions of his analysis in ways that further illuminate its importance as a reflection on the paradox of law.

Part I

Lead essay

1

Law and violence

Christoph Menke
(Translated by Gerrit Jackson)

Preface

Any attempt to understand the relation between law and violence must begin with two observations that are at odds with each other, if not even contradictory. The first observation is that law is the opposite of violence; legal forms of decision-making are introduced to disrupt the endless sequence of violence and counterviolence and counter-counterviolence, which is to say, to dispel the compulsion to answer violence with new violence. The second observation is that law is itself violence; legal decisions, too, use violence – external violence, which assails the body, as well as internal violence, which injures the soul, the being of the convict.

The antithesis between these two observations is that between the law's hostility to violence and its violent quality, between the law's aspiration to end the "wild violence" of the natural state of "external lawless freedom"[1] – the "expectation that law can transform the weak force of uncoerced, intersubjectively shared convictions into a socially integrating power that is ultimately capable of overcoming every instance of sheer violence in whatever form it disguises itself,"[2] – and the violence that inevitably returns in *how* law realizes that aspiration. The problem of law and violence is the problem of how these two observations relate to each other: the legitimation of law as the overcoming of violence, and the critique of law as the use of violence. Both observations are antithetical to each other, but neither is disputable; both are true. Recognizing the truth of both observations is the first prerequisite for an adequate account of the relation between law and violence.

The task would seem simple. That the use of violence is among the actions the law has at its disposal is the claim with which any theory seeking to legitimize the law begins: The "possibility of the conjunction of universal reciprocal coercion with the freedom of everyone" constitutes the *concept* of law.[3] Coercion (which addresses the will as arbitrary discretion) is exercised through the administration or threat of violence that assails the body and the soul. Violence, as the Latin roots of the term indicate, is a form of action that injures the victim's physical or psychological integrity; to administer violence means to violate. Law, its legitimation avers, operates on the basis of the fact that its judgments are justified, which is to say, normatively valid. If its judgments are justified at all, they are justified in the eyes of anyone, including the individual being judged. In this sense judgements aren't passed even against the person's will, which is to say, they are not acts of violence and violation against her or him. Law must be able to use violence only when this justificatory nexus is broken. It uses violence only by way of substitution: *instead of* the justification on which it rests. So if violence served the traditional law as "a means of presentation and substantiation of expectation,"[4] which is to say, as a means to reinforce its legitimacy, it has lost that function in modern law, whose rational legitimation is neither in need of nor amenable to corroboration by violent means. Its only function is now to counter the ever-present "risk of dissension": It serves to secure the *factual* existence of the consensus whose *normative* existence is implied by law.[5] The use of violence in law, the argument for its legitimacy says, constitutes an "unsurpassable limiting case";[6] it is at the disposal of law, whose internal organization is "symbolic" or normative, as a "symbiotic mechanism" that operates by action upon "physical-organic existence." "Physical violence accompanies law like an inescapable shadow," because only the use or threat of violence enables law to ensure that its normativity, which is designed to gain consent, "function[s] in every case and enjoy[s] confidence as such."[7]

So the critique of law says nothing new when it insists that there is no law – not even the post-sovereign law that eschews the cruel solemnities of punishment and torture – that has no need of violence;[8] by insisting on this point, the critique of law merely repeats what its legitimation already knew. But the critique of law consists not in the mere observation that law threatens or uses violence to enforce its judgments, but instead in the insight that the "limiting case" (Luhmann) of its violence is a structural condition of law. The critique concerns the subliminally operative logic that intrinsically connects the symbolic or normative dimension of the justification of legal judgments to the symbiotic mechanism of their violent enforcement. Violence consists in the "elimination of action by action."[9] This – the elimination of action, of the ability or freedom to act – is not a mode of operation linked to law only as external to it, let alone as a mere instrument of law. The critique of law shows instead that violence, as the elimination of action, is a necessary consequence of the legitimacy of law: a consequence of its justified way of judging. The critique counters the legal legitimation of violence by asserting that legal legitimation is itself violent.

That turns the problem of the interrelation between the two observations about law, which seemed easy to resolve, into a paradox. Part I of the following reflections will map this paradox of the simultaneous abolition and use of violence by law ("The Fate of Law"). It will proceed by reconstructing the legal thinking of tragedy. The aim of this reconstruction is to understand the paradoxical *union* of the legitimation of law and its violence; to understand, that is, why the normativity of law is the ground of its fateful violence. Walter Benjamin's "Critique of Violence" may be read as a summary of this insight of tragedy. The second part attempts to find the gap in the union of law and violence, of normativity and fate, in order to interpret the paradox of this union as opening up the possibility of liberation. To this end, Benjamin's cryptic idea of a "relief of law" will be explicated as framing the program of a self-reflection of law: to relieve law means neither to apply it indefinitely nor to abolish it once and for all; it means to execute it in reflective fashion, which is to say, with repugnance for its execution.

I. The Fate of Law

The genre of tragedy and the institution of law are genetically and structurally interlinked: Tragedy is the genre of law; law is the justice of tragedy. It is accordingly not only the themes and plots of tragedy that are juridical; so is its genre-specific makeup. Justice is also at issue in the pre-tragic epic. But there, justice reigns as fate, whereas tragedy, by virtue of its form, stages the fate of a new form of justice that is associated with the authority of a judge passing impartial judgment. The suit of the individual, the antagonism and the dialogue between the parties, the responsibility that comes with action, the significance and consequences of the decision, the questions and mysteries of interpretation – these are structural elements of both tragedy and law. The basic elements of tragedy correspond to the basic elements of the new theory and praxis of justice that emerge concurrently: justice as law.

But the connection between tragedy and law applies conversely as well: Not only is tragedy the form in which law is represented, law is also tragedy's form of justice. Law is the form of justice that tragedy engenders: the form of justice that tragedy, by virtue of its labor of reflection on the epic form of representation, distils from the experience the crisis of pre-legal justice (the justice of sacrifice or retribution). The law to be discussed here is the law of tragedy; not just any sort of order guaranteed by a power that establishes a minimum of reliability of expectations, but the specific form of law engendered by the tragic labor of reflection. Tragedy defines an ambitious concept of law by telling its history; tragedy defines law on the basis of its history. This tragic (or "tragedy-like") history of law is a double history: its pre-history and its post-history, the history of its genesis and its failure, of its legitimation and its crisis or critique.

That is the object of my brief look at two tragedies in the following pages. My aim will be to extract from these two tragedies a normatively ambitious concept of law that also includes, from the outset, an awareness of its paradox. I will do so in two steps: The first step – taking my cue from the Oresteia – moves from the justice of retribution to that of law and shows in which regard the reign of law, as it breaks with the violence of retribution, at once repeats it in altered form. The second step – "this time with a look towards King Oedipus" – moves from "authoritarian" law, which rules by fear, to the "autonomous" law, which is founded on the free self-condemnation of its subjects. My aim in this reconstruction of the tragic history of law is to understand how violence is perpetuated within the "autonomous" law, the law of enlightenment (from Oedipus[10] to the present): in which sense – in which sense of "critique" and in which sense of "violence" – the autonomous law must become the object of a "critique of violence."

1. *The undecidability of revenge* (Agamemnon)

The philosophical discourses on legitimation pit law against the violence of the state of nature, where everyone can do anything with impunity. This state that philosophy envisions is fictitious[11] and the same is true for the philosophical legitimation of law as its remedy. Tragedy, on the other hand, presents the violence from which law breaks as arising not from natural drives or sheer arbitrariness but, on the contrary, from an order of iron necessity: Law, as tragedy's realism indicates, results from the objection to the violence of retribution. Retribution, however, is a form of the implementation of justice. The violence that law overcomes is not the violence that, according to the philosophical fiction, constitutes the state of nature, but the violence of a first, an earlier order of justice: the violence of a normative order, normative violence. The *katastrophé* – an "overturning" by force, which, in the experience of the Erinyes, the goddesses of retribution, is what the instauration of "new laws" amounts to[12] – is not the unprecedented genesis of normativity against nature but a late transformation in the order of justice. According to the insight of tragedy, law arises from – and *against* – the experience of violence implicit in justice as retribution. Law seeks to be a normative order of justice after – *beyond* – the violence of retributive justice.

Retribution is justice for it strikes the one who deserves it. Retribution obeys the law of equality, in that it is the payment of like for like: the wife murders her husband for his sacrifice of their daughter; the son, in return, murders his mother and is then haunted by the goddesses of revenge because there is no longer a member of the family to pursue him. Retribution is just because it is justified. Retribution is not a first, groundless, deed; it is the second deed. Retribution is the answer to an offense – an answer that *must* ensue (whence it is considered to be divinely sent) because or when the offense was a boundless transgression against the just order.

> The gods are not blind to men with blood upon their hands. In the end the black Spirits of Vengeance bring to obscurity that one who has prospered in unrighteousness and wear down his fortunes by reverse.[13]

Against the excess of the offense – of fortune enjoyed "in unrighteousness" – retribution restores the balance of things, "wearing down his fortunes" and reversing them into misfortune. Retribution brings balance by turning on one who has committed a crime and committing the same crime against them in turn. The justice of retribution consists in doing the same.

Yet it is precisely in the equality of retribution, which justifies it, that its violence lies. The retributive deed answers the deed it avenges by repeating it; the retributive deed is *like* the deed it avenges. By repeating the deed it avenges, the retributive deed is at once, in one and the same regard, justified and indeed necessary and inevitable[14] – and violent. As a repetition of the offense to be avenged, the retributive deed itself is in turn an offense calling for revenge. The retribution a god –"Apollo perhaps or Pan, or Zeus" – has sent to the "transgressors" *can* only be exacted in a way that exceeds the bounds of justice; "an abomination," it arouses the "wrath" of another goddess – in this instance, of Artemis (*Agamemnon*, 55–59, 130, 135–36). So the avenging deed in turn demands an answer that does to the avenger what she or he has done. As retribution executes the law of like for like, it continues in perpetuity. Every avenging deed, however justified it is as an answer to a previous violation, is just like the violation it answers. The justification of retribution and its violence are indissolubly linked: Retribution is measure for measure *and* excess that then requires another retributive deed to restore the balance of measures. The violence of retribution consists in its necessary perpetuation: in the "frenzy of mutual murder" (*Agamemnon*, 1575–76).

Any retributive deed is ambivalent: It repays *and* repeats an excessive crime. For any retributive deed occupies two places at once in the sequence of events. There are two narratives about any retributive deed, because whenever retribution is exacted, two ways of counting are in play. In the one counting, the retributive deed occupies the second place. It expiates a first crime; the goddesses of retribution are "just and upright" judges (*Eumenides*, 312). In the other counting, the retributive deed occupies the first place. It is a boundless deed that awaits its "just punishment" (*Eumenides*, 272). The retributive deed is counted doubly, and so is subject to antithetical assessments, because it is ontologically ambivalent. Retribution is the mere execution of a fate or curse the first crime has already brought down upon itself: something that comes to pass. And retribution is an action, a first crime, which must be followed by an avenging second one.

Ethnologists who study retribution argue over what it is: either it is an "extremely elaborate and controlled form of the regulation of violence" that restores balance in the relations between different but interacting groups after an offense has been committed. It takes this form because there are no established public authorities who could intercede.[15] Or it is an infinite cycle of violence in which there is "no clear distinction between the act for which the killer is being punished and the punishment itself."[16] Retribution is neither the one nor the other because it is essentially both at once. The justice of retribution – that it restores balance against a boundless deed – and its violence-begetting violence – in which it repeats the boundlessness of the crime it repays – are two sides of the same coin. Retribution harbors an equivocation that lets its justice disintegrate into an undecidable strife between enemy parties: was it the repayment of a past boundless abomination (as Apollo argues in defense of Orestes: "Through my oracle, I directed him to exact vengeance for his father"; *Eumenides*, 203), or was it the spilling of "fresh blood" (as the Erinyes see it; *Eumenides*, 204) that cries for retaliation? The justice of retribution has no answer to this question, because it always answers it with two incompatible claims.

Just as retribution cannot give an authoritative answer to the question whether the offense was a first or a second deed, it also cannot say whether the retribution exacted for it settles the matter. The question that retribution must leave unanswered is: how can there be a just deed in answer to an offense that no longer calls for another answer, that does not initiate a new plot, but makes an end? The violence of retribution is a violence driven by justice. This violence consists in the endlessness of its operation. The question that retribution raises and must leave unanswered is: is there a deed of justice whose operation does *not* continue without end – that is not violence?

2. *The proceeding of law* (The Eumenides)

The answer of law to the question that retribution was incapable of giving is: yes, there is an end, if the decision-making hews to the right proceeding. Law does not embody a higher knowledge of the just state of affairs than the order of retribution did. Law, too, knows only that, according to the rule of justice, crime requires an answer: that be done the same to whom who committed the crime. But law knows moreover, that knowledge is contentious; every deed can be counted and recounted in two ways. Law knows that every narrative is only a narrative. And law knows that there is a counter-narrative to every narrative. When the one narrative has been told – for example, the narrative of the spilling of "fresh blood" – law knows and says:

> Two parties are present; only half the case is heard.
>
> (*Eumenides*, 428)

That is how law begins: it is the first and fundamental step of the proceeding in which law consists. Law overcomes the violence of retribution because it can first perceive and then ensure that "two parties are present" and have their say. (In tragedy too, – that is why it is the genre of law – there are always "two parties present": the history of tragedy began when "[the] number of actors was increased from one to two by Aeschylus."[17]) So law defines everyone who is present as one of two. It defines each of the attendees as a party: as someone whose narrative is partial. And it therefore defines each of them as one who faces the justified opposition of another with his or her own partial narrative. The proceeding of law consists in approaching any narrative as partial. That does not imply that law assumes that a narrative is not true. Why should not the one partial narrative possibly be the true narrative? What it does imply is that law does not presume a narrative to be true (or untrue). Approaching any narrative as partial means proceeding according to the rule that after one has been heard, the other must also be heard. The proceeding of law *distances* every narrative and thus *qualifies* it as one of two. That is why law hears both. The fact that the same (mis)deed can be told in one way or another brings the justice of retribution to its end. In the proceeding of law, by contrast, that is the normal case. That the same (mis)deed can be told in one way *and* another is simply what constitutes a legal case. And it is what renders every legal case a hard case.

How the deed is related within the order of retribution is not a question: Whether the matricide is a spilling of "fresh blood" that cries for retribution or is itself already the retribution for the earlier murder of a husband (and hence, whether that murder was a spilling of "fresh blood" that cried for retribution or was itself already the retribution for the earlier murder of a child) – for someone who understands justice in terms of retribution, that is not a question. The narratives the retributive justice enforces lack a subject; like myth, they unfold themselves. By contrast, the narratives whose antagonism constitutes the legal case are narratives related by one party. Truth thus becomes a problem and hence the result of a proceeding: The truth remains to be determined; it stands at the end of a process of examination and judgment.[18] This proceeding requires that two parties are seen to be present at the same time. The proceeding of law hears both sides. That is why the proceeding of law calls for a subject that is not a party: a nonpartisan, an impartial subject – a judge. It is with this appointment that Athena executes the "catastrophe" of retribution:

> The matter is too great, if any mortal thinks to pass judgment on it; no, it is not lawful even for me to decide on cases of murder [...] But since this matter has fallen here, I will select judges of homicide bound by oath, and I will establish this tribunal for all time.
>
> (*Eumenides*, 470–84)

Now, "just" no longer means to do what must be done, to balance the excess of the crime by repeating it against him who committed it. "Just" means now to understand the matter in a way that is not partial but sees both sides.

The break with retributive justice and the accession to the justice of law demands from both antagonists that they see themselves as parties. That means two things: it demands that they recognize both the other and the Other. It demands that they see themselves as a party and the other as another, a second, party, and that both parties are heard equally. And it demands that they see themselves and the other as parties that are incapable of just judgment on the point of contention between them and so can obtain that judgment only from another: from another who is not merely yet another, yet another party, but categorically different from them, who is not a party – the Other. Departing from retributive justice and acceding to the justice of law demands that the antagonists forgo the right to judge in their own matter and recognize the Other as judge over them. The accession to law demands the submission of both sides to the Other's power of judgment:

> ERINYES: Well then, question him, and make a straight judgment.
> ATHENA: Then would you turn over the decision of the charge to me?
> ERINYES: How not? – since we honor you because you are worthy and of worthy parentage.
>
> (*Eumenides*, 433–35)

> ORESTES: You judge whether I acted justly or not; whatever happens to me at your hands, I will be content.
>
> (*Eumenides*, 468–69)

Breaking with the retributive justice and the turning to the justice of law requires a double decentering of each party (which only becomes a party by meeting this requirement). The antagonists confronting each other must see themselves as one of two "parties" who express their mutual recognition by relinquishing – simultaneously and in equal measure – their power of judgment to a third who stands before and above them, the impartial judge. It is with this double decentering that the subjectivation required by law begins. (That subjectivation neither stops with the double decentering – it unleashes the curse of the autonomous internalization of law – nor will it ever be fully accomplished: the subjectivation by virtue of law is met by the "repugnance" of those subjected to it.)

3. *Equality and authority*

The proceeding in which law consists is defined by three positions – a first party; a second party; a third person, who wields the power of judgment – and two relations – the horizontal relation between the two parties and the vertical relation between the parties and the non-party of the judge. But to understand the meaning of these relations in the legal proceeding, we must recognize their political substance. In negative terms this means that the legal proceeding is not an arbitration procedure; the judge is not an arbitrator who weighs the relative justification of two claims. That is because the positions and relations in an arbitration procedure that weighs their relative merits are "private." They are based on the voluntary agreement of two adversaries to avail themselves of the assistance of a noninvolved third in this case and for this purpose. The legal proceeding, by contrast, establishes political relations between those involved: relations of equality and of authority. These two relations constitute the politics of the legal procedure; they define the legal proceeding *as* politics.[19]

Equality is here first and foremost the equality of the parties' subjection to the legal proceeding: The two parties are equally heard in the legal proceeding and are answerable to the same judge. Yet what realizes itself in this procedural equality is the political equality of citizens: To be an equal citizen implies to be capable of becoming an equal party in a legal proceeding. The equality the legal proceeding engenders or safeguards between the parties involved derives from the equality of all citizens. To be a "party" in a legal proceeding, someone needs to be a citizen, a "part," a *partie*, in a polity.[20]

Therein lies the political quality of law as proceeding: it is bound up with the citizenry. In contradistinction to the justice of retribution, which rules between different communities, the justice of law can exist only in a community of equal citizens. By implication, there is no law outside the polity. So when the goddesses of retribution are outraged by their disempowerment after the introduction of the legal proceeding, Athena soothes their wrath by showing them the domain in which they can continue to rule because law does *not* apply there: within the house, where – between husband and wife, between father and children, between master and servants – there is nothing but relations of inequality, and in the relations between the communities, where the "god of strife" rules: "Let their war be with foreign enemies, and without stint for one in whom there will be a terrible passion for glory; but I say there will be no battling of birds within the home" (*Eumenides*, 865–67). Once the court of law has been instituted, Athena notes, the Erinyes can no longer rule between "my citizens," among "my people" (*polítais: Eumenides*, 854, 927). For there equality reigns – equality before the law or *by virtue of* the law.

But the political equality of the citizens is the basis not only for the procedural equality of the two parties. It also defines the relation between the parties and the nonpartisan judge over them. According to Athena's insight, the judge too, is a citizen; only a citizen can be judge. Unlike the justice of retribution, the justice of law no longer finds expression in a judgment that has no subject, or certainly no human subject. The judgment of retribution was subjectless, since it was already contained in the excess of the deed to be avenged; the avenger merely observes this quality. The judgment of law, by contrast, has a subject that *produces* it by means of a procedure of examination and judging – the judge. The latter stands in a twofold relation to the parties over whom he or she judges: The judge not only *is* an equal citizen like the two parties of the dispute; but unlike the parties, the citizen-judge also speaks *in the name of* equality. The judge is the figure of equality, the representative of the equality of all citizens. The judgment of the judge is the judgment of citizens over citizens. Or more precisely, it is the judgment of a citizen (or several or many or all citizens) in the name of *the* citizen. Through the judge or judges, the entire citizenry judges over individual citizens.

In Athens, the question whether the legal judgment must be conceived and organized in democratic or in aristocratic terms in order to qualify as the judgment of the entire citizenry was fiercely contested for centuries.[21] Aeschylus takes a side in this debate when he has Athena say that not just any citizen can be a judge: Athena intends to select "the best of my citizens" as judges (*Eumenides*, 487). According to Athena, Aeschylus suggests, law must be constituted in aristocratic terms if it is to function: Rule of law means rule of the best.[22]

"Rule of the best" implies that an antithesis, or more precisely a hierarchy, establishes itself within law on the basis of its equality. In this instance, in Athena's aristocratic discourse, it is designated by the hierarchical distinction between the best citizens and ordinary ones. But it points to the relation of authority that is part and parcel of all law, no matter how it appoints its judges. The aristocratic terms for the hierarchy between the "best" citizens and ordinary ones merely lend expression to the essential authoritative or "cratic" quality of law. Whatever the organizational solution may look like, the problem is always the same: that the justice practiced by the legal proceeding consists in nothing other than the citizenry as a whole judging, through the judge or judges, over individual citizens. That is what "impartiality" means here. What speaks through law is the political union of the citizens. In the pre-legal state of retribution we saw that every individual sees themselves as an addressee of normative demands and indeed unconditional duties. Everyone is subject to the requirements of *his or her* justice (the military leader must sacrifice the daughter; the mother must avenge the daughter; the son, the father; etc.), requirements whose fulfillment a god or goddess demands. The order of retribution is characterized not by a lack of justice but by an overabundance of justices. Law puts an end to this situation by establishing and enforcing the one law. This one law is the law of equality, which constitutes the political union of the citizens. All the various and conflicting justices in whose name the acts of retribution were carried out are reduced to mere partialities. The jurisdiction of the courts, Robert Cover writes with a view to *The Eumenides*,[23] does not primarily create or implement law but first and foremost attacks and destroys it (his term is *jurispathic*); it intervenes into a field of *polynomia* and enforces the one law by suppressing the many and conflicting laws of retributive justice. Whether democratic or aristocratic, whether administered by an assembly of all or only by the best among the citizens: The practice of legal judgment executes the rule of political union over the partial individuals.

So law, in its proceeding, always realizes the political union of the citizens in a twofold way: because it lets both parties speak for themselves and equally, and because a judge judges in the name of the equality of all citizens. In the procedure of the hearing, law realizes the plurality of political equality; in the moment of decision, it realizes equality as political union. In the horizontal dimension, equality in law means plurality of the parties, which are one another's equals in being mere parties. And in the vertical dimension, equality in law means hierarchy between judge and parties; the judge's ruling executes the equality between the citizens as their collective rule over the individual.

4. *Manifest violence*

With the establishment of the court of law, Athena confirms the authoritative character of law by presenting herself as an eager student of the Erinyes. She repeats the lesson they have taught her: that justice exists only when it is supported by "fear." The cratic doctrine by which the goddesses of retribution derive from justice the necessity of their ugly and forbidding doings – the doctrine that neither a "lawless life" nor "one subject to a tyrant" is good because the citizens *fear* only a master (and because justice cannot rule without fear)[24] – this doctrine is not only not forgotten in the political order of law. On the contrary, the order of law takes it into account from the outset in a manner that charts a future in which it will see extreme escalation. The order of law has *internalized* the cratic doctrine of rule through fear. So Athena repeats, as though she had memorized it by rote, that the relation of the citizens to law, as a relation of "reverence," must remain one of "fear" (*Eumenides*, 691): The recognition of the validity of legal judgments – because they merely express the equality of the citizens – *implies* submission to the menacing power of the authority all citizens exercise over the individual. In fact, Athena recommends the new order of law to her city precisely because it dovetails equality and authority:

> Neither anarchy nor tyranny – this I counsel my citizens to support and respect, and not to drive fear wholly out of the city. For who among mortals, if he fears nothing, is righteous?
>
> (*Eumenides*, 696–99)

From the very outset, this repetition in law of the very terrifying rule that already legitimized the order of retribution has been interpreted as evidence that the two are indistinguishable. As early as in Euripides' rewriting of the third part of the *Oresteia* plot, his *Orestes*, the confidence that a distinction can be made between the acts or menaces of retribution and those of law has given way to an amalgamation of both phenomena: They are objects of the *same* fear. For Orestes it makes neither a differnce to his feelings, nor his grievance, whether he fears "those maidens with their bloodshot eyes and snaky hair [...] death's priestesses with glaring eyes," who seek to murder him in revenge,[25] or the impending vote of the citizens of Argos, who will sentence him to "death by stoning at the hands of the citizens" (*Orestes*, 442) in the murder trial against Electra and him. (Both, the justice of retribution and that of law will accordingly be repealed by the court on the Rock of Ares, which Euripides, unlike Aeschylus, describes no longer as a court of citizens appointed by Athena but as a divine tribunal promised by Apollo: *Orestes*, 1643–51.) To Euripides' *Orestes*, the aspiration of law to be categorically (which is to say, catastrophically) different from retribution has become incomprehensible; law's aspiration to be different now falls silent before the phenomenal evidence that law looks just like retribution, and the violence of legal punishment like the violence of the act of revenge.

The difference between retribution and law is "a quality imperceptible to the senses" because it is – *merely* – a difference of form, of the form of their judging. What Hans Kelsen writes about the "fact that an act is the execution of a death sentence and not an act of murder" also holds for the difference in form between retribution and law: It "is imperceptible to the senses" and "becomes recognizable only after a process of reflection."[26] This non-sensible, formal difference fades into the background when the facts of legal reality come to the fore with irrefutable power: when the "realistic" perspective, from Euripides and the contemporary Sophists to today's Critical Legal Studies, reveals law to be a violence in disguise that helps enforce the interests of the ruling class. Given the simple statistical fact that more than 11 percent of Afro-Americans between the ages of twenty and thirty-four are in prison – which is more than ten times the average incarceration rate and still almost four times the rate for whites in the same age bracket – it is feckless to point out, however correctly, that every individual legal act of judging that contributes to this statistic is formally distinct from an act of retribution. Law and retribution do not just seem to be the same; their manifestations are the same.

5. Law and non-law

But by the same token, the realistic perspective, in which we see only what is manifest, is not enough to understand the violence of law: it takes a "process of reflection" (Kelsen) to recognize that it is the violence *of law*. Contrary to the fundamental assumption, that the realistic perspective on law shares with its idealistic opponent, the violence of law is not the other of its form (and the form of law is not, idealistically speaking, the other of its violence). Instead the violence of law emerges from its form – from the very legal form that breaks with the violence-reproducing undecidability of retribution. All violence appears the same: for the one who suffers it, it makes no difference why and how it is exercised. But not all violence is equal in form and, hence, in essence: The different forms in which actions have violent effects differ in terms of their finality and hence also their causality. We can only understand the violence of retribution as much as the violence of law if we cease to see them in the indistinction of their manifestations and instead trace each back to its form – to the particular form justice takes in each.

Retribution was just in that it restored the right state of the world against an excessive deed. Retribution proceeded from an idea of the just state of the world; it understood the justice it asserted in objective terms. In the order of retribution, there can and indeed must always be two antithetical narratives about whether a deed restored or, on the contrary, disturbed the just state of the world. The bitter antagonism of retribution is about justice against injustice. But injustice here always means a contrary conception of justice. The injustice against which retribution turns is a counter-justice (not non-justice). In the order of retribution, both sides see justice prevail; both are agents of justice.

The justice of law, by contrast, is not about the right state of the world but about the right "political" relation: it is about equality among citizens. This civic equality is what the judge asserts in their judgment. The relation of equality among citizens defines their political union, as that of parts of a polity. It is in their name, in the name of the equality and union of the citizens, and not in the name of the order of the world, that the judge passes legal judgment. A judge speaks for, that is he or she represents, the political union of the citizens. By rendering the judgment of justice subjective and procedural and thus tying it to the political union, law at once engenders a possibility that is without precedent, and indeed was inconceivable in the order of retribution: the possibility of an *outside* of justice; the possibility of non-justice – of wills and actions wholly divorced from the normative guidance of justice at large. Because if the juridification of justice implies its subjectivization, its proceduralization, and therefore its politicization, then justice in law is tied to an order that – unlike the just order of the world that retribution restores and that encompasses everything and everyone – knows an other, a counterpart or an outside. No one can stand outside the justice of retribution, because everyone is *either* just *or* unjust – he or she disturbs or executes or restores the just order of the world. But one can stand outside the justice of law: the polity in whose name law judges is defined by the fact that it confronts a state – the state of "nature" – in which the equality of the citizens does not count. For someone to stand outside of law, it is not enough that one believes to be inadequately represented as a "particular" individual by the generality of its propositions and judgments. Someone who stands radically outside law *no longer* looks to the norm of law, the norm of civic equality, for guidance *at all*; he or she no longer looks to *any* norm of justice for guidance (because due to the instauration of law, there no longer is any justice other than the political-procedural justice of civic equality). So if justice gains a procedure, a subject, and hence a political substance in law, it faces an entirely new problem as well: how to enforce law not only against one who is unjust, but also against one who is non-just – against one who stands outside, and is alien to, the justice of law.

Hence the equivocal significance of the authority the judges exercise and the fear they arouse. It is only at a first glance (through rose-tinted glasses) that the hierarchical difference between the best citizens and the ordinary ones, between those citizens who judge and those who are parties, is about the insight into what the equality of the citizens requires, as though the injustice of partiality were merely a misapprehension, an incompetent and therefore mistaken view of what law demands.[27] If that were so, law would not need to rule or spread fear. Law would merely need to explain and exhort the citizen to understand and ("reverently") accept the higher insight of the judges. Yet the rule of law must arouse *fear* – indeed, there can be no law without fear – because any act of injustice may contain a spark of the extra-legal and even counter-legal. Law must apprehend a departure from, and even rebellion against, law as such in any infraction against the equality of the citizens. Because law merely realizes the political union of the citizens, it can never be sure that the parties over whom it judges see themselves as parts of this union rather than as confronting it from outside it. Law must be alert: In any act of injustice it may face a non-legal, extra-legal, or even counter-legal act. Faced with an extra-legal actor, however, the judges cannot bring to bear what legitimizes their judgment over the "ordinary" citizens: that they, the judges as the best citizens, possess higher insight into what they share with the ordinary citizens – their equality as citizens. That is because neither the equality of the citizen nor the graduation of insight connects the judge to the extra-legal actor: the extra-legal actor is unequal and misses insight. So the judges can bring their judgment to bear upon the extra-legal actors only by enforcing it *against* them; faced with one who stands outside, and is alien to law, the judgment of the judges can rule only by fear.

That is why violence is not only part of the manifestation of law but also of its essence: the violence of law comes from its political-procedural form of judgment. And this perspective reveals in which regard retribution and law truly resemble each other – why they must equally manifest themselves as law and what their violence actually consists in. The violence of retribution, we have seen, did not consist in the acting-out of a blind affect, an irrational and even hysterical thirst for revenge (as it appears in the psychologizing perspective of opera). The violence of revenge consisted in its executing the restoration of justice with an act that a second narrative described as an excessive abomination that disrupted the just balance and so called for another restoration of justice.

The violence of retribution, that is to say, consisted in the fact that its restoration of justice must repeat itself endlessly: the violence of retribution is always exerted in an act of the exact same kind as the one against which it is directed. Put more precisely, it is against its own nature as an act that retribution, seeking to preserve the just state of the world, is directed. What retribution seeks to banish as an abomination from the world, which it brings back time and again into the world itself: the act, the deed. What retribution seeks to restore – the just state of the world – and what it is in itself – a necessarily excessive act – are irreconcilable.[28] The violence of retribution is the compulsion of its repetition.

The situation in law is the same and yet utterly different: Law, too, must perpetually repeat its own violent enforcement. But that is not because law, like retribution, engenders within itself that against which it is directed; it engenders it outside itself as its counterpart. By tying justice to the political union of the citizens, law engenders its own other. From now on, there exists an outside of justice: the instauration of law at once and inevitably engenders the possibility of the extra-legal, of non-law. Law must accordingly secure its decisions not only against other, conflicting, interpretations of the civic law of equality. Law must also secure its rule against the possibility of the extra-legal or non-law that it has itself engendered and reproduces with each of its acts. Doing so does not just require violence as an instrument – as it must be employed against "ordinary" citizens who cannot or do not want to understand and accept the higher insights of the best among them who judge. Securing the rule of law against the possibility of the extra-legal is *essentially* violence, is violence through and through. The relation between law and non-law is not normative and hence not cognitive. It is an antagonism that no insight can bridge, no reasoning can reconcile. It is a relation of pure enforcement – of pure violence.[29]

6. *The curse of autonomy* (King Oedipus)

There is perhaps no text that has more thoroughly thought through the externality of law than Sophocles' tragedy of Oedipus. By dramatizing the inexorable logic with which the judge Oedipus unleashes the violence of law against himself, Sophocles demonstrates that the problem of the externality of law, which is rooted in its very being, leaves only one direction for its historical evolution: The externality of law compels its unceasing progressive internalization. Law must engender the autonomous subject. For the sake of its rule, authoritarian law must transform itself into autonomous law: into a law that, as conceived, anyone is capable of practicing. As *King Oedipus* illustrates, everyone then becomes the authority that can and wants to turn the violent action of law against the lawless individual as that individual's own deed against him- or herself.

King Oedipus begins with a reminder: The citizens of Thebes, who are suffering under a plague, are reminded by an oracle of the old practice of cathartic sacrificial rituals that served to expiate a "pollution." Creon, who has been sent to Delphi as a messenger, reports that "King Phoebus bids us straitly extirpate / A fell pollution that infests the land, / And no more harbor an inveterate sore."[30] Such rituals implement the justice of retribution: justice as balance is brought about by countering an abomination with another (equal) violation.[31] Yet as Oedipus' interrogation of Creon about the purport of the oracle immediately shows, law already rules in Thebes. One no longer pays for abominations and excess with retribution or sacrifice in Thebes; one investigates and adjudicates cases. And so Oedipus complies with the oracle's command to purify the city by initiating a murder trial: "I will start afresh, and once more make dark things plain" (*Oedipus*, 132). Oedipus believes he can be a judge not only because he has proven himself a master at solving complicated riddles (which earned him his office as king, or more precisely, "tyrant," who rules not because of his ancestry but because of his accomplishments). He also believes that because he, as a foreigner who is impartial, having no kin in the city, will lead the investigation solely for the sake of the victim, the city, and the god. As the subsequent action will illustrate, that requires strict adherence to the precepts of legal procedure. As judge, even Oedipus, however superior his insight may be, must abide by the rule that the legal determination of the facts demands that the parties (who have the right to contradict others who speak in court and ask counter-questions, a right Creon asserts against Oedipus' overbearing manners: *Oedipus*, 543–44, 574–75, 626–27) acknowledge them.

Yet the rule of law in Thebes is just as, or even more, evident in the fact that no one has bothered to investigate the murder until now, which is to say, in decades, even though the Thebans agree that the oracle – which, as oracles are wont to do, only makes vague reference to some "fell pollution that infests the land" – can only be about this very murder. Their lame excuse, which Creon offers in response to Oedipus' charge of inaction, is that they simply had more important things to do. The imperative call of retribution has been supplanted in Thebes by a legal order whose externality is manifest: once retribution has been replaced by law, one can choose to worry about one's own "distress" rather than resolve a murder case. In this perspective, the rhetoric of the Erinyes that spilled blood cries for retribution appears as no more than embarrassingly extravagant – well, rhetoric.

The Erinyes had already forecast that this was how justice would fare once the bond between it and fear had been severed by the establishment of a court of law founded solely on the equality of the citizens, to whose insight and decision justice was thus entrusted. They had forecast that no sort of justice at all would rule then. That is what things have come to in Thebes, where an act of murder remains unpunished for lack of interest. For justice to be done, it must be compelled by means external to law: An oracle must demand it, and a king must attend to the matter.

Yet the very first thing Oedipus learns in the legal procedure he leads is that his attending to the matter alone is no use either. Oedipus endows his office as judge with all the power he wields as ruler, only to learn that the passivity the Thebans bring to judging recurs in their unwillingness to participate in the proceeding. So Oedipus must set the murder case aside to prosecute another infraction first: The withholding of knowledge, the non-participation in the legal proceeding, becomes the primary object of the measures he takes. In a first step, Oedipus promises exemption from punishment, sentence mitigation, or a reward to persuade the perpetrator, accessories, and witnesses to reveal what they know. And yet, as though convinced from the outset that these attempts will be fruitless, Oedipus then says what he will do when all his measures fail: He will "charge" and "condemn" the offenders to exclude themselves from the religious and political community of the city. In order to enforce the law, or more precisely to compel participation in the legal proceeding, Oedipus regresses to before the law, invoking the oracular prophesies of ritual, speaking "in priestly fashion"[32] as a judge, and *curses* those who try to elude the legal proceeding – to stand outside law, to remain uninvolved – condemning them to punish themselves for doing so with exclusion from the citizenry:

> But if ye still keep silence, if through fear / For self or friends ye disregard my hest, / Hear what I then resolve; I lay my ban / On the assassin whosoe'er he be. / Let no man in this land, whereof I hold / The sovereign rule, harbor or speak to him; / Give him no part in prayer or sacrifice / Or lustral rites, but hound him from your homes. / For this is our defilement, so the god / Hath lately shown to me by oracles. / Thus as their champion I maintain the cause / Both of the god and of the murdered King. / And on the murderer this curse I lay / (On him who stays hidden, may his actions be his own or shared by others): – / Wretch, may he pine in utter wretchedness! / And for myself, if with my privity / He gain admittance to my hearth, / I shall suffer the curse I laid on others.
>
> (*Oedipus*, 233–51, translation modifed)

A curse is not a threat: A threat is directed at someone who has wishes and, more importantly, fears, and deliberates how they can attain their wishes and avert what they fear. A curse functions very differently: without mediation by further deliberation – immediately; a curse is something one "suffers" (*Oedipus*, 251), that falls upon one. The curse robs the one upon whom it falls of the subjectivity the threat presupposes. A curse is violence in the sense defined above because it "eliminates action by action" (Luhmann). This, Oedipus' recourse to the curse seems to say, is the only way law can rule: when its subjects suffer it like a curse. The rule of law subjugates by robbing its subjects of their subjectivity. But by the same token, what the rule of law demands with the inexorable violence of the curse is precisely *self*-condemnation in accordance with law: the law curses the subject to self-confiction, to be the subject of judgment, to judge him- or herself in accordance with the law. It is the form of *legal* subjectivization to which law condenms the one of whom it robs its subjectivity.

Oedipus' experience, which proves strikingly true in his own case, tells him that this is the only way the justice of law is capable of ruling: if law is to prevail, it cannot rely on fear of its threats alone. That was the answer of the authoritarian law that Athena advocated and that had already stopped functioning in Oedipus' Thebes. Ever since its instauration, law has been at risk of succumbing to the indifference of those who are outside the law, those who are extra-legal, though it has engendered the very possibility of their existence. Oedipus' new insight is that the rule of law can be ensured only when it is exercised from within: when it enforces the legal manner of judging as the own judgment of the subjects it subjugates; when law *and* the subjects become autonomous at one stroke. It is not enough that the adversaries redefine themselves as parties, as the Erinyes and Orestes did in *The Eumenides*, and submit to the power of another who judges over them. The subjectivation compelled by the rule of law must reach further and deeper: law rules by compelling its subjects to be autonomous; law rules by compelling, by means of its curse, that its subjects freely judge themselves in accordance with the law. That is the "curse of law" that Plato speaks of: The "curse of the law" is that the individuals become law's own subjects, that they become its self. The "curse of the law," which, according to Plato, falls upon him who has "failed" to execute it[33] – in other words, the curse that law inflicts on one who stands outside law – is fulfilled by power not of authoritarian rule but of autonomous self-judgment. It is precisely not the logic of sovereignty (as Giorgio Agamben says) but of *autonomy* that defines the form of the rule of law.[34]

Oedipus utters the curse of autonomy in order to assert the rule of law. But the curse of the law condemning the subject to autonomy is not merely an external means of its enforcement: the curse of the law describes the way law rules only because it springs from the way in which law legitimizes itself. In the step Oedipus takes beyond Athena's authoritarian law by introducing the autonomous law, the rule of a king prepared to use violence coincides with the normative justification of law: law is justified because its judgment is impartial and issued in the name of the equality of all citizens. That is the only aspect in which the violence associated with the punitive judgment of law differs from the violence exerted by the retributive counter-violation. And so – this is the consequence the autonomous law draws – the judgment of law, unlike that of retribution, is also the judgment each party must render if it sees itself as one of two parties and hence as an equal citizen. The legal judgment is everyone's own judgment.[35] So law demands of the one whom it judges, and even of the one whom it convicts, that she share its judgment of her. Therein, and only therein, lies the legitimacy of law that sets it apart from retribution. The insight of the tragedy of Oedipus is that the violence-exerting rule of law, too, consists only therein. It is not that law, despite its claim to be justified, must resort to additional coercive measures in order to rule. Rather, it must realize its claim to be justified *as* the exercise of violence: in the aspiration from whose fulfillment it draws the justification of its judgment – the aspiration to be the own judgment of the one being judged – it must repeat the violence of the curse that secured the rule of the pre-legal justice of retribution in altered, and indeed heightened, form. The cratic doctrine of the Erinyes that there is justice only for one who is neither "lawless" nor "subject to a tyrant" is fully implemented only when everyone has become their own master and hence his or her own servant. That is why law has declared the autonomy of the subject to be the first legal duty ever since it became autonomous itself. The commandment "Be autonomous; be a person!" marks the beginning of law.[36] But since this first commandment of the autonomous law is addressed to one who cannot even understand it because he or she stands outside the law, the commandment of autonomy is itself not a commandment prompting autonomous compliance: it is a compulsion – an imperative of the ruling power, a curse; the aspiration of law to be justified falls upon its subjects as a curse.

Oedipus issues the legal curse of autonomy only as a proxy, in his role as judge: He curses not in his own name but in that of law. So the obligation to apply the curse to himself as well is part of its purport from the very outset: "I pray / The curse I laid on others fall on me" (*Oedipus*, 251). And that is how it will turn out: No one but Oedipus himself will convict him of murder and incest,[37] and no one but Oedipus himself will sentence him to blinding and exile. Under the rule of law we must condemn ourselves, and this self-condemnation under the rule of law is a curse. Precisely because it is a condemnation we inflict on ourselves, it is a condemnation in which we are not free, and more importantly, *from* which we will never be free. We remain forever caught up in the self-condemnation to which law curses us precisely because we have inflicted it on ourselves; nothing can dispel it. In his legally imposed self-condemnation, Oedipus is caught up in the question of his guilt and is incarcerated in the prison of his self-consciousness. The subject makes the legal judgment her or his own and by doing so renders herself or himself law's own subject. The subject *identifies* itself by virtue of its legal judgment.

7. The fate of law (Benjamin 1)

Even by its own concept, law is violence: justified violence. In its judgments, and *a fortiori* in its punishments, law violates the violator. (Counter)Violation of the violator is the shared definition of justice in retribution and law. By its own concept, law is entitled and indeed obliged to judge and punish because it does so in the name of a universal that is the condemned and punished subject's own. Law judges and punishes in the name of justice not as a state of the world (whose disruption by excessive deeds retribution and sacrifice aim to counteract) but as the equality of the citizens. Law – already the authoritarian law – violates the violator in his or her own name: in his or her own name as an equal citizen. Hegel's assertion that the punishing "injury […] which is inflicted on the criminal" is "also a *right for the criminal himself*," which is to say, "*his* right" is not an eccentric exaggeration;[38] it follows from law's claim to legitimacy.

From the outset, it has been a fundamental challenge for law to bring about this legitimate assertion of form (that, in return, allows its experience). Observing the violence of the injury law inflicts, how are we to see that it is justified because it is inflicted in the violator's own name? At a minimum – that is the fairly obvious answer of the autonomous law[39] – law should renounce some instruments of criminal procedure (such as torture) and no longer inflict "cruel and unusual" punishments. But not only does the question whether a particular punishment (such as the death penalty) is "cruel and unusual" remain contentious: even the most liberal and humanitarian reform of penal law cannot resolve the fundamental doubt whether the counter-violations law inflicts in the name of political equality are justified or in fact execute the rule of existing social and economic inequalities. The formal difference of law, in which alone its legitimacy consists, is forever liable to be perceived as *merely* formal; law can always be seen as class justice or the victor's justice.

But as Walter Benjamin has pointed out in trenchant terms,[40] the critique of the violence of law, which aims at its manifest appearance (which is to say, its means), suffers from one of two weaknesses. It must "proclaim a quite childish anarchism" that "[refuses] to acknowledge any constraint toward persons and [declares], 'What pleases is permitted' " ("Critique", 241). This critique of the violent means of law proceeds "in the name of a formless 'freedom' " ("Critique", 242) in whose perspective any constraint or mere stipulation appears as violent privation and injury; yet as Benjamin argues, this critique does not accurately address the question even of the death penalty. Or the critique of the violent means of law must proceed in the name of its just purpose. To do so, it must distinguish the justice law purposes from the violent means it employs – so that the former may serve to both justify and delimit the latter.

This second form of the critique of violence – its critique as the simultaneous justification and delimitation of violence as means in the name of justice as its purpose – is the line of reasoning in which, Benjamin writes, natural law and positivism agree. They "meet in their common basic dogma: Just ends can be attained by justified means, justified means used for just ends" ("Critique", 237). Benjamin objects that "justified means on the one hand and just ends on the other [are] in irreconcilable conflict" (*ibid.*), and this objection is no longer about the violent manifestation of law – or in other words, no longer about the means of law whose violence supersedes the justness of their purpose. Benjamin instead rejects the logic of purpose and means in which the legitimation of the form of law and the critique of its manifestation meet: the violence of law cannot be understood by this logic at all. The violence of law is not a means, however just its purpose. Or: the violence of law that truly calls for a critique does not consist in its means – nor in the fact that law, too, constrains, threatens, and violates. Rather, the violence of law is "violence crowned by fate" ("Critique", 242), which is to say, the violence of law consists in its operating as – *like* – fate. Another term Benjamin uses to express this idea is: law is "mythic" violence ("Critique", 248).

In a central passage of his essay, Benjamin explains this as follows:

> For the function of violence in lawmaking is twofold, in the sense that lawmaking pursues as its end, with violence as the means, what is to be established as law, but at the moment of instatement does not dismiss violence; rather, at this very moment of lawmaking, it specifically establishes as law not an end unalloyed by violence but one necessarily and intimately bound to it, under the title of power. Lawmaking is powermaking, assumption of power, and to that extent an immediate manifestation of violence. Justice is the principle of all divine endmaking, power the principle of all mythic lawmaking.
>
> ("Critique", 248)

It is not the fact that law is applied and enforced by violent means – not the fact that law uses violence as a means at all – that is the problem of law and the legitimation of its violence. Rather the violence in law, unlike, say, the violence implicit in technology, cannot *remain* a mere means, that it does not "abdicate," and instead becomes the secret purpose of law itself is the problem.[41] According to Benjamin, the violence of law, which he calls "fateful" for this reason, consists in the fact that law's violent means obliterate its just purposes because its self-preservation becomes its only purpose. Law is purely about power, yet not about the power of the ruling class or the victor: it is about *its own* power, the power of law. The "fateful" violence of law is the violence of its pure self-preservation.

We should note two aspects that will contribute to our understanding of the relation between law and violence. First, we must distinguish between two uses of the term "violence." We ordinarily use it to designate actions with obstructive or injurious effects.[42] It is obvious that law resorts to such actions. That is a consequence of its nature as political power, since power depends on violence as a "symbiotic mechanism" (Luhmann). The injurious violence of law is lamentable because it causes suffering. Still, it may be justified, even, Benjamin is convinced, as violence against life. Law as mythic or fateful violence, on the other hand, is always reprehensible. Taken in this sense, the concept of violence designates not the injurious effects of legal acts, which are especially prominent in judgments and punishments, but their mode of operation: the mythic or fateful violence of law consists in the fact that the acts of legal judgment and punishment are opaque; no purpose is evident in them other than the mere preservation of law's power to judge and punish. "Violence" in the second sense of the word – which is the true object of critique – designates an operation that is concerned with itself; an operation, that is to say, in which purpose and means coincide. That, Benjamin argues, is what makes the violence of law reprehensible: not that law, too, threatens, violates, and coerces, but that (or when) law is executed in such fashion that it operates purely for its own sake, for the sake of the preservation of its order, the establishment and enforcement of its categories, perspective, and language – for the sake of its pure power. Like fate, such an operation that is solely about its power to operate is destined to continue forever.

Second, Benjamin explicates the violent and fateful operation of law as a repetition of the instauration of law in its preservation. In the acts of the latter, law's perspective on justice – the equality of the citizens – is specified in laws and applied in judgments. "Preservation of law" is Benjamin's term for the normative implementation of law. However, according to Benjamin, there is no preservation of law in which the "origins" of law do not manifest themselves in law: the preservation of law always performs a "repetition" of the original lawmaking; the preservation of law is never solely about the framing or application of this or that law, but about the reaffirmation of "law itself." This observation – that such reaffirmation of "law itself" is forever and continually necessary – adumbrates what is "rotten" in law ("Critique", 242): law is "rotten" because it is "violence" in the second sense of the word explicated above – because it must endlessly repeat its instauration in its implementation. This necessity follows from the very logic that governs the instauration of law: the instauration of law installs it in opposition to the extra-legal or non-law (which Benjamin describes as "mere life" – life outside law: "Critique", 251). Because law itself installs this opposition between law and extra-legal or non-law, between legal and "mere" life, it remains caught up in it. Law can never be conclusively enforced, can never prevail over non-law, because law itself engenders what it aims to prevail over in its enforcement. By consequence, law can never be purely preservative, proceeding in accordance with its normative logic; it must again and again oppose its power to the extra-legal in acts divorced from all normativity. Law cannot leave the act of its instauration behind. To be compelled to repeat it endlessly is the fate or the violence of law.

* * *

(1) The violence of law consists in its endless compulsion to repeat the violent enforcement in which it prevails over the extra-legal. The violence of law is not simple but potentiated violence: the violence of violence; the violence of the repetition of violence.

(2) The root of the violence of law is that law must prevail over non-law. Faced with non-law, law can only prevail by overwhelming and

> violating force, not by force of persuasion and justification. And law must forever and continually prevail over non-law because it presupposes the non-law over which it prevails.

These are the two central hypotheses of Benjamin's critique of law. The experience of law in tragedy, with its sequence of shifts from retribution to authoritarian law to autonomous law, complements this double hypothesis with two insights. The first insight is that law's engenderment of the non-legal or extra-legal follows directly from its political-procedural character: because law breaks with the violence of retributive repetition by virtue of its procedure of equality; and because this legal procedure of equality is the expression of a politics of equality; because, that is to say, this procedural equality between the parties ensured by the legal proceeding is founded on the political equality of the citizens in whose name the judge judges; because the justice of law is therefore due to the political union of the citizens, which, as a created union, maintains its difference from what is not part of it – for these reasons law must again and again prevail by violent means over the extra-legal or non-law. Yet law's political-procedural quality is the source of its legitimacy vis-à-vis the violence of retribution. So the violence of law and its legitimacy are directly bound up with each other. They are rooted in the same structure.

And the second insight with which the experience of law in tragedy complements Benjamin's double hypothesis on the violence of law – the hypothesis that this violence is the ("fateful") violence of violence – is that the union of legitimacy and violence that constitutes law finds its consummate manifestation in the figure of the subjectivity that the curse of the autonomous law condemns its addressees to develop.

II. The relief of law

1. *The relief of law (Benjamin 2)*

Benjamin's concept of fateful violence[43] allows us to define the experience of law in tragedy more closely, because it shows what the violence of law consists in beyond its manifestation as constraint and violation. But the inverse is also true: the experience of law in tragedy allows us to define Benjamin's concept of fateful violence more accurately. Benjamin discerns in "violence crowned by fate" what law *has in common* with the justice of retribution (and its curse-like operation), which precedes law and which law promises to supplant. That is the object of Benjamin's consideration of law in the perspective of the "philosophy of history" ("The critique of violence is the philosophy of its history": "Critique", 251): it is meant to show that law's claim to be the other of retribution and curse is mere semblance. Law is not the other of fate but merely another period in the age of its reign. The central critical concept in Benjamin's reflections – the concept of the mythic or fateful – cannot and is not designed to capture the difference of form between retribution and law. In Benjamin's view, law and retribution are *equally* fateful.

Tragedy, by contrast, begins with their distinction: with the engenderment of law *against* retribution. If tragedy subsequently shows that law is essentially violence, then it's not to demonstrate a simple identity between law and the old order of retribution. It's to point out the paradox that constitutes law's essence, or to put it in procedural terms: to highlight the reversal into its opposite that takes place within law.[44] Law breaks with the curse-like operation of retributive justice in which every violation demands a counter-violation in return by establishing a new form of judging: the impartial juridical proceeding in the name of the equality of the citizens. But this new way of judging likewise rules with the violent force of the curse. So law, that is the experience of tragedy, *is* not fateful violence, like retribution. Law is at once the break with fateful violence *and* the return of fateful violence (in a different guise and on a different scene: in the guise and on the scene of the subject).[45]

The experience of tragedy thus accentuates the problem of how there can be a critique of the violence of law at all. "Critique," Benjamin writes, is the title for the "discriminating and decisive approach" ("Critique", 251). The critical "discrimination" being sought is one between the fateful violence that continues and repeats itself ad infinitum and an agency (or "violence") that breaks with fate by sublating itself in its purpose. But as tragedy demonstrates, in law, the two – the break with fate and the catastrophic reversal into fate – are paradoxically interlocked: the break with the fateful violence of retribution in law is brought about by the establishment of the new political-procedural form of judgment that for its part then rules in fateful fashion, through the curse of self-condemnation. The "discriminating and decisive approach" of critique, then, cannot be taken with regard to law: *within law*, the break with fate and the catastrophic reversal into fate are inseparable. The legal break with fateful violence and the legal transition into fateful violence share the same root: the legal form of judgment. This nexus, which tragedy unfolds, makes it impossible to discriminate and decide between consent to law and its rejection, between the instauration of law and its destruction. Both sides repress one of the two paradoxically interlocked sides: Consent to law represses the curse of self-condemnation imposed by the establishment of law's political-procedural form of judgment; rejection of law represses the fact that to abandon law's new political-procedural form of judgment is nothing other than to fall back into the order of retribution.

Benjamin offers an alternative to consent or rejection, instauration or destruction, an alternative he calls "relief of law" (*Entsetzung des Rechts*):

> On the breaking of this cycle maintained by mythic forms of law, on the relief of law with all the forces on which it depends as they depend on it, finally therefore on the abolition of state power, a new historical epoch is founded.
>
> ("Critique", 251–52, translation modified)

Benjamin formulates this program of the "relief of law" in the concluding paragraph of his treatise, where he also seems to sketch, under the titles of "divine" or "pure" or "revolutionary" violence, a mode of action and agency that, in contradistinction to law, knows how to break with the violence of fate such that the latter does not return in a different guise. Benjamin thus reframes the idea of critique on a higher plane. This would be a critique of law that, rather than discriminating two sides within law, discriminates – divorces – us *from* law. Yet the price to be paid for this higher critique is the false concept of law that identifies it with the violence of retribution; a concept of law, in other words, that understands it as *nothing but* the repetition or continuation of fateful violence. But law itself already contains the break with fateful violence (into which it at once falls back). So even the higher critique that Benjamin's terminology –"divine" or "pure" or "revolutionary" violence – heralds by promising a divorce from law must resolve the paradox whose unfolding constitutes the experience of law in tragedy. According to the latter, not only does law *already* implement a break with fateful violence, a break from fateful violence can only take place *by way of and through* law.[46]

Yet Benjamin's program of a "relief" of law allows for a second reading, in which it purports something other than a critical discrimination within, or divorce from, law. This reading comes into view when we follow Giorgio Agamben's insight that the real opponent of Benjamin's idea of the "relief" of law is Carl Schmitt's ideological program of its "suspension," with which many commentators (and most translations) confuse Benjamin's idea: "relief" is the *counter*-program to the call for a "suspension" of the law.[47] By "suspension" of the law, Schmitt means that "the norm is destroyed in the exception." The application (or, as Benjamin puts it, the "preservation") of law is disrupted and supplanted by the instauration of law by virtue of an "absolute" decision unrestrained by any norm:

> The decision frees itself from all normative ties and becomes in the true sense absolute. The state suspends the law in the exception on the basis of its right of self-preservation, as one would say. The two elements of the concept *legal order* are then dissolved into independent notions and thereby testify to their conceptual independence. Unlike the normal situation, when the autonomous moment of the decision recedes to a minimum, the norm is destroyed in the exception.[48]

What Schmitt describes (and legitimizes, even champions) as the "suspension" of the law, then, is the very regression from the preservation of law to its instauration whose incessant repetition is, in Benjamin's view, what is "rotten" in law.[49] By contrast, the "relief" of law Benjamin speaks of is the "breaking of this cycle" of law's preservation and instauration that ties the two together by "governing their oscillation." Schmitt wants to release the violence of lawmaking from any norm by suspending the law; Benjamin, by contrast, discerns in this very release, in the repetition of the violence of lawmaking, the fateful necessity that rules law. The relief of law is meant to disrupt this mythic cycle in which the suspension of the law is caught.

* * *

Benjamin's term "*Entsetzung*" (translated here as "relief") has a history of technical legal uses as well as more general non-legal ones. In both fields it blends two different contexts of meanings. The first contexts includes "dismissal (from an office), removal," "loss (of civil rights), disenfranchisement," and, more generally, "degradation of a nobleman into a commoner." The second meaning recorded by Grimm's *Deutsches Wörterbuch* is the raising of a military occupation or the liberation of a city ("*liberatio urbis*").[50] So the "*Entsetzung*" or "relief" of law implies both its abrogation and its liberation. Whilst Schmitt's suspension of the law is meant to free the power of the state at least temporarily from the regulations and barriers of law, Benjamin's relief on the other hand aims at disempowering the law, calling for nothing less than a liberation of law itself. By the same token, Schmitt wishes to see the norm of law obliterated, Benjamin its "historical function" ("Critique", 249). This historical "function of violence in lawmaking" – that is Benjamin's central claim (see above, p. 30) – is "powermaking", and power is "the principle of all mythic lawmaking." Schmitt wants to suspend the law for the sake of the power of the state, whereas to "relieve" law requires it to be enacted in such a way, that law is removed from its office, its historical function of powermaking is expunged, and law itself is thereby liberated. Is there such a form of law enactment?

2. *Self-reflection of law*

We may put the question a different way: How far do we have to go back into the conceptual construction of law to access the possibility of the other mode of its implementation? The answer can only be: to the beginning of law (which is to say, not to a point *before* the beginning of law[51]). The beginning of law, that is the insight of tragedy, consists in the introduction of a procedural form of judgment that ties legal judgment to a political subject – the judge who speaks in the name of the equality of the citizens. From the very beginning, that is to say, a difference intervenes between law and the extra- or non-legal. So to be valid, law must not only assert one authoritative interpretation against other, deviating interpretations; it must also prevail over attitudes and forms of behavior that are lawless or extra-legal: attitudes and forms of behavior that do not look to the idea of law for guidance in the first place. Faced with these attitudes and forms of behavior, law cannot rely on the normative power of conviction and justification; it must resort to violence, asserting its power with threat, stricture, and violation. With its political-procedural form of judgment – which breaks with the order of retribution in the name of equality – law, from the very beginning, faces an impossible challenge: it must secure not just this or that law but the law of law; it must secure not just this or that norm but the very normative character of the norm, against the lawless and norm-free. To solve this impossible problem, law must time and again "suspend" itself (Schmitt), for "a situation in which legal prescriptions can be valid must first be brought about."[52] The suspension of the law is its way of wielding power – as violent rule over the extra- or non-legal. The relief of law, by contrast, is the relief *from* its suspension: the relief of law consists in a form of the implementation of political-procedural judgment that is liberated from its violent rule over the extra- or non-legal.

How is that possible? There is both a regressive and a reflective answer to this question. The regressive answer is: sublation of the difference between law and non-law, reconciliation of law with the non-legal. This answer has its model in a teleological (or "aesthetic") concept of pedagogy: According to the regressive answer, the violence of law is overcome by pedagogy, because pedagogy is concerned with the "soul of the living," as even Benjamin still notes, it implies the "absence of all lawmaking" ("Critique", 250). Pedagogy puts an end to the violence of law because it transmutes "mere" life, which confronts law and all normativity as external to it, into ensouled and hence formed life. And "with mere life, the rule of law over the living ceases" (*ibid.*).[53] Yet with the paideic sublation of the violent rule of law, law itself disappears as well. Because what then disappears is the political character of judgment: in the teleological (or aesthetic) concept of pedagogy, the polis becomes a second nature that no longer confronts anything external to it. Once pedagogy takes the place of law, as the violence of law disappears, so does the political difference, the political itself disappears, who's emergence had been tied to law's rupture with the subjectless and mythical justice of retribution.

The regressive answer demands that law be released from its difference from the extra- or non-legal. Because this difference is the crack through which fateful violence infiltrates law, so the argument, the violence of law can only be overcome if its difference from the non-legal is sublated. The reflective answer, on the other hand, demands rather than releasing law *from* its difference, that difference itself must be released; which is to say, the difference between law and the non-legal. Rather than being sublated by means of pedagogy, the difference itself must be allowed its full expression. That is what, according to the second, the reflective answer, "relief of law" means: "Relief" means liberating law's difference from the non-legal, from law's rule over the non-legal. The possibility of another mode of the implementation of legal judgment lies not in overcoming the difference of law from the non-legal by means of pedagogy, but in realizing this difference non-cratically, non-violently.

This second answer to the question concerning a different mode of the implementation of legal judgment is "reflective" because it is realized only by law changing itself: by a law that reflects on itself in its difference from the non-legal; by a law that has become self-reflective. If the "relief" of law is not to be regressive, if it is not to subvert the possibility of law (and thus jeopardize its break with the retributive violence), it can only assume the form of a self-reflection of law in its difference from the non-legal. "Self-relfective" doesn't refer or point to a law that lays its own foundations, but to one that differentiates and by doing so delimits itself from the non-legal. So the self-reflective law is not distinct from the non-legal, it does not simply suffer that distinction as applying to it. Rather, it *implements* its distinction from the non-legal as its own operation of distinguishing. The self-reflection of law consists in reenacting within law the contradistinction between law and the non-legal with which law engenders itself. The self-reflective law "knows" – what the non-reflective, ordinary law of "normal legal procedure" perpetually forgets – that it has brought about the non-legal in the first place, over which it must prevail. The self-reflective law therefore contains within itself the non-legal from which it distinguishes itself. The self-reflective law is constituted by a paradox: the self-reflective law contains its *other within itself*. Yet this paradox does not lead to the dissolution of the self-reflective law; on the contrary, the latter consists only in the implementation or enactment of that paradox.

But how can law contain its other, the non-legal as the "infinite space of otherness,"[54] within itself? Does that not turn the extra-legal into a matter of stipulation within law, which is to say, into something law rules as its own? And how does the "relief" of law via self-reflection, the release of law from its own rule over the non-legal come about?

3. *The release of the lawless* (The Broken Jug)

It is an act of "relief," or more precisely, an act of double relief, with which Kleist's "comedy" of *The Broken Jug* seals its departure from the tragedy of its distant source, Sophocles' *Oedipus Rex*, and sets course for the happy ending of a comedy.[55] Once the guilt of Judge Adam has become obvious – though not, as in *Oedipus*, by his own doing, nor in a legal proceeding, but only after the end of that proceeding – he immediately puts into action what Oedipus proclaims he will do: Adam escapes from the city (though his polis is merely a village near Utrecht). When those he leaves behind observe Adam's escape with bitter glee,

Walter responds with a gesture that is as legally equivocal – is it a judgment, a legal measure, or an act of mercy? – as it gives a crucial twist to the story:

WALTER: Hurry, Clerk, go at once and fetch him in
Before he makes a bad thing worse.
True, I remove him from his office here
And lend you, until further notice,
The authority to hold it in these parts
But if, as I hope, the accounts are right
I will not force the man to desert.
Hurry, be kind enough to fetch him back.
(*The Broken Jug*, 65; translation modified)

This act on Walter's part is a "relief," an "*Entsetzung*," first, in the precise technical sense of the term, the only sense it still has in the General State Laws for the Prussian State: the removal of a public servant – in this instance, a judge – from his office.[56] Yet it is a "relief" also in the wider sense that, as we have seen, was formerly part of the word's usage: an act of "releasing" Adam from the very curse of the law that Oedipus, in the destructive judgment he inflicted upon himself by sending himself into exile, had enforced on himself. Walter's anti-tragic act consists in a half-solution – a legal sanction that only partly affects Adam – indeed, that divides him into two parts: he is suspended from his judgeship without being compelled to desert the polity. This partition of the sanction against Adam implies the departure from the total significance the self-imposed judgment had for Oedipus – the departure from tragedy. The legal sanction affects Adam in his legal person, but not in his existence. "Get him back": He may stay.

It is tempting to understand Walter's double act – of imposing a sanction and limiting that sanction – as an act of justice that is itself again or still legal. It is, after all, an archetypical demand of legal justice that the punishment correspond to the crime. And since Adam's offense is fairly minor in comparison to that of Oedipus (although, then again, not entirely minor: abuse of office, sexual assault and extortion, and, lest we forget, the breaking of the jug – still, Adam did not commit patricide or incest), his punishment, pursuant to the equivalence demanded by legal justice, must not be all-encompassing either. Yet this interpretation of Walter's act of double "relief" fails to appreciate one very important point: Walter is not a judge who hands down sentences and imposes punishments by applying laws or legal rules. Walter is an assessor inspecting the courts; he is an auditor who observes how others judge. It is because of Walter's function, to observe law within law, and not from the application of a legal rule, that the double act of "relief" ensues.

For an indication of how Walter's double act of relieving Adam should be understood in this sense, we may look to Eve's central scene. At that moment, Adam and Eve not only confront each other as perpetrator and victim, they also have something in common – their non-participation in law: these two are the only ones who could offer information about the facts of the case, but both refuse to do so (for antithetical reasons) – a refusal both successfully maintain until the end of the trial.

Eve, speaking to Walter, explains her refusal to answer her mother's insistent questioning and the court's inquiry on what actually happened in her room the night before:

EVE: Please, in your goodness, sir, and in your mercy,
Do not let me be forced to say what happened.
And do not think amiss of this refusal.
It is the strange determining of heaven
That in this matter lays a finger on my lips.
That Ruprecht never knocked against the jug
If you require me to I'll lay it down
On the holy altar with an oath.
But for the rest of yesterday's event
In every detail it belongs to me
And Mother can't demand to unknit it all
All for the sake of one sole thread

> Belonging to her that runs through everything.
> Who it was who broke the jug I mustn't say here
> Or I'd be bound to touch on secrets
> Not mine, and wholly not to do with the jug.
> Sooner or later I will confide in her
> But here, before the court, is not the place
> Where she's a right to interrogate me for it.
> (*The Broken Jug*, 42–43; translation modified)

Everything changes with this explanation, because the reason Eve offers for her refusal to provide information to the court introduces nothing less than a new idea of law: Eve declares that law *must not* interrogate her and that she has the *right* to refuse to answer.[57] Her speech proclaims a limitation of law: law may not ask everything. And her speech asserts a new right: a right against the law.

Eve invokes her right to remain silent.[58] Its significance in legal procedure lies in that it protects the defendant from incriminating herself. However, the right Eve proclaims in her speech has an impact that goes far beyond that purpose: it becomes a right to what "belongs to her" without being "hers"; to what is, to her, a tightly knit whole of which any individual can claim only a limited part; a right to have "secrets" before the public sphere of law. Yet what Eve thus claims is exempt from communication in court, or more precisely what she claims she has the *right* to exempt from communication in court, is at once what she is willing to disclose in a different communication in which the secrets withheld from law may be "confided." This other, non-legal communication commences immediately after the conclusion of the legal proceedings; out of court, she may speak and say straightforwardly what she absolutely must withhold before court: "Judge Adam broke the jug" (*The Broken Jug*, 63). So the point of Eve's proclamation on having a right (against law) to silence is to make a non-legal communication possible that obeys different laws: confidence (between Eve and Ruprecht), support (which Walter promises Ruprecht), forgiveness (which even Adam asks for, using a conventional formula). The right to remain silent is the right to a different kind of communication. If there is an entitled form of communication besides the law, in which may be said what can be kept secret from law, the law itself is just another form of communication: one form of communication among others. The right to remain silent before the law renders law relative: The latter is considered as different and in this difference. And even more: by acknowledging the right to remain silent before the law, law renders *itself* relative; it reflects on itself in its difference from the right of other forms of communication and delimits its right vis-à-vis them.

In light of this central scene, the partitioned sanction imposed on Adam takes on a different aspect as well: it appears not as the application of a legal rule of the equivalence of offense and punishment, but as a liberating "relief" of law meant to spare Adam the fate of Oedipus. Walter wants to break the compulsion to desert that provoked Adam's escape. This compulsion, however, is, as we know from Oedipus (and from Adam's fellow judge at Holla, who tried to take his own life after he was suspended: *The Broken Jug*, 7), an internal compulsion imposed by law. It is the compulsion to judge oneself. The "relief" of law implied by Walter's partitioning of Adam's sanction consists in releasing Adam from the compulsion to be his own judge, just as Eve has been released from the compulsion to speak in court. Like Eve, Adam is no longer compelled to participate in law. Walter's partitioning of Adam's legal sanction is thus anything but half-hearted – it is not an act of leniency, not putting mercy before justice, not looking the other way or turning a blind eye. In truth, Walter's partitioning of Adam's legal sanction implies his *total* suspension from judgeship. Adam is to lose not only his office, which authorized him to be judge over others; henceforth, Adam shall not be obliged to judge at all anymore, also and especially not over himself. Walter's revision of law ends Adam's nightmare of self-judgment:

ADAM: – I dreamed a plaintiff had seized hold of me
And hauled me up before the bench, and I
None the less I was seated on that bench

And homilied, lambasted and badmouthed me
And handed down the iron on my own neck.
LIGHT: What! You did that to you?
ADAM: True as I'm honest.
Then both of us were one and ran away
And had to hole up in the woods all night.
(*The Broken Jug*, 13)[59]

Walter's relieving of Judge Adam is neither an application of the law nor its suspension for the sake of order; it is an act of liberation – of releasing Adam from the law as much as law from its power. By relieving Adam, Walter protects Adam from Oedipus' fate; he will not live the nightmare of calling his curse upon himself.

* * *

Adam and Eve are released from the compulsion to participate in law. Yet they are released not only to different degrees and in different respects – Eve is released from the duty to speak the whole truth in court; Adam, from the Oedipal curse of having to convict himself – they are also released for different reasons. In Eve's case, the law delimits itself by recognizing the (contra-legal) right to remain silent here, in court, and to speak elsewhere and in a different manner. This (contra-legal) right to non-legal communication may be asserted, and it may be integrated into a reflectively transformed law (see below, II.4). Adam, by contrast, does not claim anything; he runs away. The second to the last thing he says is "Forgive me"; his last word is a question: "What?"[60] It is to this question, rather than to a legal claim, that Walter's partitioning of the legal sanction is the answer. But what is Adam's question about? He is not asking about anything, not about anything particular. He does not know what he is asking, and not even that he is asking. Adam's last question, like many of the questions he had asked earlier, during the proceedings,[61] is the question of an absent-minded man suddenly jolted out of the abstraction into which he had sunk amid the tumult of the action. The reason, or at least the occasion, that leads Walter, the court assessor, to release Adam from the obligation to convict himself is his absent-mindedness or, quite literally, his distraction: a dissolution of the unity that renders an individual a self, makes out of sounds words and sentences, lets movements become actions – such distraction is the force of disintegration that dissolves the unity of the subject, of meaning, of action. Walter releases Adam from the duty to convict himself because Adam is *incapacitated*. Or: by releasing Adam from the compulsion to judge and convict, he releases him into his incapacity. The act of "relief" that is the culmination and destination of Kleist's drama as a whole consists in the reflective self-delimitation of law – in the (paradoxical) recognition of legal incapacity.

* * *

But where and how does one who is incapable of law find themselves when law releases them from the compulsion to judge themselves, and by the same token, releases itself, law, from the compulsion to prevail over them? Kleist's comedy, if it is to remain a comedy,[62] must refrain from offering any answer to this question. A few lines for Walter that can be found in one manuscript of the play but were struck before it went into print hint at what is in store for Adam:

> WALTER: But if, as I hope, the accounts are right
> one will, I reckon, be able to retain
> him somewhere or other.[63]

One who is incapable of law, that much is clear, cannot be a part of and participant in law, in the sense explicated by Rousseau (see above, p. 14), since the legal order's turning of every individual into a part of a social whole, into an equal citizen, is what gives rise to the curse or nightmare of self-judgment from which the revisionary relief of law is meant to release Adam. But doesn't this inevitably lead to the fact, that for the one who is released into legal incapacity, the law is once again just an external and fateful power to which he or she submits "[as one submits] to illness or misfortune or death"?[64] And what sort of existence does one released into legal incapacity lead if, from now on, he is merely "retained somewhere or other"? So will Adam after all just be brought back to "bare life" (*The Broken Jug*, 7; translation modified), like the judge at Holla, who wanted to hang himself but was cut down at the last moment. -> Im Original steht nichts vom Dachsparren . . . ? One might almost think Oedipus' existence as a man cursed to perpetual self-condemnation and excluded from the community is preferable to Adam's future as a man who has been released from law because he is incapable of law, though included in the community. Or how should one imagine the life of one recognized as incapable of law, a life without legal autonomy, though released into freedom?

4. *Excursus: The dilemma of rights*

The Prince of Homburg, who has been challenged by the Great Elector to convict himself, similarly asks himself what sort of life he would lead if he were to refuse to do so. His answer is that a life released from the rule of law would be a life of labor, of labor for its own sake:

> I shall go to my property on the Rhine
> And there I'll work at building and unbuilding
> And there I'll sweat and there I'll sow and harvest
> As though for wife and child, enjoy alone
> And when I've harvested I'll sow again
> And keep life rushing through a ceaseless round
> Until, come evening, it lies down and dies.
> (*The Prince of Homburg*, 176; translation modified)[65]

The life of one who no longer conceives of herself or himself as a participant in law is a life in the senselessly accelerating cycle of labor for labor's sake. No longer part of law and hence an equal citizen, they finds themselves in the unnatural natural state of unbridled economic activity.

The Prince of Homburg's answer to his own question is Kleist's reconstruction of how the bourgeois society that is just establishing itself institutionalizes the self-reflective delimitation of law, its releasing of the non-legal: in the form of the "subjective right." Adam already resorts to this figure to interpret Eve, when he remarks about the speech in which she asserts her right to remain silent that "the girl knows what the rules are well enough" (*The Broken Jug*, 43). In German, he uses a peculiar trope: "Die Jungfer weiß, wo unsre Zäume hängen," "the girl knows where our bridles hang." *Vinculum iuris*, the bridle, fetter, or tie of law, is the Roman legal term for the obligation "by which we are reduced to the necessity of paying something in compliance with the laws of our state."[66] This necessity incumbent upon one side corresponds to the legal claim to the payment the other side can assert. It becomes a "subjective right" in the modern sense when, as in Adam's interpretation of Eve's speech, it becomes a right vis-à-vis the state: a right not yet to some benefit afforded by the state – that does not exist until the invention of "subjective public rights" (Georg Jellinek) – but a right to the existence of a sphere of "private," which is to say, social, relations unencumbered by state regulation. These relations are defined by spaces of personal discretion one private citizen reserves vis-à-vis another, and every private citizen vis-à-vis the polity of which he or she is a member. The modern figure of the subjective right thus introduces a fundamental discontinuity into the classical definition of law as the normative order that establishes the equality of the citizens. According to the classical definition, the institution of a legal order transforms "each individual [*individu*] … into a part [*partie*] of a larger whole" (Rousseau). The figure of the subjective right, by contrast, is the figure of a right vis-à-vis – being a part of, participation in – the law: a right to be allowed to act, within certain limitations, "at one's own discretion," without having to answer for one's actions and without responsibility for the consequences; a right to be not entirely and not in every respect an equal "part," but an "individual" released from such participation. The figure of the subjective right (Marx summarizes this discontinuity between the modern doctrine of private law and the classical concept of law) implies the "division of the human being into a public man and a private man," a "dualism between individual life and species-life."[67]

The details of this figure, of its description and its rationales, are of no importance to the present context. What matters is that liberalism or bourgeois society (both are the same: they are the theory and practice of subjective or private law) are defined by a double trait: first, the freedom from participation in law; second, the dualism of state and society, public and private, *citoyen* and bourgeois, subject and individual, and so on.

(1) The liberating impulse of liberalism lies in its questioning and delimiting participation in law: being part of, being an equal citizen, being a member in the legal realm and affirming that membership – in the highest, the autonomous form of law – by free submission to the compulsion to judge oneself. In the eyes of liberalism, these are not the definitions of freedom but the roots of what, in the last consequence, amounts to terror. Revolutionary terror, which, according to Robespierre, is "nothing other than prompt, severe, unbending justice,"[68] is in the liberal interpretation merely the purest and excessive realization of the unlimited claims law, as defined by Rousseau, makes upon those who are its "parts." According to liberalism, the equality of citizens as participants in law, in its unlimited and total implementation – as practiced in the cities of the ancient world, a practice the French Revolution sought to revive under modern conditions – creates a situation in which "the individual, almost always sovereign in public affairs, [is] a slave in all his private relations."[69] This "servitude" (Benjamin Constant) of participation in law is to be broken by law limiting its power over the individual, by releasing the individual from the power of law.

(2) Liberalism or bourgeois society implements this program of liberation as a partialization of partiality, by partitioning the being-part: liberalism or bourgeois society effects a partial liberation. It does so by securing a space of private discretion protected against the intervention of legal regulation. In the liberal, self-delimiting legal order of bourgeois society, the order of subjective rights, "privilege[s] [grant] an individual autonomy to regulate, within certain limitations, his relations with others by his own transactions."[70] The liberation from law becomes, in liberalism, the legal

> protection of the "freedom of contract" vis-à-vis law. "However, this amorphous autonomy," Max Weber notes rather disilluisoned, "merits the designation of 'autonomy' only in a metaphorical sense."[71] As the legal order of "those segments of society that [are] oriented towards power in the market," which is to say, as the legal license to negotiate the terms of contracts freely and thus to take advantage of and exploit those who are without "power in the market," the legal liberation from legal regulation leads to the emergence of an ensemble of social coercions that in fact interferes with the life of every individual only more effectively because it "[carefully avoids] the use of authoritarian forms." The liberal, bourgeois program of liberation – the program of the "decrease of constraint and [the] increase of individual freedom"[72] – produces its opposite, heightened dependency: "A legal order which contains ever so few mandatory and prohibitory norms and ever so many 'freedoms' and 'empowerments' can nonetheless in its practical effects facilitate a very considerable escalation not only of coercion in general but quite specifically of authoritarian coercion."[73]

That describes the dilemma of liberalism: in the form of subjective rights, the liberation of the individual from the coercion to become in his or her entirety a part of the legal order amounts to nothing other than the liberalization of his pursuit of his private interests. Such liberalization, however, restitutes a fate-like ensemble of coercions in which not only every individual is at the mercy of someone else's discretion, but all (together) become dependant on the operation of uncontrollable laws of the market. The liberal liberation from legal "servitude" (Constant) ultimately leads to a "very considerable escalation" of economic and social coercion.

Liberalism wants to break the power of fate that the autonomous law exercises in the subject by limiting the legal autonomy of the *citoyen* with the free discretion of the bourgeois – the freedom to pursue their interests, even by taking advantage of and exploiting others. The liberation from the compulsion to participate in law, in the form of subjective rights, proceeds in dualistic fashion: it contrasts law and interest, equality and egoism, obligation and discretion. Every individual is supposed to be free to stand on both sides, to operate in both registers. But the two sides are external to each other. The dualistic fundamental assumption of liberalism that finds expression in the form of subjective rights is that there is, *on the one hand*, the autonomous conduct that internalizes the legal regulation and thus realizes the equal participation of the *citoyen* in law, and, *on the other hand*, the pursuit of private interests, released from the equal consideration due to others. Liberalism implements the program of delimiting law by distinguishing and contrasting these two sides. Yet this liberal "art of separation" (Michael Walzer) leaves what it separates unaltered. That is in fact what the liberal "art of separation" intends: to avoid or fend off fundamental change. The liberal "art of separating" the legal from the non-legal believes that it can break the violence of law merely by limiting its reach – which is to say, without having to *change how* the law *judges*.

5. *After liberalism: The paradox of law*

The dualism of bourgeois liberalism consists in confronting autonomous participation in the law and the right of free non-participation as mutually external registers. As a consequence, liberalism identifies freedom from the law without further ado with the right to pursue one's interests "at one's discretion." That is because the liberal dualism fails to appreciate the constitutive asymmetry between the two domains. In the form of subjective rights, the law and the non-legal do not actually confront each other as mutually external. As a right to the non-legal, to the freedom from participation in law, the subjective right is itself an element of law. That may seem a trivial observation, but it is not. The fact that the subjective right is a right to non-participation in law is a reminder that it was a process of self-reflection of law that engendered the form of the subjective right. The form of the subjective right is the *effect* of an *act* – of a legal act of a new and paradoxical form:

an act by virtue of which law relates *within* itself *to* itself *as different from* the non-legal.[74] The bourgeois-liberal dualism fails to see that it presupposes a new mode of operation of law without thinking it: The external contrast between law and the non-legal presupposes that law no longer merely seeks to prevail over the non-legal, but now relates to the non-legal from which it distinguishes itself – and thus contains the non-legal as distinct within itself. Therein lies the critique of bourgeois-liberal dualism: in revealing the self-reflective operation of law that underlies this dualism even as it is concealed and repressed by it. This disclosure of the self-reflection of law will show how the "relief" of law may be understood and implemented beyond liberalism.

* * *

"Self-reflection of law", sc. the reflection of law – objectively and subjectively; reflection on law by law – as different from the non-legal. The difference from the non-legal, as we have seen (I.3/5), is constitutive of law: law always already differs from, which is also to say relates to, the non-legal. Relation to the non-legal is not something that begins only with self-reflective law: even law in its "day-to-day operation," law as it is commonly practiced, relates to the non-legal. The accomplishment of the self-reflection of law is (merely) to highlight that and how law in its ordinary operation does so, and (merely) by highlighting this fact, the self-reflection of law changes ("relieves": disempowers and releases) law.

Law is antithetical to what is unlawful: it is antithetical to whom who, or that which, breaches the equality of law for the sake of what is particularly his or hers or its. But law is antithetical also to the non-legal: it is antithetical to whom who, or that which, evades the judgment finding him or her or it to be lawful or unlawful; to whom who or that which is oblivious of law, refuses it, or is incapable of participating in it. Any act of legal judgment is accordingly guided not only by the pretension to validity within law, which is to say, it not only seeks to combat what is unlawful; it also seeks to prevail over the non-legal, over obliviousness or refusal of law or the incapacity to participate in it. This pretension of law to prevail over the non-legal leads to the cycle of violence to which fate seems to doom law; because it is law, as established by the polity, that engenders the non-legal and presupposes it as its counterpart, it cannot ever prevail over the non-legal. Yet law cannot abdicate its pretension to prevail, which is to say its rule over, the non-legal. That is because the pretension to prevail over the non-legal follows from law's very pretension to validity. It is the *right of law* to prevail over the non-legal; it is the very right of law that is the root of its fateful violence.

Yet what applies within law must also apply to the right of law vis-à-vis the non-legal: that there is no right against something or someone that isn't a right *for* that something or someone. It defines the justice of law that its judgment is valid only because it is in the end always the judgment of the something or someone being judged. That is why the autonomous form of law, which ties its obligatory application to the freedom of self-judgment, is the purest form of legal normativity. So if law prevails over the non-legal and, in doing so, proclaims its right – the right to assert law against the non-legal; if, more precisely, law prevails over the non-legal because that is the pretension, the right, of law; then law must maintain that it has the right to do so by the non-legal's own measure – because its doing so is the "own right" (Hegel) of the non-legal. The *right of law* to prevail over the non-legal is, according to the concept of law, at once the *right of the non-legal*: the right of the non-legal to be involved in law that prevails over it, to be taken into account and bring itself to bear in law.

In its ordinary operation, law assumes that these two pretensions are identical: it is the right of law that it not merely must, but also may prevail over the non-legal; at the same time, law's prevailing over the non-legal is considered to be the realization of the non-legal's own right. This assumption of identity constitutes the ideology of law in its ordinary operation: the right of law and the right of the non-legal are one and the same; one is realized at once in the realization of the other. The self-reflection of law, however, shows that these two claims are mutually contradictory precisely because they are dialectically interlocked. And even more: both claims are self-contradictory. By asserting its right against the non-legal, law at once proclaims the right of the non-legal. But the *only* way for law to realize the right of the non-legal is by violating that right.

That is due to the manner in which law can only realize the right of the non-legal that it must assert: it can only be by means of law's "own (and always only its own!) operations"[75] that law seeks to bring the right of the non-legal to bear. Law can only relate to the non-legal in legal form. As with any claim, law turns the claim of the non-legal into a legal claim; it makes the non-legal a party in a legal proceeding. The legal proceeding consists in bringing the equality of the parties to the dispute as citizens to bear in an impartial consideration of both. So for law to execute its proceeding of impartial hearing, examination, and judgment, it must always already have executed a pre-proceeding: a procedure before the procedure, in which the non-legal has been rendered legal, the non-citizen a citizen, the unequal equal – in which law has engendered the elements that it can use in its proceeding. A pre-proceeding of juridification takes place in any legal proceeding. So if law seeks to realize the right of the non-legal that it asserts, it must lend legal form to the non-legal, or in other words, it must juridify what is not juridical. That is to say, it must strip the non-legal precisely of the difference from law that constitutes it and to which it maintains its right. Realizing and violating the right of the non-legal in law are one and the same thing.

The self-reflection of law reveals the contradiction between the two pretensions – the right of law to prevail over the non-legal, and the right of the non-legal to be taken into account in law that prevails over it – whose identity law maintains in its ordinary operation. It further emerges in the self-reflection of law that this contradiction cannot be dissolved: no one of these rights can be thought without the other that contradicts it. The contradiction of law that erupts in its self-reflection is accordingly not a crisis that is capable, or in need, of a decision – not one to be resolved by a critical approach, which is to say, a "discriminating and decisive approach" (Benjamin). The contradiction of law constitutes a paradox that needs to be given full expression.

That happens in an implementation of law that tries to satisfy two mutually exclusive demands at once.[76] This must be an implementation that realizes law *and* disrupts it; an implementation that enacts the equality of the citizens *and* realizes the difference between citizen and non-citizen, between participant in law and one who is oblivious of, refuses, or is incapable of law; an implementation that executes an impartial proceeding *and* goes back to before the pre-proceeding of juridification from which the legal proceeding emerges. The self-reflective implementation of law realizes the right of law *and* the right of the non-legal by not turning the non-legal into an element – a party, a case – in a legal proceeding, but instead bringing it to bear against its juridification. Implementing law in a self-reflective manner means meticulously executing the proceeding of impartial-egalitarian examination, consideration, and judgment *and* releasing the non-legal forces of "distraction" – of obliviousness, refusal, and incapacity. In this counteraction of the forces of distraction, the identity of self and law to which the autonomous law curses us – the identity of self and law that every one of us must perpetually assert against him- or herself as a non-citizen in order to thereby subject themselves afresh into citizenship as equal participation in law – breaks apart. The self-reflective implementation of law bursts the autonomous identity of self and law and lends full expression to the contradiction, which is to say the unity of unity and contradiction, of citizen and non-citizen, of participation in and obliviousness, refusal, incapacity of law.

Does such a liberation from the legal curse of autonomous self-judgment by virtue of the self-reflective expression of the paradox of law and non-law exist?

6. *The utopia of equal possibility* (Volokolamsk Highway I)

In the short play *Volokolamsk Highway I: Russian Opening*,[77] Heiner Müller stages the following plot. A Soviet battalion is stationed just outside Moscow with instructions to defend the city against the superior and rapidly advancing German troops, which strikes fear into the soldiers' hearts; more and more desert. The commander, convinced that "only terror drives out fear," feigns a German attack ("I yelled alarm and To arms"), which only turnes fear into panic; the soldiers flee into the forest in a stampede. One of them, an officer, shoots himself in the hand as he flees to make himself unfit for action. The man is arrested, and a lieutenant brings him before the commander. The commander asks the lieutenant: "Why didn't you shoot him?" – "I don't know" – "And I'm supposed to know / Bring him in." The officer apologizes, making the excuse that it was an accident and the whole thing was only an exercise anyway. The commander calls him a coward and "traitor of the homeland" and sentences him to be shot by his own men in front of the battalion an hour later.

> The lieutenant asked Do we have the right
> I said My order will be obeyed
> And if it was unjust let me be shot
> You write the report comrade lieutenant[78]

The officer who became a traitor to his battalion and homeland, who proved unable to lead his troops "because he could not command himself," *must* be convicted. "How should I have ordered otherwise?"

The conviction of the traitor is an "order" of the commander, and it remains unclear whether he has the right to issue it; the lieutenant raises the question, and the commander does not give an affirmative answer. The commander does not *assert* that he is right. He leaves the question of his right unanswered, submitting it to a later reader of the report. Just as the lieutenant did not know why he did not shoot the officer on the spot, the commander does not know why he now orders him to be shot. The order does not flow from a knowledge of law and unlawfulness, right and wrong. A margin separates the knowledge of the law and the act that executes it, an unclear relation – just as the commander will later say, in retrospect, that "I had [him] shot and in accordance with martial law." The commander's order is issued – *and in accordance with* martial law. That the order is issued in accordance with martial law does not mean that it *issues from* martial law. The commander orders the execution – "How should I have ordered otherwise?" – without claiming to know that the law orders him to do so. It is an order, without knowledge of the law, and in that sense is a law-free (not a lawless) order; an order that disengages from knowledge of the law and so, because it does not presuppose law and knowledge of the law as its basis, does not issue from law and knowledge of the law; an order counter to law: not counter to this or that law, but counter to law as such; counter to the right of law to make a binding determination of what will hold among us.

The distance separating the commander's order from knowledge of the law, the "and" that separates them by tying them together, is capable of two antithetical interpretations. The commander's order initially appears to be an act of the "suspension" of the law, in the precise sense of that term elaborated by Schmitt (see above, p. 36). The commander has the officer shot without having conducted a formal legal proceeding to the point where a verdict follows. The objective is clear: so that "this pile of humans / Becomes a battalion before the first battle." The commander strips one of his right – his right to law: his right to be a party in a proceeding, and hence his right to be an equal citizen – to introduce a setting, where the questions of right and wrong, of lawful und unlawful, also in regards to the commander's own actions, can still and again be asked at all; a setting necessary for there to even *be* equal Soviet citizens. This necessary condition for law is the successful defense against, and victory over, the Germans.[79] Securing this prerequisite of law is the objective of the commander's order counter to the knowledge of the law. By having the one shot, the commander wants to establish unity among the rest of the soldiers, who are the executors and spectators of his execution:

> Does it take a dead man
> Or the sight of such a death
> For a battalion to become a battalion[80]

But also the commander's question regarding the impact/efficacy, just like the lieutenant's concerning the lawfulness of the execution remains unanswered: Does it take a dead man or the sight of such a death for the unity, for the order upon which law rests law to be established? "The soldiers' backs and the swaying / Of their rifles asked me Why."

Since the commander doesn't have an answer to this question, he suddenly retracts his order and lets the officer, who had asked for forgiveness, live:

> … not opening my lips I spoke
> Put on your coat again and I He asked
> The coat So I shall not be shot
> And I Resume your post You'll fight won't you
> And Yes sure I shall fight said he
> And tried to put his coat on couldn't find
> With his bandaged hand the way into the sleeve
> He laughed with us freed of the awful burden
> Which had been pressing on him for an hour
> With all the weight of earth to cover him
> Ten hands were grabbing at his coat and pulling
> So his hand would search into the sleeve And back
> And forth and there was no end to their laughter[81]

Until, in a second sudden twist, this "film" is ripped apart by the commander's order to fire, wiping out the image of deliverance: "And the volley cracked / From twelve rifles like a single shot." The order prevails over the "wishful image of the pardon," as Müller put it in a note accompanying his play.[82] But once the film of pardon and liberated laughter has played, it is no longer the same order: it is still the order to shoot the officer, "and in accordance with martial law"; an order that accords with the law without following from it; but it is no longer an order that "suspends" the legal order in the Schmittian sense of the term.

The order that suspends the law is at once legitimized by law: it secures the order which law presupposes. By contrast, the act of pardoning the convicted offender, that other traditional form of sovereignty,[83] is not concerned with the order of normality as the prerequisite of law. It is concerned instead with a justice beyond the rule of law. This possibility, the "wishful image of the pardon," appears in the "film" that plays – where? not only in the commander's mind, but on the stage, in the reality of the play – only to be abruptly cut short by the order to fire. In a note on the staging of the play, Müller insisted that the pardon and execution should be performed in such a manner that they have the same "degree of reality": "The wishful image of the deserter being pardoned needs the degree of realism of the execution for a war to be conceivable in which the pardon is the realistic solution. In the shadow of nuclear war, the alternative to communism, it would seem utopian."[84] Therein, says Müller, lies the moment's utopian aspect. It is *not* the pardon *instead of* the execution that is utopian, but the idea that that the pardon is the "realistic solution." "Realistic" means possible, even probable, but not necessarily the sole possibility. What is utopian in Müller's view, is that the pardon has the "degree of realism of the execution," that it is *just* as realistic, which is to say, possible or probable, as the execution.

By implication and conversely, the execution order is just as possible as the pardon. The order to execute, "and in accordance with martial law," is not a necessity either, but one of two possibilities. That is the new quality the order gains – or to put it more precisely, that is the new interpretation the doubt and lack of knowledge that surround it gain – by the confrontation with the possibility of a pardon. It is revealed that the order is merely one possibility that carries the other possibility within itself, just as, from now on and all the way from Moscow to Berlin, the commander will have the executed officer with him as his "other I." Implicit in them is this other possibility that negates their own possibility: implicit in the order is the possibility of a pardon; implicit in the commander is the possibility that it is he who was executed ("And always the dead man walks my step"). A "war" rages between these two possibilities, a war in the mind of the commander, who acted "and in accordance with" the law: and "in my mind the war no longer ends."

The fact that the execution order is issued in accordance with martial law but does not issue from knowledge of the law; the fact that the lieutenant's question "Do we have the right?" remains without answer; the fact that the order is without a sufficient basis in the law: these do not imply the hard necessity of preserving the legal order by suspending conclusive resolution of the legal question. On the contrary, they indicate the possibility of utopia. Yet utopia is not the realm of mercy beyond law. The promise of a realm beyond law, as Shylock learned,[85] merely leads to the inversion of law into unlawfulness. For the rule of law is the equality of citizens; beyond law, inequality rules. The utopian idea that emerges in the doubt whether the execution is founded on the law, whether it is necessary by law, and that opposes its suspension, is not about transcending law but about depotentiating it: by seeing law and its application become one possibility. Utopia is the equality of possibility between the legal equality of citizens *and* their non-legal inequality as non-citizens. This utopian equality is not a criterion or basis for anything. It does not define a yardstick for decision-making, instead demanding that every decision – the decision in accordance with the law as much as the one counter to the law – issue from the self-reflection of law, its self-reflection in the relation that constitutes it.

Yet because the commander's execution order – the order to execute "and in accordance with martial law" – does exactly that, it takes on a utopian aspect, its obvious violence notwithstanding. It is issued *in accordance with* martial law *and* in relation to non-law. In the commander's execution order, both have become equal possibilities; both have gained the same "degree of reality." Law ultimately prevails over non-law, the commander orders not to pardon but to execute, yet even in doing so, he no longer maintains and enforces the right of law against non-law. The utopian aspect of his order lies in how it is enacted: in the fact that he relieves law itself in its relation to the non-legal into something non-legal. That is why the commander does not exonerate himself of the responsibility for his decision by passing that responsibility to the law. And it is also why the commander does not demand the condemned man's consent to his order as one would to a legal conviction. His order lets the execution appear exactly as what it is – frank violence – whereas law eternalizes all frank violence by rendering it fateful. That is why the war in the commander's mind, the war between law and the non-legal, between the right of law and the non-right of law, no longer ends.

* * *

The relief of law is neither the end of law nor the beginning of non-violence. It is the disruption of the fateful violence law exercises because it believes it is right, because it believes in its right over the non-legal. The relief of law puts an end to the war law wages on non-law by starting this war within law. "Relieved," both disempowered and liberated, law is at war with itself.

7. A law against its will

Relieved by its self-reflection, law is at battle with itself. The relief of law does not mean that we are "done with judgment"[86] – because the self-reflective implementation of law retains the possibility of judgment ("and in accordance with" the law); the self-reflective implementation of law means being done with being done with, be it being done with judgment or with judgment upon judgment. Nor can the relief transfigure law into a "toy," opening the "[gateway] to a new happiness"[87] – for the self-reflection of law leads into a paradox that does not promise a realm beyond the contention, violence, and suffering against which law takes a stand and that it ends up reenacting within itself. The self-reflective implementation promises nothing more than a law that knows as much about itself.

That is why the self-reflective implementation of law consists in law's "reacting against itself" – as Adorno put it of aesthetic taste[88] – and recognizing itself to be without law. The self-reflective, relieved law is a law that feels *repugnance* for itself, whose flesh creeps at the thought of itself; a law against its own will – the law of the unwilling.

Notes

I would like to thank Thomas Cannaday for his assistance with the final corrections and the index for this volume, C.M.

1 I. Kant, *Metaphysical Elements of Justice*, pt. 1 of *The complete text of the Metaphysics of Morals*, trans. J. Ladd (Indianapolis: Hackett, 2nd edn, 1999), 115.

2 J. Habermas, *Between Facts and Norms*, trans. W. Rehg (Cambridge: Polity, 1996), 391.

3 Kant, *Metaphysical Elements of Justice*, 31.

4 N. Luhmann, *A Sociological Theory of Law*, trans. E. King-Utz and M. Albrow (London: Routledge & Kegan Paul, 1985), 85.

5 Habermas, *Between Facts and Norms*, 28–41. As Habermas notes, the legal theory of what is called "political liberalism" systematically disregards this problem: "Rawls concentrates on questions of the legitimacy of law without an explicit concern for the legal form as such and hence for the *institutional dimension* of a law backed by sanctions. What is specific to legal validity, the tension between facticity and validity inhabiting law itself, does not come into view" (ibid., 64, original emphasis). The exclusion of the question of violence is explicit in Ronald Dworkin, who distinguishes between the "grounds" and the "force of law" – see R. Dworkin, *Law's Empire* (Cambridge, MA: Belknap, 1986), 108–13 – so he can then limit himself to a discussion of the grounds, the – nonviolent – justification, of the law. It is not surprising that he would conclude with the claim that law is, "finally, a fraternal attitude, an expression of how we are united in community though divided in project, interest, and conviction" (*ibid.*, 413).

6 N. Luhmann, *Macht* (Stuttgart: Enke, 1975), 64; trans. G. Jackson. Luhmann discusses not law in particular but, more generally, the interrelation between power and violence, which, like Hannah Arendt – see H. Arendt, *On Violence* (New York: Houghton Mifflin Harcourt, 1970), 50–52 – he strictly distinguishes with regard to their mode of operation: power is "the transfer of operations of selection" (Luhmann, *Macht*, 11 and see also 60) and so presupposes alternatives; violence, by contrast, is an "avoidance-alternative" (*ibid.*, 64). On the following, see *ibid.*, 61f.

7 Luhmann, *A Sociological Theory of Law*, 86, 89.

8 For a good summary of this critical description of law (with which the author's own position by no means coincides; see below, p. 16), see Robert Cover, "Violence and the Word," in *Narrative, Violence, and the Law: The Essays of Robert Cover*, eds M. Minow, M. Ryan, and A. Arat (Ann Arbor: The University of Michigan Press, 1992), 202–38.

9 Luhmann, *Macht*, 64.

10 In the original plan for the *Dialectic of the Enlightenment*, it was not Odysseus but Oedipus who was its hero.

11 The state of nature is "fictitious" in the sense that it is made, invented, or produced: it is made by the very state of law that presents itself as the answer to it. The state of nature does not precede the state of law (as the philosophies of legitimation aver); the former is the latter's own product. See section I.5 below.

12 Aeschylus, *Eumenides*, in *Aeschylus*, trans. H. W. Smyth (Cambridge, MA: Harvard University Press, 1926), 490–91. Cited in the following as *Eumenides*. In this as in all crucial passages, what tragedy says about law is at once said about tragedy itself: the *katastrophé*, the "reversal toward demise," quotes the *strophé*, the turning of the chorus in its dance towards one side of the stage (and the section of the choral song sung in this direction), which is followed by the *antistrophé*, the reversal in the other direction.

13 Aeschylus, *Agamemnon*, in *Aeschylus*, trans. H. W. Smyth (Cambridge, MA: Harvard University Press, 1926), 461–66. Cited in the following as *Agamemnon*.

14 It does not matter at whose hands, how, or by which means retribution is exacted: "The case now stands where it stands – it moves to fulfilment at its destined end. Not by offerings burned in secret, not by secret libations, not by tears, shall man soften the stubborn wrath of unsanctified sacrifices" (*Agamemnon*, 67–71).

15 Marcel Hénaff, *The Price of Truth: Gift, Money, and Philosophy*, trans. J.-L. Morhange and A.-M. Feenberg-Dibon (Stanford: Stanford University Press, 2010), 215.

16 René Girard, *Violence and the Sacred*, trans. P. Gregory (London: Continuum, 2005), 15. Girard writes that that is how it appears "in Greek tragedy, for instance" (*ibid.*). The connection is much closer: it is only in (not before and not outside) tragedy that retribution appears in this light. Hénaff rightly points this out (*The Price of Truth*, 279), but his explanation for the nexus is that tragedy sides with the polis against retribution. Yet the negative

assessment of retribution in tragedy is already a consequence of the logic of its representation: It is only in (not before and not outside) a mode of representation that (re)counts everything it represents not once but twice that retribution can appear in this light.

17 Aristotle, *Poetics*, trans. M. Heath (New York: Penguin, 1996), 49a.

18 See Heidegger's remark on the concept of procedure in Plato: M. Heidegger, *Parmenides*, trans. A. Schuwer and R. Rojcewicz (Bloomington: Indiana University Press, 1998), 128. See also M. Foucault, "Truth and Juridical Forms," in *Power*, ed. J. D. Faubion (New York: The New Press, 2000), 6–89. On the uncertainty of the outcome as a fundamental requirement of all procedures, including the legal proceeding, see N. Luhmann, *Legitimation durch Verfahren* (Neuwied: Luchterhand, 1969), 40, 116.

19 That is a fundamental hypothesis in C. Meier, "Aischylos' Eumeniden und das Aufkommen des Politischen," in *Die Entstehung des Politischen bei den Griechen* (Frankfurt am Main: Suhrkamp, 1980), 144–246. See also the explication of equality as isonomy in C. Meier, *Entstehung des Begriffs "Demokratie"* (Frankfurt am Main: Suhrkamp, 1970), 36ff.

20 "He who dares to undertake the establishment of a people [*d'instituer un peuple*] should feel that he is, so to speak, in a position to change human nature, to transform each individual (who by himself is a perfect and solitary whole), into a part [*partie*] of a larger whole from which this individual receives, in a sense, his life and his being; to alter man's constitution in order to strengthen it; to substitute a partial [*partielle*] and moral existence for the physical and independent existence we have all received from nature. In a word, he must deny man his own forces in order to give him forces that are alien to him and that he cannot make use of without the help of others" (J.-J. Rousseau, *On the Social Contract*, book II, chapter 7: "On the Legislator," trans. D. A. Cress (Indianapolis: Hackett, 1987), 39).

21 For a brief overview of the back-and-forth between the two views in Athens, see C.-M. Zeitler, *Zwischen Formalismus und Freiheit: Das Rechts- und Richterbild im attischen Recht am Beispiel des Prozesses gegen Sokrates* (Baden-Baden: Nomos, 2010), 17–51. See also Meier, "Aischylos' Eumeniden und das Aufkommen des Politischen," 214ff.

22 Much later, Tocqueville shares this view. In the chapter of his book about America being dedicated to "that which tempers the tyranny of the majority in the United States," he writes: "One therefore finds, hidden in the depths

of lawyers' souls, some of the tastes and habits of aristocracy. The legal profession shares aristocracy's instinctive preference for order and natural love of formalities, as well as its deep distaste for the actions of the multitude and secret contempt for popular government [...] in a society in which no one contests the right of lawyers to occupy the high position that is naturally their due, their spirit will be eminently conservative and anti-democratic" (A. de Tocqueville, *Democracy in America*, trans. A. Goldhammer (New York: Library of America, 2004), 304–305). On the anti-democratic character of the rule of law (and its legitimation in the legal philosophy of liberalism) see M. Walzer, "Democracy and Philosophy," *Political Theory*, 9 (1981), 379–99. For a neat example, note Dworkin's assertion that "the courts are the capitals of law's empire, and judges are its princes"; see Dworkin, *Law's Empire*, 407.

23 R. Cover, "Nomos and Narrative," in *Narrative, Violence, and the Law*, 139–40; and see the succinct summary of his argument: "Judges are people of violence. Because of the violence they command, judges characteristically do not create the law, but kill it. Theirs is the jurispathic office. Confronting the luxuriant growth of a hundred legal traditions, they assert that this one is law and destroy or try to destroy the rest" (*ibid.*, 155).

24 "Who, if he did not train his heart in fear, either city or mortal, would still revere justice in the same way? Do not approve of a lawless life or one subject to a tyrant" (*Eumenides*, 522–28).

25 Euripides, *Orestes*, in *The Complete Greek Drama*, vol. 2, trans. E. P. Coleridge (New York: Random House, 1938), 256, 261. Cited in the following as *Orestes.*

26 "The fact that an act is the execution of a death sentence and not an act of murder, this quality – which is imperceptible to the senses – becomes recognizable only after a process of reflection: after the confrontation with the criminal code and the code of criminal procedure" (H. Kelsen, *Reine Rechtslehre: Einleitung in die rechtswissenschaftliche Problematik* [Studienausgabe, 1st edn, 1934], ed. Matthias Jestaedt (Tübingen: Mohr Siebeck, 2008), 19).

27 That is Hegel's description of "unintentional" (or "ingenuous": *unbefangen*) wrong; see G. W. F. Hegel, *Elements of the Philosophy of Right*, trans. H. B. Nisbet (Cambridge: Cambridge University Press, 1991), §§ 84–86.

28 For the retributive justice, "there is as yet no performance of an act" (G. W. F. Hegel, *Phenomenology of Mind*, trans. J. B. Baillie (London: MacMillan, 1931), 267–68).

29 Giorgio Agamben has described this structure of the relation between law and the non-legal or extra-legal – where law must both forever generate and suppress again and again; which thus accompanies law and at once confronts law as its other – in his critical engagement with Schmitt's concept of the exception; see G. Agamben, *State of Exception*, trans. K. Attell (Chicago: University of Chicago Press, 2005), 22–24. Law cannot be brought to bear against the extra-legal by legal process; *ibid.*, 41, 59–60.

30 Sophocles, *Oedipus The King*, trans. F. Storr (San Diego: ICON Classics, 2005), 95–98. Cited in the following as *Oedipus*. On the following, see C. Menke, *Tragic Play: Irony and Theater from Sophocles to Beckett*, trans. J. Phillips (New York: Columbia University Press, 2009), part I: "The Excess of Judgment: A Reading of *Oedipus The King*."

31 The (only) difference between retribution and sacrifice is that sacrifice is a violent deed reestablishing justice that is not followed by an answer, because it is for its part not experienced as excessive, not as a deed. The sacrifice is "an act of violence without risk of vengeance" (Girard, *Violence and the Sacred*, 13), with which it is finished. Tragedy commences with the experience that that is no longer believed of any sacrifice: Agamemnon's sacrifice of Iphigenia must be avenged, and so on.

32 F. Hölderlin, "Remarks on 'Oedipus,'" in *Essays on Letters and Theory*, trans. T. Pfau (Albany: State University of New York Press, 1988), 103.

33 "[…] and the man who fails to prosecute him when he ought, or fails to warn him of the fact that he is thus debarred, if he be of kin to the dead man on either the male or female side, and not further removed than a cousin, shall, first, receive upon himself the defilement and the wrath of the gods, since the curse of the law brings also upon him that of the divine voice, and, secondly, he shall be liable to the action of whosoever pleases to punish him on behalf of the dead man" (Plato, *Laws*, in *Plato in Twelve Volumes*, vols 10 and 11, trans. R. G. Bury (Cambridge, MA: Harvard University Press, 1967 and 1968), 871 a–b).

34 That is the difference between the curse of the law and the "ban" that – as Agamben argues, following Jean-Luc Nancy – the sovereign imposes on the extra-legal ("life") in the name of law he or she simultaneously suspends; see G. Agamben, *Homo Sacer: Sovereign Power and Bare Life*, trans. D. Heller-Roazen (Stanford: Stanford University Press, 1998), 23. The curse of the law consists in the fact that law condemns everyone to impose this ban *on themselves* (which is to say, to become an autonomous "subject" of law):

that is the central hypothesis of M. Foucault, *Discipline and Punish: The Birth of the Prison*, trans. A. Sheridan (New York: Vintage, 2nd edn, 1995), which Agamben fails to appreciate due to his fixation on the concept of sovereignty. Note also Gilles Deleuze's suggestion that, with the rise of Christianity – but "perhaps *Oedipus* prefigures this new state in the Greek world" – "dividing oneself into lots and punishing oneself become the characteristics of the new judgment or modern tragedy" (G. Deleuze, "To Have Done with Judgment," in *Essays Critical and Clinical*, trans. D. W. Smith and M. A. Greco (London and New York: Verso, 1998), 129).

35 That is already Creon's take on law when he says to Oedipus: "Then next, if you have found that I have planned anything in concert with the soothsayer, take and slay me, by the sentence not of one mouth, but of two – by my own no less than yours" (*Oedipus*, 605–607). And it is still this understanding of law that the Great Elector of Brandenburg demands of the Prince of Homburg when he puts the judgment of the latter's insubordination into the defendant's own hands: "How should I / Oppose the opinion of such a soldier? / I have in my heart, as you must surely know, / Respect in the highest degree for what he feels. / If he can hold the judgment to be unjust / I will annul it: he is free" (Heinrich von Kleist, *The Prince of Homburg*, in *Selected Writings*, trans. D. Constantine, Indianapolis: Hackett, 2004, 181).

36 "The commandment of right is therefore: *Be a person and respect others as persons!*" Hegel, *Elements of the Philosophy of Right*, § 36. The theory of the autonomous law reads the first of the three precepts of law enumerated by the Institutes of Justinian – "to live honestly, not to injure another, and to give to each one that which belongs to him" (book I, title I) – as the precept of autonomy and declares it to be the foundation of all law: "*Be an honest person* (*honeste vive*). Juridical honorableness consists of this: maintaining in relation to others one's own worth as a human being. This duty is expressed in the proposition: 'Do not make yourself into a mere means for others, but be at the same time an end for them.' This duty will be explained later as an obligation resulting from the right of humanity in our own Person (*lex iusti*)" (Kant, *Metaphysical Elements of Justice*, 37).

37 It is true: According to the law, Oedipus would not have had to convict himself. Of course he knows (better than anyone else: *Oedipus*, 124–25, 244ff.) that he is not legally guilty of murder and incest because he did not commit them knowingly (he did knowingly commit murder, but not patricide).

And so, we might further argue against Oedipus' self-condemnation, he does not meet the conditions to which his curse is tied, since that curse is inflicted – only – on those who withhold their knowledge; and that is a crime one can only commit knowingly. Still, the very moment Oedipus is identified as the perpetrator, it is also clear to him that he has been condemned because he has cursed himself. That (I would suggest) is not only due to the severity of his crimes. It is also due to the form of judgment: legal judgment is directed at subjects; what they have done to whom. But legal judgment, as it is now revealed, rests – still – on a pre-legal judgment that is directed at events or that judges through accounts of events: that judges that what happened as bad or good. Why must the legal judgment still and forever resort to this pre-legal judgment? Because the latter is the basic form of normativity from which the law's knowledge of right and wrong continues to flow. Law assumes a pre-legal form (in Oedipus' self-conviction) when it is not the application of one or another legal regulation or the enforcement of one interpretation of the law over another, but the law of law – the normativity of law at large – that is at issue. Oedipus judges in pre-legal fashion precisely because law as such is at stake: because, in his self-condemnation, he subjects himself as a lawless person to law. Faced with the lawless person, law assumes pre-legal form: its judgments about acts appear as determinations of fact. In his self-conviction, Oedipus punishes himself for having been, ultimately in the exact sense of his curse, extra-legal.

38 Hegel, *Elements of the Philosophy of Right*, § 100.

39 See C. Beccaria, *On Crimes and Punishments*, trans. G. R. Newman and P. Marongiu (New Brunswick: Transaction, 2009). Michel Foucault has reconstructed the gradual adoption of this answer; see Foucault, *Discipline and Punish*, 104–34.

40 W. Benjamin, "Critique of Violence," in *Selected Writings*, vol. 1: *1913–1926*, eds M. Bullock and M. Jennings (Cambridge, MA: Harvard University Press, 1996), 236–52. Cited in the following as "Critique".

41 According to Arendt, violence that, "having destroyed all power, does not abdicate" is terror (Arendt, *On Violence*, 55).

42 See the preface above.

43 "*Schicksalhafte Gewalt*," rendered by Edmund Jephcott as "fate-imposed violence"; see Benjamin, "Critique of Violence," 247, Translator's note, G.J.

44 Retribution and law correspond to two different forms of fate: mythic and tragic fate, fatality and catastrophe, curse and irony.

45 On the dialectic of the break with and the relapse into myth, see M. Horkheimer and T. W. Adorno, *Dialectic of Enlightenment: Philosophical Fragments*, trans. E. Jephcott (Stanford: Stanford University Press, 2002). In a remark that may be read as a critique of Benjamin, they relate this dialectic to law as well: "In Odysseus's patience – quite clearly after the death of the Suitors – vengeance is already turning into judicial procedure: the ultimate fulfillment of the mythical impulse becomes the objective instrument of domination. Law is vengeance which is capable of renunciation. But since this judicial patience is generated by something outside itself, the longing for the homeland, it takes on human traits, almost a quality of trust, which point beyond vengeance postponed. In fully developed bourgeois society, however, both are annulled: with the idea of vengeance longing, too, is tabooed – thereby, of course, enthroning vengeance, mediated as the self's revenge on itself" (*ibid.*, 262, note 12).

46 That is a condensed summary of Jacques Derrida's extensive critique of Benjamin's program of a "critique" of law; see J. Derrida, "Force of Law: The 'Mystical Foundation of Authority,'" trans. M. Quaintance, *Cardozo Law Review*, 11 (1990), 921–1045, especially part two. For the ensuing controversy, see A. Haverkamp (ed.), *Gewalt und Gerechtigkeit: Derrida – Benjamin* (Frankfurt am Main: Suhrkamp, 1994). On the possibility of reading Benjamin's figures of "divine," "pure," or "revolutionary" violence *with* Derrida, see B. Menke, "Benjamin vor dem Gesetz: Die Kritik der Gewalt in der Lektüre Derridas," *ibid.*, 217–75.

47 See Agamben, *State of Exception*, chapter 4. (This should put an end to the obscure murmurings about an alleged "concurrence of the extremes" between Benjamin and Schmitt.)

48 C. Schmitt, *Political Theology: Four Chapters on the Concept of Sovereignty*, trans. G. Schwab (Cambridge, MA: MIT Press, 1985), 12.

49 See above, p. 32.

50 See *Deutsches Rechtswörterbuch* (http://drw-www.adw.uni-heidelberg.de/drw/) s.v. "Entsetzung"; J. Grimm and W. Grimm, *Deutsches Wörterbuch* (Leipzig: Hirzel, 1854–1960), vol. 3, cols 623–25: "1) *abrogatio, dejectio de gradu, ademtio muneris:* entsetzung eines edlen zů einem unedlen. MAALER 106a.b; excommunicatio, [...] 2) *liberatio urbis, exercitus:* damit

der kriegsherr, wenn er von ihnen, wie die besatzung so wol versehen, auch wie das volk darinnen so beherzt sei, erfehrt, ein entsetzung darob empfahe. FRONSPERG 1, 96."

51 That is Heidegger's response to the violence of law, which he clearly indicated; see Heidegger, *Parmenides*, 40–42, on the commanding or "imperial" character of law, and M. Heidegger, "Anaximander's Saying," in *Off the Beaten Track*, trans. J. Young and K. Haynes (Cambridge: Cambridge University Press, 2002), 242–81, on the idea of a pre-legal – pre-subjective, non-procedural, and non-political – justice. See also E. Wolf, *Griechisches Rechtsdenken*, vol. I: *Vorsokratiker und frühe Dichter* (Frankfurt am Main: Klostermann, 1950), 218–34 (Wolf's argument builds on Heidegger's).

52 Schmitt, *Political Theology*, 13. Schmitt regards the "normal situation," conceived as the absence of chaos, as an order before the legal order, as the "presupposition" for the application of law. The "normal situation," however, must properly be understood to be normativity, that is, the willingness and ability to conduct oneself in accordance with norms.

53 Cover shares Benjamin's aesthetically utopian view of pedagogy; see his opposition between the "paideic" and the "imperial" law ("Nomos and Narrative," 105–106). For a different concept of pedagogy in Benjamin (which corresponds to the reflective model of the relief of law sketched in the following), see G. Agamben, *The Open: Man and Animal*, trans. K. Attell (Stanford: Stanford University Press, 2004), 83.

54 N. Luhmann, *Law as a Social System*, trans. K. A. Ziegert (Oxford: Oxford University Press, 2004), 180. On the self-reflection of law, see C. Menke, "Subjektive Rechte: Zur Paradoxie der Form," in Gunther Teubner (ed.), *Nach Jacques Derrida und Niklas Luhmann: Zur (Un-)Möglichkeit einer Gesellschaftstheorie der Gerechtigkeit* (Stuttgart: Lucius & Lucius, 2008), 81–108. I have developed this further in "Materialism of Form: On the Self-Reflection of Law," in Kerstin Blome (ed.), *Contested Regime Collisions: Norm Fragmentation in World Society* (Cambridge: Cambridge University Press, 2016), 281–97.

55 H. von Kleist, *The Broken Jug*, in *Selected Writings*. For some details of the following interpretation, see C. Menke, "Nach dem Gesetz: Zum Schluß des *Zerbrochnen Krugs*," in M. Groß and P. Primavesi (eds), *Lücken sehen …: Beiträge zu Theorie, Literatur und Performance*, Festschrift for Hans-Thies Lehmann (Heidelberg: Winter, 2010), 97–112.

56 *Allgemeines Landrecht für die Preußischen Staaten von 1794*, introd. H. Hattenhauer (Frankfurt am Main and Berlin: Alfred Metzner, 1970), part 2, title 10: "Of the rights and duties of public servants," §§ 94–103: "Demission, removal [*Entsetzung*], and dismissal" (p. 541). Title 17, which treats the juridical institutions, among other subjects, notes under the heading "juridical abuse": "Whosoever abuses his jurisdiction to press those subject to it shall be declared to have permanently forfeited that jurisdiction for his person, in addition to any penalty otherwise imposed on him" (§ 85, p. 623). Section 8 of title 20 ("Of the crimes of public servants") specifies the "Penalties imposed on judicial officers who are in breach of their duties" (§§ 366–408). See also T. Ziolkowski, "Kleists Werk im Lichte der zeitgenössischen Rechtskontroverse," *Kleist-Jahrbuch* 1987, 46–47.

57 Eve's refusal to answer reminds of Shylock, who declared, also in court: "You'll ask me why I rather choose to have / A weight of carrion flesh, than to receive / Three thousand ducats: *I'll not answer that!* / But say it is my humour, – is it answer'd?" *The Merchant of Venice*, ed. J. R. Brown (London: The Arden Shakespeare, 2006), IV.1, 40–44; emphasis added. That is Shylock's explanation of how he understands "your charter and your city's [i.e., Venice's] freedom" (*ibid.*, 39).

58 The right to remain silent is the product of innovations in procedural law in the sixteenth and seventeenth centuries. On the origins and significance of this legal institute, see M. Constable, *Just Silences: The Limits and Possibilities of Modern Law* (Princeton: Princeton University Press, 2005).

59 Kleist's Adam is quoting Kant, who speaks of a "double self" whose destiny is, "on the one hand, [to have] to stand trembling at the bar of a court of justice entrusted to one, but, on the other hand, [to possess] the judgeship by innate authority." "I, the accuser and likewise the accused, am the very same man (*numero idem*)." I. Kant, "Metaphysical Principles of Virtue," in Ethical Philosophy, trans. J. W. Ellington (Indianapolis: Hackett, 2nd edn, 1994), 101; I am grateful to Marina Martínez Mateo for bringing this to my attention. It is important to note that man's duty to be "judge of himself" is a duty of virtue, not a legal obligation, which is to say it cannot be conceived as the substance of a judicial law. But that is not because law does not need this duty; on the contrary, it is because there is no law at all without it; it is not *a* judicial law because it is the law of law.

60 "ADAM: Forgive me, gentlemen. (*He runs away*) / EVE: Be sharp! / RUPRECHT: Grab hold! / EVE: Quick! / ADAM: What?" (*The Broken Jug*, 63; translation modified).

61 It is said of Adam that he is "strangely distracted" (Kleist, *The Broken Jug*, 22). But that is true not only of him: Time and again the inquiry gets off track because the person under interrogation talks about all sorts of things that are "not germane to the matter" (*ibid.*, 25; translation modified), that are "foreign to [the] suit" (*ibid.*, 26), or because the interrogator forgets what he wanted to know or doesn't listen carefully in the first place (*ibid.*, 21–22). The participants often get sidetracked into an unending series of secondary quibbles or are lost in thoughts, reveries, and stories, from which they awake with a baffled start: What? How?

62 But it cannot, as the brief final scene 13 hints, in which Frau Marthe threatens to demand that "justice [be] done" to the jug (Kleist, *The Broken Jug*, 65) by turning to the "administration in Utrecht." This might be the beginning of a new plot (one unsuitable for a comedy): the story of Marthe Kohlhaas.

63 H. von Kleist, *Der Zerbrochne Krug*, in *Sämtliche Werke*, vol. I/3, eds R. Reuß and P. Staengle (Basel and Frankfurt am Main: Stroemfeld and Roter Stern, 1995), 414. (In the printed version, quoted above, Walter merely promises that he "will not force the man to desert"; translation modified.)

64 F. Nietzsche, *On the Genealogy of Morality*, II.15, ed. K. Ansell-Pearson, trans. C. Diethe (Cambridge: Cambridge University Press, 2007), 56.

65 H. von Kleist, *The Prince of Homburg*, in *Selected Writings*.

66 *The Civil Law*, ed. and trans. S. P. Scott, A.M., vol. 2: *The Enactments of Justinian*, I. *The Institutes* (Cincinnati, Ohio: Central Trust Company, 1932), book III, title XIII (www.constitution.org/sps/sps02_j1-3.htm).

67 Karl Marx, "On the Jewish Question" [1844] in *The Marx-Engels Reader*, ed. Robert Tucker, (New York: Norton & Company, 1978), 26–46.

68 M. Robespierre, "Sur les principes de morale politique qui doivent guider la Convention nationale dans l'administration intérieure de la République" [February 5, 1794], in *Écrits*, ed. C. Mazauric (Paris: Messidor, 1989), 300.

69 B. Constant, "The Liberty of the Ancients Compared with That of the Moderns," in *Political Writings*, ed. B. Fontana (Cambridge: Cambridge University Press, 1988), 311. The "political liberty of the ancients" is nothing other than what Rousseau described as the equality of the citizen as participant in law.

70 M. Weber, *Economy and Society*, eds G. Roth and C. Wittich (Berkeley: University of California Press, 1978), vol. 2, 668; translation modified.

71 *Ibid.*, 699.

72 *Ibid.*, 729–30.

73 *Ibid.*, 731; translation modified.

74 See Menke, "Subjektive Rechte: Zur Paradoxie der Form," 95ff. For a critique of liberal dualism, see J. Habermas, "Natural Law and Revolution," in *Theory and Practice*, trans. J. Viertel (London: Heinemann, 1974), 82–120. It is obviously *not* a solution to seek to overcome the "dualism" that, in the bourgeois-liberal conception, is an integral component of the figure of subjective rights by interpreting the "concession of a subjective right" as the "granting of participation in the generation of law" instead (Kelsen, *Reine Rechtslehre*, 61). This interpretation is doubly false: It misconstrues the functioning of subjective rights, and it abandons the originally liberal impulse towards liberation from law. On this point, see C. Menke, *Kritik der Rechte* (Berlin: Suhrkamp, 2015). A thorough discussion of this problem would require a critical engagement with Habermas's revision of Kant's distinction between morality and legality (Kant, *Metaphysical Elements of Justice*, "Introduction to the Metaphysics of Morals," 22–25). Unlike classical liberalism, Habermas emphasizes that recognition of the "private autonomy" released from normative restrictions as the content of the law also requires a redefinition of "political autonomy" as the *ground* of law. The latter, too, must be split within itself: into legal-political and moral autonomy (Habermas, *Between Facts and Norms*, 104–18). Habermas describes this as the "moral division of labor" (*ibid.*, 117) between law and morality, which is meant to ensure that the participants in law are exempt from the "undue expectations" (Habermas) of autonomous self-judgment that Oedipus experiences as a curse. In the final analysis, it seems to me, this assurance calls the normativity of law itself into question. See also note 59.

75 Luhmann, *Law as a Social System*, 118. (In the original context, the observation refers to the way in which "the system," not only the legal system, by internalizing the distinction between system and environment "in the form of the distinction between self-reference and external reference, [...] gains the freedom to change 'leadership' [...] [shifting] from self-reference to external reference and back.")

76 See the analysis of the "aporias" of legal decision-making in Derrida, "Force of Law," 961–73. The following account differs from Derrida's (only) in that it understands the aporia of legal judgment as the self-reflective unfolding of the difference between law and the non-legal within law.

77 H. Müller, *Wolokolamsker Chaussee I: Russische Eröffnung*, in *Werke*, vol. 5 (Frankfurt am Main: Suhrkamp, 2002), 85–96. I would like to thank Hans-Thies Lehmann for bringing this text and its significance to my attention, and Robin Celikates, Thomas Khurana, Daniel Loick, and Katrin Trüstedt for their critical responses to a first version of my interpretation.

78 *Ibid.*, 93.

79 Müller's *Wolokolamsker Chaussee II: Wald bei Moskau*, in *Werke*, vol. 5, 195–205, notes about this conditional relation: "The Soviet order I thought where will it be / When the Soviet Union has disappeared" (204). The conditional relation justifies – and indeed, the commander believes, necessitates – "that [. . .] someone take the law / In his hands and cut the knots of its constraints" (202) if that is what it takes to secure the continued existence of the Soviet Union, the only polity *in* which the law of the Soviet order can be in force.

80 Müller, *Wolokolamsker Chaussee I*, 93–4.

81 *Ibid.*, 95.

82 H. Müller, "Zur Inszenierung," in *Werke*, vol. 5, 97.

83 The pardon is the other form of sovereignty that is systematically absent from Schmitt's theory; see C. Menke, "Mercy and Law: Carl Schmitt's Concept of Sovereignty," in *Reflections on Equality*, trans. H. Rouse and A. Denejkine (Stanford: Stanford University Press, 2006), 177–98.

84 Müller, "Zur Inszenierung," 97. At this point, Müller departs from his novelistic source, where the pardon must, in the commander's eye, always remain a *mere* "dream," a "wish" born of "compassion" – understandable but wrong, proven wrong by the knowledge of what is necessary in war and thus right according to the law of war: "I wanted every man to know: if you funk, if you betray, you will not be forgiven, much as we may want to forgive you. Write this down, let everyone read it who has put on, or is about to put on, a soldier's uniform. Let them all know: maybe you were all right, maybe before this you were loved and praised; but whatever you may have been, for a military crime, for cowardice, for treachery, you will

be punished with death" (A. Bek, *Volokolamsk Highway* (Moscow: Foreign Languages Publishing House, 1956), 40–41).

85 See J. Derrida, "What Is a 'Relevant' Translation?," *Critical Inquiry*, 27 (Winter 2001), 183ff.

86 As Gilles Deleuze demanded; see above, note 34.

87 G. Agamben, *Profanations*, trans. J. Fort (New York: Zone, 2007), 76.

88 "Taste is the most accurate seismograph of historical experience. Unlike almost all other faculties, it is even able to register its own behavior. Reacting against itself, it recognizes its own lack of taste. [...] In repugnance for all artistic subjectivism, for expression and exaltation, the flesh creeps at the lack of historical tact, just as subjectivity itself earlier flinched from bourgeois conventions" (T. W. Adorno, *Minima Moralia: Reflections on a Damaged Life*, trans. E. Jephcott (London: Verso, 2005), 145).

Part II

Responses

2

Between law and violence: towards a re-thinking of legal justice in transitional justice contexts

María del Rosario Acosta López

In the already extensive literature connecting philosophy and law, there is a long tradition of framing this encounter in terms of what I will provisionally call a "negative critique." As it is clear in Walter Benjamin's canonical essay, a philosophical critical perspective seems to be capable of bringing to light the main paradox at the core of the law, namely, that its foundation coincides with its violence. Violence exists not only outside the law, as a means of its enforcement and conservation, but also lies at the center of what the law is, at the ground of its own presupposition and legitimation. What grounds the normativity of the law, that is, its capacity to oppose, interrupt, and/or suspend violence, is what simultaneously denies its legitimacy. The violence of the law, its unavoidability and its foundational character, becomes one of the main features pointed out by a philosophical critical engagement with the sphere of right.[1] And this goes hand in hand with a (Hegelian–Marxist) tradition of critique attentive to exposing the contradictions at the heart of the law.

These are contradictions that reveal the need to either abolish the sphere of law altogether, namely, to overcome it in a sort of *an-archic* gesture, or to bring about its limitations and the need for another perspective, different and beyond the law, that may become the standpoint for its critique. These are also, in a way, the two main trends that Benjamin's critique has produced in the tradition of its interpretation, the two main sides, one would say, of a *philosophical critique* of the violence of the law. So, on the one hand, such a philosophical critique has had as its main task a conceptual analysis that can effectively make visible the violent structures that lie at the ground not only of specific political and historical forms of the law as right, but moreover, of the law as a concept, that is, of the *very form* of the law. On the other hand, by bringing these structures to light and, more importantly, by making them *intelligible*, such an inquiry seeks to produce alternative modes of resistance to the law, showing the limits of the kind of justice offered by a legal framework, and indicating forms of interruption of the historical and political effects of the structures subject to critique.

In his essay "Law and violence," however, Christoph Menke decides to take a different approach. He retraces the tradition of a philosophical critique of violence – paradigmatically represented by Benjamin's methodology and his philosophical-historical critique of the law – but reframes it in the context of a *genealogy* of the foundation of law as right. Faithful to Benjamin's original claim that a critique of violence requires a philosophy of its history, Menke proposes to look at the history of law as it is told by tragedy. As he argues throughout the first part of his essay, such a history reveals that the violence of the law is not the mythical violence of its pre-history, but rather the violence that returns as a curse in law's explicit attempt to overcome its original mythical and fateful structure. As Menke shows, the history of the tragic origin of the law reveals that it is the law itself that, already in its foundation, defines itself as a break with and in opposition to fate, and hence, that a critique of an original, cyclical, and "mythical" violence has already taken place *within* the sphere of the law.

By doing this, Menke is not only able to distance his critique from Benjamin's most fatalistic diagnosis, namely, his identification of the violence of the law with the broader sphere of mythical violence. This identification, Menke argues, leads Benjamin to ascribe all legal violence to the same vicious circularity of fate, and hence, to the same self-contradictory and inescapable mythical structure. However, if legal violence responds to a more sophisticated form of violence, or at least, to one that complicates the structure of its own fateful repetition, by including within itself the possibilities of its own interruption, as

Menke proposes to show, then what is needed is both a more nuanced and sophisticated *mode of critique*, as well as a different *conception of the law*, or at least a different understanding of its operation.

On the one hand, then, Menke's analysis puts forward the need for a form of critique attentive to the differences between a pre-legal form of violence and the kinds of violence that result from law's own attempts to distinguish itself from its antecedent's violent fate. On the other hand, such a critique allows him to envisage an alternative task for the philosophical analysis. Rather than demanding a divorce *from* the sphere of the law, as has been the case with at least one of the possible – and more usual – interpretations of Benjamin's call for an *Entsetzung* of the law, Menke argues for an understanding of the violence of the law from *within*, and thus for an understanding of the possibilities the law brings with itself of *judging otherwise*.

As Menke will show, retracing the steps taken by Benjamin (and, following Benjamin, by authors such as Agamben, Nancy, and Derrida), the violence of the law is indeed paradoxical in its structure and inescapable in its foundation. Such a paradox, however, does not call inevitably for a radical suspension of the law altogether, nor for its limitation by a non-legal sphere of justice, external to (even if indissociable from) the law. "The promise of a realm beyond the law," Menke reminds us, "merely leads to the inversion of law into unlawfulness" (p. 60). Any attempt to escape the paradox leads immediately to its reenforcement. What is needed is rather to take up the paradox in its "full expression" (p. 39), that is, to take it to its limits and force us to understand it from within. For Menke, this does not only mean, as in Derrida, tarrying with the aporia of legal judgment. It goes further; it means tarrying with this aporia precisely from the perspective of the law, from law's self-reflective capacity to unfold in itself and by itself the difference between the law and the non-legal that gives expression to its own paradoxical structure.

By going beyond a negative critique of the law, or rather by situating his critique in a different relation to Benjamin's critique, Menke is able to propose a different interpretation of Benjamin's notion of *Entsetzung*.

He writes: "to *relieve* law means neither to apply it indefinitely nor to abolish it once and for all; it means to execute it in *reflective* fashion, which is to say, with repugnance [*Widerwillen*] for its execution" (p. 6; emphasis added). Menke therefore speaks in this context of a "depotentiation" of the law, an attempt to render it inoperative from within (in its self-reflective capacity) and taking to its limits the contradictions at the heart of its own paradoxical structure. Rather than abolishing the law by way of bringing to light its internal contradictions, Menke brings forward the philosophical task of thinking the law differently (also thinking differently the way the law can think of and reflect on itself) by changing the relationship it displays with its own foundational violence; thus, to broaden law's specter and make it *judge differently*, rather than to limit its sphere vis-á-vis a kind of justice that acts counter to the violence of the law. And hence, to explore the possibilities that still lie at the center of the law, its self-critical and emancipatory capacity, in order to avoid a utopian perspective that has tended to move too quickly from the need for a transcendental critical perspective to the demand to transcend (overcome and suspend) historically the very realm of law and the sphere of right.

***

Let me go now to what I find particularly interesting and fruitful in Menke's analysis. My own commentary wants to situate his proposal in connection to a context that is legal, historical, and political, but also philosophical and critical, in which the self-reflexivity of the law can show one of its most productive aspects, namely in transitional justice processes.[2]

On the one hand, these processes become privileged sites for rethinking the sphere of the law, and in particular, the specific connections between law and violence. This is the case because it is in these contexts, more than any others, that the idea of *legal justice* is put to the test. The capacity to engender and produce justice under the law not only becomes one of the central goals of the transition, but also one of the features that is being interrogated *as part of* the transition, that is, as one of the concepts that, in a way, needs also to be put *in* transition.

On the other hand, it is precisely in these contexts that the law becomes both the *object* of critique and the *tool* that guarantees the effectiveness of the process. The expression "transitional justice" points, therefore, not only to the transitional form that legal justice attains in such a context, but also to the fact that justice itself is also *in* transition, and with it the sphere of law, as its requirement and justification. Consequently, transitional justice processes must seek to interrogate what kind of connections between law and justice have been and are still complicit with the forms of violence and injustices implemented in the past. They must also provide new forms of legal justice that will be able to address and produce an adequate representation of, and more importantly, a satisfactory response to, the forms of violence that have so far been legally implemented and endorsed.

Thus, transitional justice processes call for an exploration of a broader conception of the law, from within the law and in connection to its own paradoxical and transitional structure; one in which, without trying to escape the sphere of law and denounce the restrictions on its effectiveness, what is needed more than anything is an account of both the possibilities and limits of the law to engender a critique of itself, namely, to acknowledge and be accountable for its own forms of violence, while simultaneously transforming its own mode of operating and judging. This is where I believe Menke's perspective becomes most fruitful, because it highlights the role the law can play in a transitional context. By distancing himself from a "negative critique" of the law and an anarchic interpretation of Benjamin, Menke is able to present an alternative, self-reflexive critique of the law, one that is performed by the law itself, within the sphere of law as right. This also allows Menke to dispense with two different and narrower critiques of the role that law and legal violence play in transitional justice processes.

In what follows, I want to show how these critiques of the law and its violence, usually related to a negative critique of its structure, correspond to two misunderstandings of the role the law plays in transitional justice processes. These critiques point not only to the limitations of the law to provide and guarantee "justice" (each one of them presupposing a particular definition of what justice is), but even more so to the way in which, in its inadequate response, law reproduces the violence it is supposed to overcome. In this sense, these critiques are framed by the very same approach to the law that Menke's proposal is both taking on and displacing. By pointing to the limitations of each one of these conceptions, while also bringing to light a more complex version of the kind of curse represented and reenacted by the violence of the law, Menke's own genealogical exploration turns out to be a particularly productive entryway into discussions about the role, the limits, and the possibilities of the law and legal justice in transitional justice contexts.

***

There are, as mentioned before, at least two critiques of the role law plays in transitional justice contexts. In both cases, what is pointed out is the incapacity of legal justice to respond satisfactorily to the forms of violence tacitly condoned by the law or executed as legitimate in the past. Each one of them, however, as Menke's analysis helps to show, presupposes a conception of the law, and of *legal justice*, that undercuts the complexity of its structure. By doing so, these criticisms also simplify the kind of violence at the core of the law, while narrowing down, correspondingly, the capacity of the law to deal with its own structural forms of violence. Each one of these perspectives is also, from Menke's standpoint, a misunderstanding of the nature and the object of law's violence. Each one of them also, at the same time, demands too little of the law, thereby undermining its own emancipatory potential.

The first criticism is related to a conception of legal justice as *retribution*. Transitional justice processes bring to light more than ever the incapacity of the law to provide retribution for the quality and sometimes the sheer quantity of the harms that are to be addressed by the legal process. In these contexts, it is often argued that the law needs to "sacrifice" its capacity to punish, and sometimes also its capacity to fully repair, for the sake of a broader conception of justice, one that, beyond retribution, seeks to achieve as much knowledge of the truth as possible, with a view set on the future rather than on the past. Memory initiatives and an accurate account of the atrocities of the past are promised in exchange for a diminished justice. But justice is understood narrowly here, as punishment and/or compensation for the harms of the past.

The history of the law as it is told by tragedy, in Menke's analysis, helps to show the inadequacy of this first type of critique. The problem does not seem to be the incapacity of the law to adequately function as a retributive entity, but rather a conception of the law that narrows it down to a retributive operation. Justice as retribution, according to Menke, belongs to the *pre-history* of the law. It is not *yet* legal justice, since it is still driven by a logic of retaliation. It is, in a way, a sophisticated, procedural version of what otherwise manifests itself in terms of vengeance. Even though it conceives of itself as an interruption of vengeance and therefore as an alternative to an irrational response, it ends up being nothing but the enactment and application of the "law of equality, in that it is the payment of like for like" (p. 8).

As Menke explains, it is easy to confuse retributive justice with a legal act, since in its *form* it presents itself as violence driven by justice. It acts *as if it was* the law, even though it only acts in substitution for the law's absence. It seeks to restore the "just state of the world," but it can only do so every single time with an excessive act, bringing about a new imbalance that can only repeat and perpetuate the violence of the original act. In its operation, therefore, retributive justice enacts the contradictions at the core of its own conception. Or, put in Hegelian terms, each one of its actions corroborates the irreconcilability between its concept and its truth. The equation of the crime with a comparable response – a reproduction therefore of violence rather than a radical interruption of its effects – marks retributive justice's essential ambivalence or equivocation. "Retribution," Menke writes, "harbors an equivocation that lets its justice disintegrate into an undecidable strife between enemy parties" (p. 10). Retribution has no answer to this undecidability, because it can only take into account one of the two sides at a time. By doing so, retributive justice is incapable of interrupting the cycle of vengeance it was set up to suspend. Its violence is therefore not merely the violence of its reproduction, but even more so the compulsion of its repetition.

The question that retribution raises, but leaves unanswered, also sets the stage for the beginning and the origin of the law, the task and the challenge that will be taken up by the sphere of law as right: "is there a deed of justice whose operation does not continue without end – that is not violence?" (p. 10) Law, according to Menke, begins with this question. It is the sphere that must conceive of justice in its *narrative* character, namely, in its capacity to hear both sides and produce a *judgment* that can account simultaneously for incompatible claims, avoiding thereby the equivocation proper to the pre-legal conception of justice as retribution. "Justice," in this sense, no longer means "to do what must be done" to redress the excess of the crime. It rather means to "understand the matter in a way that is not partial but sees [hears] both sides" (p. 12). To demand justice in terms of retribution, or rather, to point to the limitations of the law precisely in its incapacity to produce an adequate retributive response, is therefore to remain tied to a misconception of the law and to deny the fact that right and legal justice have by definition already moved beyond a logic of mere retaliation.

Hence, what transitional justice processes do, in a way, and following Menke's argument, is to bring to light a truth about the law that is always operative under its structure but perhaps only visible in limited cases, namely, that if there is a violence of the law, this violence has nothing to do with the pre-legal reproduction of the violence of the past, but rather with the concept of justice that is put to the test in the *hearing*, and with the promise this conception of legal justice brings with it of being able to universally represent all the parties. To remain tied to the demands of retribution is therefore not only to misunderstand the role of legal justice, but even more so, to cover up a more nuanced and sophisticated kind of violence that can only come to light under an analysis that recognizes the difference between retributive and properly *legal* justice.

***

This brings me to the second critique of the role law plays in transitional justice processes, a critique that is related precisely to law's capacity, and its failure, to *represent*. More exactly, legal justice in many transitional justice situations is confronted with what looks like an impossible dilemma: on the one hand, it behaves as the only sphere capable of generating representation where nothing else seems to be able to do so. Law's capacity to judge, therefore, and to produce justice, is measured in terms of the promise it carries to provide a narrative and a meaning where the unspeakable and meaningless seem to pervade every other account of the events.[3] On the other hand, given that such events are usually related to traumatic forms of violence and mass atrocity, critical reactions arise, pointing to the limits of the law to become the site for a satisfactory representation where an adequate hearing can actually be provided.[4]

Here again, I believe, Menke's genealogy can be helpful for understanding both the origin and nature of these criticisms, as well as the limits of the conception of the law that serves as a presupposition for these critical reactions. Because, as much as this step into justice as representation becomes the entryway into the history of right and the sphere of law, the understanding and self-understanding of the law at this stage also reduces its possibilities to a one-sided – or, at least, not yet self-critical – notion of justice, thereby limiting the law ultimately to a mere act of domination (something that the law indeed is, at the beginning of its history, as Menke argues, but certainly not everything that the law *can* be).

As a response to the multiplication of "justices" through acts of retribution, which is characteristic of the pre-legal stage, the beginning of the legal sphere coincides, according to Menke, with the establishment and enforcement of one law (p. 16). Such a move requires a step from the "overabundance" of particular viewpoints (and narratives) to the possibility of a *universal* perspective, capable of listening to, and representing, all the parties in conflict. With this, Menke recounts, "justice gains a procedure" and a "political substance" (p. 20). It becomes the stage for a universal language, providing representation, understood both in terms of a fair hearing for each one of the parties, as well as in terms of a meaningful and intelligible narrative of what otherwise would remain entirely partial, or even more so, unintelligible (un-representable).

There is, however, an element of betrayal in this step from particularity to universality – a betrayal that is at the center of certain criticisms of the legal procedure that remain only at this first stage and narrower definition of the law. As Menke points out in his analysis of the kind of violence entailed by this move from pre-legal to a first form of legal justice, the imperative to provide a fair hearing becomes the *imposition* of a universal perspective. The universality of the law, its capacity to provide representation to each one of the parties under its command, is therefore at odds with the possibilities (and the power) of its enforcement. Once again, put in Hegelian terms, the concept of the law as universality meets the other of its truth in the process of its implementation, revealing at the ground of its operation a presupposition-less kind of violence, namely, the violence of domination (*Herrschaft*).

This moment of the argument needs to be taken slowly, since it seems to me that Menke is introducing here, as a second logical step of this "violence of domination," the nuances and complexities of what authors like Agamben, to name just one of Menke's most explicit references, have analyzed as the violence of *sovereignty* as *inclusion by exclusion* (the violence of the *ban*, in Nancy's terms).[5] On the one hand, the violence of domination means that anything outside the law must be included under its command in order for the *one* law, its universality, to be preserved over and against the multiplication and undecidability of pre-legal forms of justice. "The violence of the law," Menke reminds us, "emerges from its form – from the very legal form that breaks with the violence-reproducing undecidability of retribution" (p. 19). Such is the violence as a *means* implied in law's application, the violence of the promise of representation, which betrays any form of particularity that does not confirm the universality of the law.

On the other hand, however, a second step is needed here – a new mode of operation of the law, Menke argues, that is presupposed rather than knowingly pursued (p. 50). Because such an operation of the law in its universality can only be ultimately secured if it is the law itself that engenders what remains outside of its domain, namely, the non-legal, which will be included under law's domain only as the other of itself. The problem here is not only that law seeks to "prevail over the non-legal," but even further, that it "now *relates* to the non-legal from which it distinguishes itself – and thus contains the non-legal as *distinct* within itself" (p. 52, emphasis added). Only then can the law guarantee, beyond its universality, the legitimacy of its form, over and against anything that attempts to escape its logic of domination. "The law," Menke writes, "must also secure its rule against the possibility of the extra-legal or non-law that it has itself engendered and reproduces with each of its acts" (p. 22). Violence, therefore, is no longer only violence as a means with which to dominate something outside the law. It is rather violence as an end in itself – violence as the self-assertion of the law, namely, violence as "a relation of pure enforcement," "violence through and through" (p. 22).

At this point, the manifestation of the law as violence appears to be the same as the violence in a pre-legal, retributive, stage. The situation in the law, at least as it is enforced and hence understood in its first constitution (as universal and sovereign), is similar to the repetition in the case of retributive justice: "Law, too," Menke writes, "must perpetually repeat its own violent enforcement" (p. 22). The difference, however, is the structure that lies at the ground of this operation. Since, unlike the logic of retributive justice, which engenders that against which it will then be directed, the sphere of the law engenders its object "outside itself, as its counterpart," while, at the same time, including it *within* the legal sphere by asserting its domination of the non-legal (p. 22). The violence of the law coincides at this point with its tragic origin. It is the doubling of the original staging of the hearing that ultimately leads to the law's manifestation as pure violence. Only, this time, it is not a hearing between two parties under the law, but one that confronts the law with the other of itself, with what is external to the law and yet still included within it. "From the very beginning," Menke writes, the law "faces an impossible challenge: it must secure not just this or that law but *the law of law*; it must secure not just this or that norm but the very normative character of the norm, against the lawless and norm-free" (p. 38, emphasis added).

This is related to what Menke describes later in his analysis as the true *paradox of the law*, since, on the one hand, the law, in its commitment to a fair and equal representation, must provide the staging for an impartial hearing, examination, and judgment. However, the only way in which the law can guarantee this staging – and hence this universal possibility of representation – is by having already executed "a procedure before the procedure, in which the non-legal has been rendered legal, the non-citizen a citizen, the unequal equal"; a pre-procedure, therefore, in which the law "has engendered the elements that it can use in its proceeding" (p. 54). To do so, however, "it must strip the non-legal precisely of the *difference* from the law that constitutes it and to which it maintains its right" (p. 54, emphasis added). The law, Menke argues, "can only relate to the non-legal in a legal form" (p. 54). This is its paradox, and the curse at the heart of its structure. It can only realize and guarantee the right of the non-legal – and hence remain faithful to its impartiality and promise of universal representation – by simultaneously violating this right (p. 54). It is then the promise of representation as a measure for justice that coincides in the end with its betrayal. The violence of the law coincides with the legitimate exercise of its justice, which is to say, its legitimation coincides with its violence.

The violence of the law remains ultimately, therefore, the "secret purpose of law itself" (p. 31). This is the reason why, Menke reminds us, a critique of this violence, as Benjamin had already stated, cannot be executed in terms of the justice or injustice of its means. The violence of the law, Benjamin writes, is a "violence crowned by fate." This means it is not only, and not essentially, the kind of violence that constrains, threatens and/or violates. It is also not only, in the light of Menke's analysis, a violence reduced to a mythical cyclical reproduction of itself. Furthermore, it is not really to the "injurious *effects* of legal acts" (p. 31, emphasis added) that a critique of legal violence should be directed, nor to its incapacity to judge adequately, to its failure to represent, or the threat produced by its own imposition. The violence of the law lies ultimately in its *mode of judging*, in the *mode of operation* of its judgments: the "fateful violence of law consists in the fact that the acts of legal judgment and punishment are opaque; no purpose is evident in them other than the mere preservation of law's power to judge and punish" (p. 31).

A traditional and liberal reaction to this attestation has been, as Menke points out, to limit the sphere of law's authority, and to liberate the individual – the ultimate object of this violence – from the power of the law. "The liberal 'art of separating' the legal from the non-legal," Menke writes, "believes that it can break the violence of law merely by limiting its reach – which is to say, without having to change *how the law judges*" (p. 51, emphasis added). Such is also the case with those criticisms, which arise more often in transitional justice processes, against the incapacity of the law to provide and secure an adequate representation and thus a narrative and a meaning for the horrific truth of the past. The only way out of these criticisms is either to radically question the capacity of the law to address what is ultimately un-representable, potentially stripping the legal procedures of their legitimacy and falling back into the kind of lawless violence that the transition is attempting to interrupt, or to acknowledge the limitations of the legal procedure from within, preserving, however, the very same conception of the law and legal justice (and thus its structural forms of violence) that the transition is supposed to put into question.

As Menke points out in his quote, however, this should not be the end of the story. His suggestion is to begin precisely where the liberal critique seems to end. Because if what needs to be interrupted and relieved (*entsetzt*) is the way in which the law, since its beginning, has dealt with the difference between the law and the non-law, the critical gesture cannot risk simply reproducing this structure – namely, reproducing the movement that suspends the law in order to deal with this difference in the first place. Hence, what is needed, Menke states, is not so much a suspension of this violence, of the violence that sustains and is sustained by this difference, but a *counter-suspension*. If a *relief of the suspension* is possible at all, it will have to be done through a self-reflective gesture, not by "releasing law *from* its difference," but rather by releasing that difference at the center and mode of operation of the judgment of the law (p. 39, original emphasis).

This is the heart of Menke's proposal, and the point where his idea of a self-reflective law comes most clearly to the fore. What is rendered inoperative, in Menke's critique, is not the violence of the law, but rather the mechanism or operation through which the law *hides* its violence from itself; hence, the mechanism that allows the law to present itself and its judgments as unquestionably legitimate. The violence of the law is ultimately unavoidable, Menke would claim. This recognition, however, does not need to lead to the dissolution of the law altogether, nor to its limitation by another (non-legal) sphere external to the law. On the contrary, it can lead to a modality of the law in which each of its judgments turns into a self-reflective enactment of its paradox (p. 40). An implementation, Menke suggests, that simultaneously "realizes law *and* disrupts it" (p. 55, original emphasis), and in which whoever judges can no longer disburden themselves of the responsibility for their decision, nor pass that responsibility on to the law (p. 60).

Menke sees in law's self-reflective capacity the potentiality of the law to *judge differently* while being sustained by the very same operation that makes its violence unavoidable. The difference here is not in the *effect* of the judgment, neither in the very nature of the law –its promise and its failure, nor better yet, the necessary failure given the nature of its promise. It is rather a difference in the way the law relates to its own process of legitimation. Menke writes:

> The relief of law is neither the end of law nor the beginning of non-violence. It is the disruption of the fateful violence law exercises because it believes it is right, because it believes in its right over the non-legal. The relief of law puts an end to the war law wages on non-law by starting this war within law (p. 61).

Nothing could be a better description of the situation in which law finds itself precisely at those moments when, as is the case in a transitional justice process, the law is itself on trial. It is precisely in these contexts, more than ever, that the law is at odds with its legitimacy, but the acknowledgment of this fact – of the fact of its violence, and hence of its arbitrariness as a mechanism of justice – is not realized through the suspension of its judgment, but rather in the execution of this judgment as a powerful way of making explicit and subjecting to critique its own arbitrariness. "The self-reflective implementation of law means being done with being done with" (*der selbstreflexive Vollzug des Rechts macht Schluss mit dem Schlussmachen*: p. 61). I wonder if such a conception of the law would not be the most fruitful way of relating to legal justice precisely in those situations where justice should never be the equivalent to bringing definitive closure, but rather the opening of a promise that legal justice should never give up on.[6]

Notes

1 In English it is necessary to clarify the use of the notion of "right." When mentioned here, I will be using it as equivalent to "*Recht*" in German or "*droit*" in French.

2 While I mostly speak here from my own experience with the theoretical and political discussions currently taking place in Colombia, I will be basing my comments on a more general description of transitional justice situations. The literature on this is extensive and I will not be referring specifically to any particular theoretical posture, since my interest in what follows is to draw exclusively from Menke's own analysis. I am interested in pointing out the similarities between his genealogy of the violence of the law – the stages that go from its pre- to its post-history and the ways in which, according to Menke, the law can take up its own historical (and foundational) fate – and the usual criticisms that come to the fore in transitional justice contexts regarding the capacities and limits of the law in providing effective justice in relation to the harms of the past. I believe that Menke's own take on this subject, and the kind of critique that is performed by his proposal, can be a productive alternative for reflecting on the *legal task* as well as on the *task of the legal* in transitional justice contexts.

3 I take these ideas mainly from the work of my colleague Esteban Restrepo at the Law School in the Universidad de los Andes. For a more detailed account of his hypothesis, namely, that it is because of this promise and this commitment to provide representation that law also produces a specific

"fascination" in transitional justice contexts, see his "Justicia de las imágenes, justicia por las imágenes: apuntes para pensar la relación entre el derecho penal y la representación de la atrocidad masiva," in Jorge Contesse Singh *et al.* (eds), *Derechos Humanos: posibilidades teóricas y desafíos prácticos* (Buenos Aires: Libraria, 2014), 336–52. In relation to the classic literature on transitional justice, I consider Restrepo's position to be very original in understanding precisely this theoretical side of the problem, which has nonetheless, as his work very well shows, very concrete practical effects.

4 The concept of *representation* here refers both to the idea of being "represented" by the law, as one of the parties in a hearing, as well as to the question of the possibility that the law itself brings with it of producing representation (a meaning, an image and/or a grammar) to a claim that otherwise cannot seem to find a language of its own – and hence cannot enter the realm of the intelligible. From my perspective, these two different meanings are tied together in the history of law as told by tragedy, since it is the possibility to become a narrative that constitutes one of the conditions of possibility for becoming a party at a hearing, and these are both conditions guaranteed by a certain understanding of justice as legal, as engendered by, and sustaining, the sphere of law.

5 It is not clear to me whether the violence of domination in Menke's analysis entirely coincides with or includes what Agamben refers to as the violence of sovereignty. However, what seems to be clear is that both of them belong to a previous stage of what Menke considers the ultimate violence of the law, namely, the violence (and the curse) of autonomy: a self-imposed ban of the subject to itself – a subject simultaneously produced and presupposed by the law – rather than the ban imposed by the sovereign's foundational act. Menke's criticisms of Agamben are not so much a disagreement with the latter's assessment of the violence of sovereignty, but rather a disagreement with the centrality this violence should play in a philosophical critique of the law. Beyond the violence of sovereignty, Menke is interested in a more Foucauldian conception of the violence of the law, represented by Oedipus' story. "The curse of the law," Menke writes, "consists in the fact that the law condemns everyone to impose the [sovereign] ban on *themselves* (which is to say, to become an autonomous "subject" of the law): that is the central hypothesis of [Michel Foucault], which Agamben fails to appreciate due to his fixation on the concept of sovereignty" (p. 66–67, note 34). For the time

being, I will have to leave aside a detailed description of this third stage of Menke's account of the history of tragedy. It is indeed an important step in Menke's argument, but one that deserves a commentary on its own. In what follows, I will just presuppose this step as one of the sides (and nuances) of a complex operation of the violence of the law, in order to concentrate on Menke's own proposal of a self-reflective critique.

6 I thank my friend and colleague Colin McQuillan at St. Mary's University in San Antonio, for going patiently and thoroughly through several versions of this chapter. Not only did he help me to convey my ideas in a much better English, but also his insights into my arguments and Menke's were really helpful during the process. Any discrepancies with Menke's original argument, or any unnecessary density in the presentation of the ideas, is, however, entirely my own.

3

Law without violence

Daniel Loick

"Law is itself violence" (p. 3) – this claim is not only an "observation" about forms of law existing hitherto, but a thesis about the very concept of law as such. According to Christoph Menke, there never was and never can be any law without violence. The reason for this dependency of law on violence lies in its need to be enforced; Menke follows Kant's definition according to which law consists in a reciprocal authority to use coercion. The aim of my essay is to question this basic assumption. While it is certainly true that the history of occidental legal forms was a history of torture and cruelty, of discipline and punishment, of police, prisons, and border control, there are at least two normative orders within the European ethical horizon that should be called "legal orders" even though they forego the use of coercion and are thus potentially nonviolent. The first one is international law, as most prominently conceptualized by Kant himself (thereby contradicting his own definition of law): international legal norms are binding, but have no distinct coercive forces at their disposal. The second one is Jewish law, developed and practiced over centuries under conditions of the diaspora, thus lacking any state-based means of enforcement. Both legal orders already informed the agenda laid out by Walter Benjamin's "Critique of Violence" (1920/21) which can therefore guide a critical interrogation of Menke's hidden premises. Benjamin's notion of deposing the law (*Entsetzung des Rechts*), I argue, should not be interpreted as a "self-reflection of law," as Menke suggests, but rather as the idea of a law without violence. Only if we interpret Benjamin's philosophical-political program as the attempt to rigorously *eliminate* violence from law (instead of prolonging it against its own will, p. 61) can it guide a social transformation that truly does justice to the victims of past and present legal violence.

I will proceed in four steps. First, I will attempt to reject Menke's thesis about the necessary connection of law and violence by discussing two cases of non-coercive law: international law as presented in Kant's *Metaphysics of Morals* (1) and Jewish law as conceptualized by Benjamin, among others (2). I will then discuss an additional argument for the irreducibility of violence in law that Menke has presented in a different context, namely the claim that violence in law is necessary in order to deploy a socially transformative force (3). Finally, I will argue that Benjamin's demand to "depose" law, understood as a liberation of law from violence, is not only able to serve as a common denominator of the goals of current social movements against state-sanctioned violence such as prison abolitionism or the Black Lives Matter movement, but also offers an important perspective for any future critical theory of law (4).[1]

1. Kant's "pure law"

Christoph Menke's claim that violence is implied in the very "*concept* of law" (p. 4, original emphasis) is derived from the definition of law provided by Immanuel Kant's chapter on the "Doctrine of Right" in his *Metaphysics of Morals*.[2] "Right and authorization to use coercion," Kant succinctly states, "mean one and the same thing."[3] This connection between law and coercion is conceptual and not merely historical, because it is generated by means of an a priori analysis. Coercion, for Kant, is the simple negation of a negation of freedom: since law is an order of freedom, every illegal act is a hindrance to freedom. Coercion, on the other hand, is a "hindering of a hindrance of freedom" and thus "by the principle of contradiction" automatically just.[4] Kant thus believes he can derive the authority to use coercion without regard to any empirical considerations, merely by making explicit the logical structure of law as such.

Kant's definition has been extremely influential, not only in legal and political philosophy, but also in public discourse and in our everyday understanding of law and legal matters. There is a nearly unanimous consensus that all law, in order to really be law, has to be *enforced*. This widely unquestioned adoption of Kant's doctrine is astounding, since it rests on a number of problematic premises. First of all, Kant offers no argument for his claim that the "hindrance of a hindrance" must take the form of coercion. In fact, this assertion is based not on analytical, but on empirical assumptions: the idea that coercion secures the possibility of law implies expectations about the *actual* suitability of coercion to fulfill the function ascribed to it. Since law is an outer norm (as opposed to morality as an inner norm), it cannot do without a prudent consideration regarding the best means to implement it. Instead of providing such an empirical deliberation, Kant – the philosopher of autonomy, after all – uncritically accepts the traditional mechanistic notion that only force can counteract force. However, empirically speaking, major doubts can be raised against this assumption. The over 200-year-long history of bourgeois society has proven that legal coercion neither prevents breaches of law, nor does it compensate for them retrospectively, nor does it work as a reliable medium for conflict resolution at all. On the contrary, there are a number of good reasons to believe that the juridical apparatus and the police regularly tend to breach the law themselves, as recent social movements such as prison abolitionism and the Black Lives Matter movement, as well as many contemporary critical theorists, have convincingly argued.[5] (This is what Benjamin already hints at when he writes that "the assertion that the ends of police violence are always identical or even connected to those of general law is entirely untrue."[6]) The experiences from penal law in particular show that legal coercion does not actually help to hinder hindrances of law; state-inflicted punishment – paradigmatically the prison system – rather continually produces and reproduces "milieus of delinquency"[7] outside of the legal order.

Besides their empirical ineffectivity, moral objections can be raised against means of coercion on strictly deontological grounds. Once coercion and law are no longer a priori bound to each other, normative criteria are needed in order to distinguish legitimate from illegitimate hindrances of hindrances of freedom: the legitimacy of coercion can no longer simply be deduced from the law itself. This is the starting point of Benjamin's "Critique of Violence": the legal order, even if it was perfectly just, would still not contain "a criterion for violence itself as a principle but, rather, the criterion for cases of its use. The question would remain open whether violence as a principle, could be a moral means even to just ends."[8] This question is avoided by classical political theory, because it presupposes the notion of legal force as a means to the end of law. Its basic dogma is that "just ends can be attained by justified means, justified means used for just ends"[9], which means that the possibility that the principles of the ends and the principles of the means could collide with each other cannot be excluded. To even recognize such a possible collision, independent criteria for both moral spheres are needed, Benjamin concludes. In the sphere of the means, the legitimacy of state-sanctioned violence *in principle* must be addressed, and therefore a question concerning a criterion "without regard for the ends they serve"[10] arises. Kant himself has prepared the grounds for questioning the legitimacy of violence even as a means for just ends. His moral philosophy postulates that moral imperatives apply *categorically*, that is, they need to be followed without regard for the empirical consequences. This notion has crucial consequence for the evaluation of violence as a means to the ends of law. Think of the example of torture: in liberal democracies, torture is prohibited notwithstanding questions of its (in-)effectivity. Human dignity, including the criminal's dignity, is to be respected unconditionally. Benjamin's move now is to expand the scope of Kant's transcendental argument to the entire register of legally sanctioned violence: police and prisons are illegitimate independently of the ends they serve, because they are structurally incapable of treating human beings as ends in themselves.[11]

Kant's claim (which Menke adopts), according to which violence is implied in the very concept of law, is therefore problematic for both empirical and moral reasons. It is empirically wrong, because it can be shown that violence is not an effective means to hinder hindrances of freedom, and it is morally wrong, because violence, even if used as a means to just ends, violates deontological moral principles. It is remarkable, however, that Kant himself does not consistently apply his own definition of law. Despite his own original definition of law, Kant mentions one case of a normative order that he explicitly calls a legal order but that is not based on force: international law. It follows directly from the universality of reason that law cannot be limited to the territories of single states. Democratic reform of national legal orders will therefore lead to the establishment of an international law whose regulative idea is the idea of perpetual peace. This idea substantially undermines the principle of sovereignty, as Kant asserts a source of legal norms that are higher than any national law, which are binding on individual nation states, and which cannot be dispensed with. These international legal norms for Kant are not "overpositive" norms that stem from morality or natural rights; the principles of a binding international law are rather inherent to the very concept of universal law as such. It is important, however, to note that Kant does not posit a world state to enforce this law, which is, after all, the highest of all legal norms of his entire doctrine of right. Kant envisages only a dissoluble confederation of states without any authority to use coercion. International law thus becomes, to borrow Hans Kelsen's term, "pure law," a law independent of its own enforceability.

It is not relevant for these considerations that the actually existing international law is not non-coercive. My aim here is merely to prove that the connection between law and coercion is not a conceptual, but a historical one. It is therefore at least possible to imagine a non-coercive law. By allowing for a non-coercive legal order in his doctrine of right, Kant himself must have sensed this possibility to conceive of a merely voluntary rule-following. People, states even, are in principle capable of adhering to the law simply because they recognize it as reasonable.

This is what Benjamin has in mind when he refers to diplomacy as an instance of nonviolent conflict resolution.[12] For Kant, the condition for such an international order to be effective is that all member states have a republican constitution: only a just internal order disposes states to follow international law even when they are not forced to do so. If we replace "republican" with "radically democratic," we arrive at a plausible description of the conditions necessary to secure voluntary compliance with a legal order: if people themselves are the authors of a rule (the *actual* authors, not the presumed authors in a counterfactual thought experiment), the chance that they will comply with it radically increases.

Kant goes even further in realizing that the mere existence of means of violence actually *undermines* a voluntary compliance: standing armies – armies that by definition do not actually apply force, but merely represent the possibility of force – should, according to Kant's essay on "Perpetual Peace," in time be abolished altogether, for:

> they incessantly threaten other states with war by readiness to appear always prepared for war; they spur states on to outdo one another in the number of armed men, which knows no limit; and inasmuch as peace, by the costs related to it, finally becomes even more aggressive than a short war, a standing army is itself the cause of an offensive war, waged by a state in order to be relieved of this burden; in addition, being hired to kill or to be killed seems to involve a use of human beings as mere machines and tools in the hands of another (a state), and this cannot well be reconciled with the right of humanity in our own person.[13]

The right of humanity, Kant states, is not only injured by a violent act, but has already been injured by the threat of and the readiness to resort to violence. Kant therefore deems it to be our duty to create the political and institutional conditions necessary for this constant threat of violence to end. All of these arguments, however, also hold true against the existence of police and prisons: they are institutions which in principle pervade society with violence, thereby constantly undermining the possibility of a just and free life. Nobody has expressed this more pertinently than the Marburg neo-Kantian Herman Cohen (who taught Kant to Benjamin): "Coercion represents, logically as well as ethically, the end of reason."[14]

2. Jewish diasporic law

The concept of international law in Kant proves at least that much: violence is not a *constitutive* part of law, but its specific historical *attribute*. The idea of a non-coercive law expresses the hope to liberate the rational capacities aggregated in law by eliminating its violent dimension. Besides Kant's idealistic notion, there is at least one other legal order that foregoes its own coercive enforcement: Jewish law. Over centuries, Jewish legal traditions have not only theoretically reflected, but also reliably practiced, a law without any recourse to state-sanctioned violence. They also were among the most important sources of inspiration for the young Benjamin (as well as for his teacher Cohen).

The social, political, and cultural circumstances to which any legal system is subject also contribute to determining the form and content of this system. As far as Judaism is concerned, this means the conditions of the diaspora; since the destruction of the Temple in AD 70, Jewish law has had to preserve itself in hostile environments, without being represented in a state form. These conditions have thus shaped a legal order that is fundamentally different from all other European legal orders: it created a law without sovereignty. Due to our preoccupation with the state, legal scholars and philosophers even today have difficulty with actually recognizing it as a legal order at all. According to the centuries-long Jewish legal tradition, however, Jewish law is certainly not merely a religious normative order but a proper *law* – it entails scope, content, and function typical for a legal regime. Interestingly though, due to the conditions of the Diaspora, Jewish law cannot have recourse to any governmental apparatus of power by way of an enforcement agency. Its reference in the life of the members of the legal community must therefore be ensured without the use of force.

For this reason, Jewish law has had to develop very different resources as its means of persuasion, resources that were simply not available to the Roman-Christian tradition. Among the most important features of Jewish law is their pedagogical character: it is not to be understood as imperative commandment, but as *teaching*. It cannot secure its own relevance through police and court houses, but through schools and academies. In this respect the absence of executive agencies is connected with the idea, already set out in the Bible, that mankind will have to account for its interpretation of law before God, which excludes any application based purely on passive obedience. Because it does not address its members on an authoritative basis, therefore, but is directed towards a mature understanding, Emanuel Lévinas has rightly referred to Judaism as a "religion for adults."[15] To connect law with coercion would mean to preclude its study and thus any authentic responsibility. This is also the case because in Judaism, study is always essentially conflictual and not made for a naive application. This leads to a particular appreciation and nurturing of the controversial and dissenting exchange of different legal opinions and thus to the creation of a *community of interpreters*.

It is important to note that this is not a utopian image to be realized in a faraway future, but an already existing practice that has proven its capacity to reliably solve conflicts and regulate human behavior over centuries. Jewish legal practice has always been a legal practice in distance to the state and thus a legal practice in which Kant's analytic connection between law and coercion was never appropriate. Besides his own radicalization of Kant's categorical imperative, it was the Jewish legal tradition that inspired Benjamin to search for a nonviolent form of obligation. Against previous forms of law and law enforcement, which Benjamin refers to as "mythical," his aim is to defend a non-statist form of commandment that can be seen as opposing or distancing itself from the state. This becomes clear when Benjamin discusses the question whether a critique of violence as a means of law undermines the very validity of any legal rule. "This," he responds with explicit reference to "Judaism," "cannot be conceded. For the question 'May I kill?' meets its irreducible answer in the commandment 'Thou shalt not kill.'"[16] The irreducibility of this commandment, Benjamin insists further, is not dependent on its violent enforcement. On the contrary, violent enforcement prevents us from truly taking responsibility by, as Benjamin puts it, "wrestling" with the law (an activity that can never be skipped because we always need to find an interpretation of the law's meaning for the situation at hand). Rather, Benjamin says in his essay on Kafka: "Law which is studied but no longer practiced is the gate to justice."[17] This notion, which is a reference to the idea of the Talmud (Hebrew for "study") entails Benjamin's political program in a nutshell: neither the abolition, nor the (however "self-reflective") perpetuation of the law, but the suspension of its violent application.

At this point, an objection could be made that the study of law is not nonviolent, but rather simply based on *another form of violence*: educational violence. It is not only since Foucault's *Discipline and Punish* that we have learned that education, even under the guise of humanism and enlightenment, is based on a variety of disciplinary strategies. This objection is thus indeed an important reminder that violence can take unexpected forms and that we therefore should not be too quick with self-congratulatory gestures: even the study of law can entail traces of violence, be it in the form of repressive teaching methods or in more subtle forms of moralism and conformism. It does not follow from this, however, that the relation between law and non-law is *always or necessarily* a relation of violence, much less, as Menke claims, of "pure violence" or "violence through and through" (p. 22). Menke's claim that the gap between the legal and the non-legal can *in principle* never be bridged through reasoning or insight (p. 22) and, furthermore, that legal rule-following must always be based on fear (p. 21), is based on two hidden premises: Menke first naturalizes the antagonism he observes between the members of bourgeois society to an eternally irreconcilable conflict between human beings, and second, he follows Kant in adopting a mechanistic notion of cause and effect according to which only force can move force. Both premises are problematic: we already know forms of nonviolent conflict resolution that can reconcile adversaries without recourse to the threat of violence (Benjamin hints at this possibility when he mentions the "conference, considered as a technique of civil agreement"[18]), and there are ways to increase rule-following behavior other than by invoking fear (for example, by making rule-following behavior *more attractive* than rule-breaking behavior). The notion of the study of law is well equipped to accomplish both: since it addresses all members of the legal community as participants of an interpretative process and thus treats them as subjects rather than objects of the legal procedure, it hopes to reconcile the adversaries with each other and at the same time with the legal rule. If we then again replace the religion-based motivation to enter into such a strenuous study with the illocutionary binding energies set free by radically democratic and participatory processes of deliberation, we arrive at a notion of law as a voluntary agreement that is based precisely on rational insight and that Benjamin has therefore called "the gate to justice."

3. Violence and social transformation

So far, I have tried to refute Menke's claim that a nonviolent law is *conceptually* impossible. In a recent response to Andreas Fischer-Lescano (who has presented a critique in a similar vein as mine),[19] Menke has introduced an additional argument in favor of law's violent application that is not yet fully developed in "Law and Violence." Even if law without violence was possible, he argues, it is not *desirable* from the perspective of a critical theory of law. Menke certainly does not follow the mainstream of political philosophy in basing the need for violent enforcement of law on a Hobbesian anthropology: law's authority to use coercion is not derived from a need to protect men from each other. Rather, Menke discovers a genuinely *emancipatory* reason not to get rid of the violent dimension of law. His basic argument is that only a law that has material forces at its disposal can be a tool for the struggle against social domination: "The law needs to remain violence," he writes, "in order to critically intervene into society."[20] The reason for this, according to Menke, is that in order to transform society, law needs to keep a distance to it. If it opens itself up towards non-legal practices too much, it will be absorbed by forces of social domination and thus lose its critical edge.

By introducing an argument concerning the strategy of social transformation, Menke leaves the terrain of legal philosophy in favor of a philosophy of history. This turn is quite welcome, as it is precisely the domain in which Benjamin's "Critique of Violence" is situated. The whole point of Benjamin's essay, however, is to expose the problematic consequences of the very assumption Menke takes for granted: the assumption namely that only violence can counteract violence (an assumption that, as noted above, is based on a mechanistic notion of cause and effect). According to Benjamin, violent revolutions suffer from the same problematic as the law: they tend to justify the violence they imply by reference of the justness of their ends. This justification strategy is problematic simply because it too neglects the question whether or not violence, "as a principle, could be a moral means even to just ends."[21] By failing to ask this question, all revolutions hitherto have deemed it unproblematic to posit new law. They have thereby also reproduced the law-preserving violence of police and military as well as new revolutionary counterviolences; they have, in short, simply prolonged the historical "cycle maintained by mythical forms of law."[22] Benjamin, on the other hand, is not ready to let go of the possibility of fundamentally *nonviolent* modes of interaction. He therefore explicitly demands "a new historical epoch"[23] that has rigorously terminated the vicious circle of violence and counterviolence. To put it bluntly: revolutionary ends do not legitimize the violence in law; as Menke would have it, the violence in law rather delegitimizes its (potentially) revolutionary ends. As long as the law remains violent, all forms of social transformation that are essentially legal can never be fully just.

Is nonviolent social transformation possible? To answer this question was the task that Benjamin had set to himself in "Critique of

Violence." On the one hand, social transformation seems violent by definition, since it is a "cause that intervenes into a moral order."[24] On the other hand, Benjamin repudiates all justifications of violence based on the ends they serve. What is needed, then, is a "different kind of violence,"[25] a nonviolent (or "pure") violence: a form of political action that has manifest consequences in the world without resorting to violence as a means, or in other words, a *force that moves without force.* His prime example for such a nonviolent violence is the proletarian general strike. Unlike a mere political, extortionary general strike, Benjamin asserts that the proletarian general strike is "as a pure means [...] nonviolent" for "it takes place not in readiness to resume work following external concessions and this or that modification to working conditions, but in determination to resume only a wholly transformed work, no longer enforced by the state, an upheaval that this kind of strike not so much causes as consummates."[26] This proposal, according to which the proletarian general strike does not "cause but consummate" social transformation, is an explicit reference to the anarchist concept of direct action: Benjamin advocates a non-instrumental mode of political action which has given up any relationship to the law and its extortionary procedures.[27] This model of direct action offers an – historically at least partially successful – alternative to the law-based model of social transformation that Menke has in mind. Benjamin's essay thus provides resources to question both Menke's legal philosophical as well as his historico-philosophical basic assumptions: it is neither true that the law is conceptually bound to be violent, as the examples of Kant's pure international law as well as Jewish diasporic law have proven, nor is legal violence the only possible way to struggle against social domination, as the example of direct action shows.

4. Liberating law from violence

Menke's claim that law without violence is conceptually impossible has created a dilemma for his theory. On the one hand, Menke can no longer envision the utopia of social reconciliation (as the early Frankfurt School did), because that would contradict his claim about the irresolvable link between law and violence.[28] On the other hand, if Menke's legal theory is to remain a genuinely *critical* theory, it may not simply opt for the perpetuation of the same forms of interaction as the ones already existing. Menke solves this dilemma by proposing a new understanding of Benjamin's notion of "deposing the law" (*Entsetzung des Rechts*, translated in this book as "relief of law"). According to Menke, the task of legal criticism is not to discriminate law and violence, but to discriminate different "modes of implementation" (*Vollzugsweisen*) (p. 39 *passim*) of law. Menke beholds the establishment of a "self-reflective" mode of implementation of law, one that does not conceal but unfolds its own paradoxical intertwinement with violence, to be the proper goal of a radical transformation of law. Such a law, according to Menke, would at least do away with the "fateful" and thus the "mythical" character of all previous legal forms. "[T]he self-reflection of law," he writes, "leads into a paradox that does not promise a realm beyond the contention, violence, and suffering against which the law takes a stand and that it ends up reenacting within itself. The self-reflective implementation promises nothing more than a law that knows as much about itself" (p. 61). Menke calls such a self-reflective law "a law against its will" or a "repugnant law" (p. 61).

Given the overall brilliance and ruthlessness of Menke's essay, this seems like a rather cheerless promise. The perspective offered by Menke fails to satisfy the radicalism of Benjamin's critique. For this critique is not concerned with the law's ignorance of itself, much less with the judge's mood. Benjamin's critique demands nothing less than the deposing of law (*Entsetzung des Rechts*) "with all the forces on which it depends as they depend on it, finally therefore [...] the abolition of state power."[29] This demand was the necessary consequence of Benjamin's diagnosis about both the *structurally ineffective* as well as the *transcendentally illegitimate* character of legal violence and is supported by the possibility of nonviolent forms of conflict resolution, some of which, like international law and Jewish law, have a legal form. In addition, Benjamin has also laid out a strategy how to accomplish this goal, namely by following the anarchist concept of direct action that is situated beyond law and state power. One might find Benjamin's utopia of the abolition of state power to be too simplistic or messianic, his strategy to be naive or unrealistic. However, as I have attempted to show in this essay, there is *at least no conceptual reason* to resign and to give up the utopia of nonviolence prematurely.

It is precisely the radicalism of Benjamin's demand that allows it to serve as a common denominator of a whole range of emancipatory social struggles. In fact, at least three of the most important contemporary political movements are concerned with state-sanctioned violence: first, the insistent critiques of mass incarceration as presented by prison abolitionism; second, the vast Black Lives Matter movement triggered by the frequent racist police killings in the US, and third the refugees' struggles against state violence executed at borders or in internment camps all around the world. All of these initiatives reject the aggregation of manifest violence in the apparatuses of the modern nation state. Their vision is easy to express but hard to accomplish: to find a way of organizing our political community in a non- (or at least less) violent way. If Marx is correct in his famous assertion that philosophy represents "the self-clarification of the struggles and wishes of the age,"[30] it is the task of any emancipatory legal theory to provide for the theoretical articulation of the desires expressed by such movements.

Notes

1 In this essay, I draw on arguments that I first presented in my book *Kritik der Souveränität* (Frankfurt am Main and New York: Campus, 2012); for a conceptualization of the idea of law without violence, see especially part III.

2 I agree with Menke here that coercion is always to be understood as a form of violence: "Coercion [...] is exercised through the administration

or threat of violence that assails the body and the soul" (p. 4). However, while all coercion is violence, not all violence is coercion. Manifestations of non-coercive violence include psychological harm or injuries. This opens up the possibility that even a non-coercive law can remain (or become) violent. This threat is particularly pertinent with respect to the notion of pedagogical law as outlined below. In my opinion, critical theory has to take this *possibility* seriously, but should not elevate it to a *conceptual* feature of law.

3 I. Kant, *The Metaphysics of Morals*, trans. M. J. Gregor (Cambridge: University of Cambridge Press, 1991), 57.

4 *Ibid.*

5 For a theoretical reflection of the criticism articulated by these movements, see e.g. A. Davis, *Are Prisons Obsolete?* (New York: Seven Stories, 2003); A. Vitale, *Abolish the Police* (London and New York: Verso, forthcoming).

6 W. Benjamin, "Critique of Violence," trans. E. Jephcott, in *Reflections* (New York: Schocken, 1986), 287.

7 M. Foucault, *Discipline and Punish: The Birth of the Prison* (New York: Vintage, 1977), 272.

8 Benjamin, "Critique of Violence," 277.

9 *Ibid.*, 278.

10 *Ibid.*, 277.

11 The "minmum program" of the categorical imperative, Benjamin states, contains "too little," for it still allows people to be used as means in any respect (see Benjamin, "Critique of Violence," 252, note 2). A critique of the subordination of people under the ends of law, he says, "coincides with the critique of all legal violence [...] and cannot be performed by any lesser program" (*ibid.*, 241).

12 Benjamin, "Critique of Violence," 289.

13 I. Kant, "Toward Perpetual Peace," trans. M. J. Gregor, in *The Cambridge Edition of the Works of Immanuel Kant, Practical Philosophy* (Cambridge: Cambridge University Press, 1996), 318.

14 H. Cohen, *Kants Begründung der Ethik nebst ihren Anwendungen auf Recht, Religion und Geschichte*, *Werke*, vol. 2 (Hildesheim: Olms, 2011), 398, my translation.

15 E. Levinas, "A Religion for Adults," in *Difficult Freedom* (London: Athlone Press, 1990).

16 Benjamin, "Critique of Violence," 250.

17 W. Benjamin, "Franz Kafka: Zur zehnten Wiederkehr seines Todestages," in *Gesammelte Schriften*, vol. 2.2 (Frankfurt am Main: Suhrkamp, 1991), 437; my translation.

18 Benjamin, "Critique of Violence," 289.

19 See A. Fischer-Lescano, "Postmoderne Rechtstheorie als kritische Theorie," *Deutsche Zeitschrift für Philosophie*, 61:2 (2013), 179–96.

20 C. Menke, "Die Möglichkeit eines anderen Rechts: Zur Auseinandersetzung mit Andreas Fischer-Lescano," *Deutsche Zeitschrift für Philosophie*, 62:1 (2014), 142, my translation.

21 Benjamin, "Critique of Violence," 236.

22 *Ibid.*, 251.

23 *Ibid.*, 253.

24 *Ibid.*, 236; translation modified.

25 *Ibid.*, 247.

26 *Ibid.*, 246.

27 One could argue that both of Benjamin's demands – to find a law without violence and to find a revolution without violence – are combined in the Jewish concept of the exodus. By leaving Egypt, the Israelites "severed relations" with the Pharaoh instead of imitating him by trying to overpower him. They did so by constituting a new law in the Promised Land, but one that was structurally different from the violent Pharaonic law.

28 Another option to consider would be a world without law (and thus without violence). For reasons that cannot be discussed at length in this text but have to do with law's capacity to create normative orders of autonomy and equality, this option seems feasible neither to Benjamin, nor to Menke, nor to me.

29 Benjamin, "Critique of Violence," 251–52.

30 Karl Marx, Letter to Arnold Ruge, in *Marx & Engels Collected Works*, vol. 3 (London: Lawrence & Wishart, 2010), 145.

4

Deconstructing the deconstruction of the law: reflections on Menke's 'Law and violence'

Alessandro Ferrara

Christoph Menke's essay belongs in the number of those short interventions that often convey a much more penetrating and lasting message than ponderous and monumental volumes. In a single-handed move that ambitiously tries to bring two philosophical worlds – liberalism and deconstructionism – into dialogue, Menke deconstructs the purportedly violence-averting function of the law by elucidating its paradoxical nature, which is overlooked and glossed over by mainstream and even by deliberative liberalism, and at the same time towards the end introduces a remedy, if not a solution, to the said paradox in the form of a reflexive "law against its will" that somehow reinstates, in a peculiar form, the liberal idea of minimizing coercion.

I will group my comments under three main headings. First, some of the presuppositions underlying the thesis of the paradoxical relation of law to violence will be addressed. Second, Menke's appropriation of Benjamin's critique of violence will be discussed, with special reference to the interconnected notions of the "opacity" of law's purpose, of lawmaking as proceeding from power, and of power itself. Finally, I will focus on the *pars construens* of Menke's essay – namely, his reformulation of Benjamin's notion of "*Entsetzung des Rechts*" as a liberation or "relief" of the law that consists in its reflectively accepting its own "other" within itself without juridifying it – and will comment on its relation to the fundamentals of political liberalism.

1. The "paradox" of the law

Law, argues Menke in the first section of his essay, is inextricably bound up with a paradoxical relation to violence: aimed at curbing violent action taking place in the legal area that it regulates, law performs its function through directives backed up by a violence which is always lurking in the background and is sometimes manifestly applied. Within this classical topos – already found in Benjamin's essay "Critique of Violence" and in Derrida's revisitation of it in his Cardozo Law School lecture "Force of Law: 'The Mystical Foundation of Authority' "[1] – Menke emphasizes that law bears not simply an instrumental relation to violence, in those unfortunate cases when persuasion, deterrence, or all other means fail, but also a "structural," permanent, and ineliminable relation to violence. Law generates its own Other: that is, domains of human experience that are identified as in need of regulation and then subjected to its "rule," always backed up by the threat of violence. In other words, law does not discover an antecedently existent lawlessness, as though the state of nature really existed, but it *creates* areas of lawlessness (e.g., the state of nature *qua* mental experiment) to be violently subjected to lawful regulation. This is what Menke understands as "the fate of law."

Drawing on the history of tragedy, Menke starts out by highlighting the transition from the "justice of retribution" (exemplified by *Agamemnon*) to the "justice of the law" (exemplified by *Eumenides*). In the justice-of-retribution paradigm each party is judge in his or in her own case and the balance of retribution is in fact never achieved because what for one party counts as a justice-restoring act of retribution, for the other counts as a new offense ("the spilling of fresh blood") calling for more retributive violence. In the justice-of-the-law paradigm, however, the figure of a "non-partisan party," or the impartial judge, is introduced, who relativizes every narrative of violence as just "one side of the story," normatively inert until "the other side" is offered a fair hearing. Thus the justice-of-the-law paradigm reconceptualizes justice as a way of understanding "the matter in a way that is not partial but sees both sides" (p. 12). Indeed, what Menke calls "the order of retribution" is an equivalent of what Locke understands as a state of nature – a state in which, differently than in Hobbes' view, some rudimentary normativity exists, albeit always interpreted from the point of view of a self-interested party, and no impartial judge for a dispute can even be imagined. Here we reach a first juncture where some comments are in order concerning Menke's notion of politics and his thesis that law creates its own other.

Menke links the dimension of publicness of the justice-of-the-law paradigm with an intrinsically *political quality* of the law, which is counter-intuitive and requires a supplementary argumentation. Adjudication is no arbitration. In every legal proceeding there are two parties and an impartial third party, and each of these three poles has different relations to the other two: a horizontal relation to the other party and a vertical one to the judge. These relations are called "political" by Menke, as distinct from the "private" nature of the relations that bind the parties to an arbitrator who merely facilitates the reaching of an agreement between them. Jointly taken, Menke argues, these two relations "define the legal proceeding *as* politics" (p. 14, original emphasis) in a double sense. The first is the sense that the equality of the parties before the judge is derivative from the equality of all citizens: indeed, the judge "is the representative of the equality of all citizens." The second is the sense that the legal paradigm presupposes "citizenry," a community of equal citizens, and thus "by implication, there is no law outside the polity" (p. 14).

One wonders what concept of politics is presupposed by Menke in order to claim that the "publicly binding" quality of the relation between each of the parties and the judge turns justice into a matter of politics. Politics is contentious in a way that adjudication – the procedure of determining what the law prescribes in a given case – is not. Of course adjudication can be questioned, and for this reason we have courts of different rank, up to a Supreme Court, but it remains separate from and independent of politics insofar as it proceeds from legal principles, constitutional stipulations, legal precedents, and statutes, and not from the negotiated consensus of parties who try to co-determine either the ends to whose pursuit the not unlimited resources of their social union should be allocated or the priorities that should guide their joint action.[2] In an intuitive sense, then, the relation of the parties to a proceeding of arbitration seems much more "political" than the relation of the parties in a judicial proceeding.

Furthermore, one wonders again what concept of politics underlies Menke's claim that the presence of law within a community of equal citizens implies that there is no law beyond the borders of such community. The statement is obviously false in our time, when we are witness not only to the growth of international law, but more significantly to an incipient process of its constitutionalization, along with the constitutionalization of human rights. My point is that the claim was dubious even at the time of the "birth of tragedy," for then too there existed customary law and the embryo of what in Roman times would be called *jus gentium*. Thus at no juncture in history does it seem to have been true that the existence of law within borders has implied the lack of *any normativity whatsoever* affecting relations across borders.

Likewise, in the section on "Manifest violence," Menke asks us to take at face value two claims that in the fourth century BC had already been questioned by Plato. One is the thesis, put forward by Athena in *Eumenides*, that justice or the authoritativeness of the law is bound up with *fear* – the same point raised by Glaucon in Book II of *The Republic* through his myth of Gyges' ring and to whom Socrates replies by showing the intrinsic desirability of a life lived in pursuit of justice. The second is the revelation, for which the realist tradition from Euripides to critical legal studies is given credit, that the law is in fact "a violence in disguise that helps enforce the interests of the ruling class" (p. 18) – a plain restatement of Thrasymachus' thesis, which is indeed the real opening gambit of Plato's *Republic*, that "justice or right is simply what is in the interest of the stronger party."[3] Menke endorses this line of thinking when he intimates that:

> given the simple statistical fact that more than 11 percent of Afro-Americans between the ages of twenty and thirty-four are in prison … it is feckless to point out, however correctly, that every individual legal

> act of judging that contributes to this statistic is formally distinct from an act of retribution. Law and retribution do not just seem to be the same; their manifestations *are* the same" (p. 18, original emphasis).

This is a far from self-evident truth. On the contrary, it is a statement that requires detailed argumentation. In the history of political philosophy the "radically realist" approach pioneered by Thrasymachus has received bashing criticism not just from Socrates/Plato, but also from Locke and Rousseau and even, somewhat surprisingly, from Hobbes. One of the strongest objections, raised by Socrates, points to the inconsequential quality of generalizing Thrasymachus' view and to its undermining all capability for agency: a band of criminals systematically disregarding all concern for justice would be unable to execute any of their designed actions, for they would never keep their hands off each other. So even in such extreme cases, "there must have been some element of justice among them [the criminals] which prevented them wronging each other as well as their victims, and brought them what success they had."[4] This point will be addressed again below, in Section 2. For the time being, let me just point out that the thesis of the paradoxical relation of the law to violence would require a confutation of the points raised by normative political philosophers against such understanding of the nexus of justice and power.

Moving on to Menke's thesis that law creates its own "other," the idea is that whereas in the system of retribution no one is "beyond the reach of justice," "because everyone is *either* just *or* unjust – he or she disturbs or executes or restores the just order of the world" (p. 20, original emphasis), in the case of the "justice of the law," the law, by delimiting a legal space, a jurisdiction, and thus creating a space "beyond," in the end rules over both insiders and outsiders and is enforced against the unjust and the non-just alike. Thus, concludes Menke, because the extra-legal actor, the non-citizen, the outsider, is *not* included in the pact of equality, the judges can bring their judgment to bear upon them:

> only by enforcing it *against* them; faced with one who stands outside, and is alien to law, the judgment of the judges can rule only by fear.

> That is why violence is not only part of the manifestation of the law but also of its essence: the violence of the law comes from its political-procedural form of judgment (p. 21, original emphasis).

As in the retributive order, justice is restored through an act of vengeance that the other party describes as excessive and thus calling for further vengeance, thereby condemning final justice to be a moving and unreachable horizon; thus within the rule of law the violent enforcement of the law must be repeated over and over against the other of the law, namely against "the possibility of the extra-legal or non-law that it [law] has itself engendered and reproduces with each of its acts" (p. 22). The use of force threatened against domestic deviant conduct pales when compared to the structural violence that law exerts over non-law. As Menke puts it, "the relation between law and non-law is not normative and hence not cognitive. It is an antagonism that no insight can bridge, no reasoning can reconcile. It is a relation of *pure enforcement* – of *pure violence*" (p. 21, emphasis added).

Suggestive though these pronouncements may be, they are undergirded by some elements of unclarity. First, it seems implausible that the framework of retribution is entirely coextensive with the friend and foe divide, with no neutral position even possible. Because the chain of vengeance usually takes place within a close-knit *Gemeinschaft*, the larger context within which the community is enmeshed is inhabited by outsiders who have nothing to do with the two conflicting narratives of justice: an Egyptian or a Sicilian or a Phoenician resident would fit in neither side of the *Agamemnon* feud. The outsider's position is not a characteristic of the rule of law alone.

Second, why should the rule of law necessarily enjoin a relation of *violence* with all that stands outside its jurisdictional sphere? Again, what notion of politics must be presupposed in order to claim that a polity regulated by a legal framework must try to *subjugate* every other form of association, of human relation, or simply of human life that crosses its path? *Law* as such is externally inert: it is entirely indifferent to what lies outside its scope, whether a natural or a social world. It is *politics* –

or, more precisely, the political will of the executive power *pro tempore* in charge of ruling a political community – that is first and foremost responsible for the attempt to extend the reach of domestic law to new areas, both geographical and social, which previously were "unregulated." If Menke's statement that law "must also secure its rule against the possibility of the extra-legal or non-law" is understood as a description of the relation that liberal polities have traditionally established with the external world of foreign political communities, such an account is accurate only for the age of colonialism and aggressive expansionism. Since the 1928 Briand-Kellog Pact, signed by sixty-two states, not to mention the UN Charter of 1945, aggressive wars are banned as crimes by the international community. Of course these documents were and are far from effective in preventing the violent imposition of one legal frame over an alien context that counts as "non-law" – an imposition that regretfully continues to occur every time democracy gets forcefully "exported." However, the factual persistence of a violent imposition of the law of one place over the social life of another place bears no more normative significance than the persistence of car theft can be counted as counterevidence against the merit, desirability, or legitimacy of property laws. Crime, ineliminable though it is, is to the normative foundations of property laws as background noise is to communication – a nuisance to be duly taken into account and neutralized, but of no greater significance. Thus, from a historical point of view it seems to me far from being established that there is a necessary relation between the law and its violent imposition, let alone that there is any necessary relation between *liberalism* and such imposition. In particular, if we take Menke's essay as a reflection on law and violence intended to address *us,* the contemporary citizens of a globalizing world, I find that the suggestion that today's liberalism may not be immune from the temptation to impose regimes of legality onto recalcitrant extra-legal contexts flies in the face of even a superficial survey of today's liberal-democratic theory. To mention three obvious cases, Rawls' picture of the world *qua* political entity by no means allows for these kinds of relations: not just peoples that embrace liberalism, but also so-called "decent peoples," are envisaged as relating to one another on the basis of considerations of justice within a "Society of Peoples," and then jointly relating to far more diverse kinds of peoples out of considerations of prudence.[5] Even in the least favorable case – that of so-called "outlaw States" – such relation never includes the prospect of violent regime-change but simply contemplates containment. Habermas' idea of human rights as being on their way to global constitutionalisation, and of a world society in the process of being formed and constituting the social basis of a "world internal politics,"[6] can again hardly be associated with the law's relating to non-law in terms of "pure enforcement" or "pure violence." In his essay "Governing the Globe,"[7] Walzer outlines a desirable liberal political order for the world society that goes even further than Rawls' and Habermas' respective visions in that it avoids all reference to one central lawmaking source and allows for a number of regulatory sources cooperating in a regime of legal pluralism.

Finally, if we understand the relation of law and non-law as entirely confined to the internal space of a legal community, the meaning of the claim concerning the paradoxical nexus of law and violence appears even more counterintuitive. If by "non-law" we mean the complex of actions, relations, prerogatives, duties, sins, expectations that for a society at any given time are *not* regulated in the legal codes, then the idea that law has an intrinsic tendency to exhaust the entire life-world seems self-contradictory: it would be as if an organism were trying to envelope the shell within which it is growing. Furthermore, should Menke's thesis be construed as suggesting that by trying to regulate social life, *law* generates new dimensions of experience that appear in need of legal regulation, again that claim would find counterevidence in the fact that many other human practices – medical science for one, but also technological developments, communication technology, and economics – produce instances of conduct, action, interests, and conflicts that appear in need of legal regulation. However, more questions concerning the thesis that law is bound to generate its own other and then to violently assimilate it are raised by Menke's reconstruction of Benjamin's view of law and violence, to be addressed in the next section.

2. The tragedy underlying Benjamin's view of emancipation

In his famous essay "Critique of Violence," dated 1921, Benjamin distinguishes two kinds of criticism that can be leveled against the persisting enmeshment of law with violence. One is a rather naive critique of the *use* of violence as a means by the law in the pursuit of its ends. This critique is naive in the sense that it focuses merely on the *law-preserving* function of the violent forms of enforcement. First, it can be easily met by the creation of the legal category of "excessive" or "cruel and unusual" punishment, through which the law immunizes itself against this criticism. Second, even when articulated in more sophisticated terms, for example in the name of the categorical imperative never to treat persons merely as means,[8] the effectiveness of this critique is preempted by positive law's claim to be in the *equal* interest of every citizen: quoting Anatole France, Benjamin reminds us that "Poor and rich are equally forbidden to spend the night under the bridges."[9]

The other form of critique addresses the deeper nexus of *lawmaking* and violence. In a passage quoted by Menke, Benjamin clarifies the twofold function of violence in lawmaking: on the one hand "lawmaking pursues as its end, with violence as the means, what is to be established as law";[10] on the other hand, what gets so established is "not an end unalloyed by violence, but one necessarily and intimately bound to it, under the title of power." Thus, Benjamin concludes, "lawmaking is power making, and, to that extent, *an immediate manifestation of violence*."[11] This is the *mythical* constitution of power under the guise of law, the fate of law, and law presenting itself as fate. As Menke approvingly comments:

> according to Benjamin, the violence of the law, which he calls "fateful" for this reason, consists in the fact that the law's violent means obliterate its just purposes because its self-preservation becomes its only purpose. The law is purely about power, yet not about the power of the ruling class or the victor: it is about *its own* power, the power of the law.

> The "fateful" violence of the law is the violence of its pure self-preservation (p. 31, original emphasis).

Menke then draws two conclusions that will be examined in this section: first, over and beyond overt violence, the most problematic thing about law presenting itself as fate, or about the mythical moment of law, is the *opacity* of its purpose, which coincides with its means. Law ostensibly protects something else – the ultimate values of the polity – but in fact "operates purely for its own sake, for the sake of the preservation of its order, the establishment of its categories, perspective, and language – for the sake of its pure power" (p. 31).

Second, in every act of *enforcement* – or, in Benjamin's terms, "preservation" of the law – a "repetition" occurs of the original law-making, namely the law's forceful and violent suppression of "non-law" or "mere life" or "life in the state of nature." Thus, suggests Menke, the "law can never be purely preservative, proceeding in accordance with its normative logic; it must again and again oppose its power to the extra-legal in acts *divorced from all normativity*" (p. 32, emphasis added). The violence ultimately bound up with the law consists of its compulsion to repeat this original violent scene over and over. Mysteriously, the legal order is said to impose itself over what preceded it "not by force of persuasion and justification" – as three centuries of contract theories, from Hobbes to Locke to Rousseau and on to Rawls have argued – but only "by overwhelming and violating force" (pp. 32–33). The explanation provided by Menke is that because the legal framework "breaks with the violence of retributive repetition by virtue of its procedure of equality" (p. 33), and because the latter, in turn, is justified by its reflecting the political equality of the citizens, it follows that the "justice of law is therefore due to the political union of the citizens, which, as a created union, maintains its difference from what is not part of it" (p. 33). Here we again find the conflation of "maintaining difference" and doing so by suppressing or subjugating that – be it individual, nation, or form of life – which is other, simply not reducible to law and its forms.

It seems to me that Menke imports three dubious assumptions from Benjamin into his own argument about law and violence: (a) the conflation of boundary maintenance and violence, (b) a realist view of law-making as proceeding from power, and (c) an undifferentiated notion of power. Let me briefly comment on each of them.

Concerning (a), it is not clear for what reason a legal order's attempt to maintain itself differentiated from its non-legal environment should count as violence or, to speak in less reified language, why the attempt of the concerned (individual and collective) actors to keep the integrity of a certain multilevel practice – which includes moments as diverse as legislation, adjudication, interpretation, judicial review, and enforcement – independent and distinct from other forms of practice (e.g. the wielding of political power, the mobilization of constituencies, market behavior, administration) should count as "violence." It is implausible to identify such reason with the fact that in so doing the actors try to have law operate "purely for its own sake," that is, "for the sake of the preservation of its order, and the establishment and enforcement of its categories, perspective, and language." Why couldn't the same be said of the practice of moral judgment and moral conduct, which obviously consists of actors trying to preserve the distinctiveness of "the moral point of view" from contamination with "non-moral" or "extra-moral" considerations? Does a moral culture, an ethos, commit violence when it tries to preserve its own integrity as a system of principles and values aimed at orienting conduct? Paradoxically, couldn't the same claim be raised with respect to art and the aesthetic sphere? Since it has emerged as an autonomous sphere of human practice, guided by its own autonomous values, and even more since it has become a practice no longer dependent on political patronage but supported by the market, art has stimulated a reflection on its own independence and has striven to maintain such autonomy vis-à-vis the alien forces of commercialization, political conformism, and religious complacency. Should the museum or the academies be accused of entertaining a paradoxical relation to violence only because they programmatically try to defend the boundary between art and non-art for the sake of the preservation of art? Should the symbolist poetics of "l'art pour l'art" and the avant-garde radical reflexivity be accused of being an exercise of *artistic violence*? The nexus of law and violence cannot just reside in the tendency of law to maintain its own integrity and distinctiveness vis-à-vis the larger societal process within which it is, along with many other practices, immersed.

Furthermore, concerning (b), it is difficult to find any supporting argument in Menke's text for his acceptance of Benjamin's claim to the effect that "lawmaking is power making, and, to that extent, an immediate manifestation of violence."[12] That statement can be properly understood, in accordance with the charity principle, as linked with the political culture of the aftermath of the First World War, in a continental European context where democracy, with the exception of France, had weak roots and where totalitarian creeds held sway. The echo of Schmitt's understanding of sovereignty and the ground of legitimacy as resting on the power to suspend the law and declare a "state of exception" can be heard. Schmitt had already published *Political Romanticism* and *Dictatorship* by 1921, and the essay on the concept of sovereignty would be published the subsequent year,[13] but certainly the critique of liberalism, by then already assimilated to democracy, was part of a common humus in Germany. It is the ultimate tragedy of Benjamin to be thinking of liberation – because he seeks to transcend the mythical manifestation of law as violence through the notion of divine justice or *mystical* violence – from what he perceives as law's compulsive repetition of the initial violence and yet to be forced to think of such liberation in terms of categories partially rooted in a non-democratic political culture. Rather than tragic, it is ironic that such uncriticized assumption should reappear in Derrida's "Force of Law." After reconstructing the "mystical foundation" of the authority of law in Montaigne and Pascal, and the complex relation of law and justice, Derrida argues that:

> since the origin of authority, the founding or grounding [*la fondation ou le fondement*], the positing of the law [*loi*] cannot by definition rest on anything but themselves [sic], *they are themselves [sic] a violence*

> *without ground* [*sans fondement*]. This is not to say that they are in themselves unjust, in the sense of "illegal" or "illegitimate." They are neither legal nor illegal in their founding moment. They exceed the opposition between founded and unfounded, or between any foundationalism or anti-foundationalism.[14]

Later in his essay Derrida reiterates the point:

> The foundation of all states occurs in a situation that one can thus call revolutionary. It inaugurates a new law, *it always does so in violence.* Always, which is to say even when there haven't been those spectacular genocides, expulsions or deportations that so often accompany the foundation of states, great or small, old or new, right nearby or very far away.[15]

While an assessment of Schmitt's critique of liberalism or Derrida's view of the "force of law" exceeds the scope of my present argument,[16] it must be noted that the crucial assumption concerning the inextricable nexus of lawmaking and naked power is reflected in Benjamin, and in Menke's adoption of Benjamin's analysis, without any acknowledgment, let alone refutation, of the objections found within the tradition of normative political philosophy. To recall some of the most salient ones, for Locke the imposition of a legal order or even of a single provision through the use of force puts the lawgiver in no different position than that of a highway bandit who forces me to surrender my purse to them. Even the "Conquerour in a lawful War," cannot impose a form of government by force and violence:

> He that forces my Horse from me, ought presently to restore it, *i.e.* quit me of the Obligation of it; or I may resume it my self, *i.e.* chuse whether I will perform it. ... Nor does it at all alter the case, to say I *gave my Promise*, no more than it excuses the force, and passes the Right, when I put my hand in my Pocket, and deliver my Purse my self to a Thief, who demands it with a Pistol at my Breast. From all which it follows, that the *Government of a Conquerour*, imposed, by force, on the Subdued, against whom he had no right of War, or who joyned not

> in the War against him, where he had right, *has no Obligation* upon them.[17]

Rousseau pushes the counterfactual argument one step further. Even in the unlikely case that a violent imposition of the law – the archetypal "mythical violence of the law" – should succeed in winning the consensus of the subjects, as in La Boétie's and Grotius' patterns of voluntary enslavement, still we could not call the ensuing rule a legitimate one:

> if an individual, says Grotius, can alienate his liberty and become the slave of a master, why should not a whole people be able to alienate theirs, and become subject to a king? … Even if each person could alienate himself, he could not alienate his children; they are born free men; their liberty belongs to them, and no one has a right to dispose of it except themselves. … In order, then, that an arbitrary government might be legitimate, it would be necessary that the people in each generation should have the option of accepting and rejecting it; *but in that case such a government would no longer be arbitrary.*[18]

Finally, even one of the staunchest advocates of absolutist sovereignty, namely Thomas Hobbes, counts among the "false principles" the idea that Benjamin and Menke urge on us, namely that de facto power, victorious violence on the ground, may with time – like the alchemist used to hope of vile metals turning into gold – result into a rule of law, and reiterate symbolically this violence at every enforcement of the law. If there is a false political principle *par excellence,* Hobbes argues, that is the principle adopted by those who:

> from having observed how in all places, and in all ages, unjust Actions have been authorised, by the force, and victories of those who have committed them … have thereupon taken for Principles, and grounds of their Reasoning, *That Justice is but a vain word: That whatsoever a man can get by his own Industry, and hazard, is his own: That the Practice of all Nations cannot be unjust: That Examples of former times are good Arguments of doing the like again;* and many more of that kind: Which being granted, no Act in it selfe can be a Crime, but must

> be made so (not by the Law, but) by the successe of them that commit it; and the same Fact be vertuous, or vicious, as Fortune pleaseth.[19]

Among contemporary authors, Rawls and Habermas can certainly be mentioned as critics – Rawls through his principle of liberal legitimacy and Habermas through his "co-originality thesis"[20] – of the realist premise that legitimate forms of rule are the product of the stabilization and legitimation over time of what was once an exercise of naked power. Most interesting is Michelman's idea that higher lawmaking, even when it amounts to an exercise of "constituent power," is "always under law," that is, it always amounts to an interpretation of the *sui generis* normativity connaturate with social life itself (according to the principle *ubi societas, ibi jus*).[21] In sum, the assertion that lawmaking is an exercise of power which reflects an originary violence cannot be accepted if it does not come with a convincing refutation of the competing normative accounts.

Finally, concerning (c), in Menke's endorsement of Benjamin's critique of the nexus of law and violence, the notion of power is dedifferentiated with respect not only – as one would expect – to contemporary liberal views of a normative bent, but surprisingly also with respect to the "political-realist" theorization of power found in Max Weber. There is no trace even of the merely descriptive Weberian distinction of *Macht* – namely, power as the ability to obtain compliant behavior through the use of force or the threat thereof – and *Herrschaft* or the authority to obtain compliance by virtue of the addressee's belief in the legitimacy of the ordering authority and its being entitled to issue such a command. Even in the light of this merely descriptive approach, the enforcement of the law and its everyday operation can never be equated with exercise of violence, or the repetition of an originary act of violence, for the simple reason that the originary founding of a legal system requires a moment of "belief" or, in a different and non-Weberian terminology, a moment of "recognition" that naked power cannot impose. The replacement of this fundamental conceptual differentiation, usually crystallized in the two terms "power" and "authority," with an undifferentiated concept of "power" is one of the philosophical moves underlying Menke's essays that stands in need of most urgent justification. The reason for the urgency lies in the fact that the central claim that in every act of law enforcement a repetition of the violence perpetrated by the originary enactment of the law occurs can only make sense against the background of such dedifferentiated notion of power.

3. Law's reflective self-restraint and political liberalism

In the second half of his essay, Menke reinterprets the closing paragraph of Benjamin's essay in an original way and puts forward his own solution of the paradox of the law. While up to now the purported breaking away of the law from the mythical violence of retribution has ended up in reproducing the same mythical violence at a new level, Benjamin's project for avoiding the dual trap of either "assenting to the law" (thereby acquiescing to the violence it inflicts onto our inner nature) or "rejecting the law" (thereby relapsing into the order of retribution) rests on what he calls the *Entsetzung des Rechts*, which heralds "a new historical epoch."[22] Following Agamben, Menke reinterprets the *Entsetzung des Rechts* – usually translated as "the suspension of the law," in consonance with the Schmittian theme of the state of exception as the sovereign('s) decision – as the *relief of law.* In Menke's rendition, "Schmitt wants to suspend the law for the sake of the power of the state, whereas to 'relieve' law requires it to be enacted in such a way, that law is removed from its office, its historical function of powermaking is expunged, and law is thereby liberated" (p. 37). Further in his text, Menke details the idea of "liberation of the law" as consisting of a "form of the implementation of political-procedural judgment that is liberated from its violent rule over the extra- or non-legal" (p. 38). But how can law be really liberated from violence?

Menke elaborates on Benjamin's idea and distinguishes two ways of liberating the law from its entwinement with mythical violence. Both ways somehow entail a reduction of the hiatus between law and non-law or the extra-legal, but the first modality – a "teleological (or 'aesthetic') concept of pedagogy" (p. 38) – aims at sublating that hiatus by aligning the extra-legal constitution of subjectivity to what the law requires, and thus carries within itself a residue of the "imperialism of the law," up to the point that the ethos of the polis becomes a kind of second nature. For this reason it is called "regressive" by Menke. The second modality is called "reflective" because the bridging of the hiatus proceeds from the law's active self-transformation in the direction of "reenacting" within itself its own demarcation from the extra-legal: in Menke's words, "self-reflective law contains its *other within itself*" (p. 40, original emphasis).

To the question that immediately springs up – how can law contain the other within itself and do so without yet again *reducing* it to itself? – Menke replies that, drawing on the character of Eve within Kleist's *The Broken Jug*, a right to remain silent in court, or not to disclose significant elements of the life-world in which one is immersed, can be construed as a "right against the law," secured through law itself. Through giving up its own imperialistic pretense to rule over the whole of social life, law "renders itself relative" and self-limits itself. This view could sound like a mostly welcome translation into the vocabulary of contemporary continental philosophy – and much of the work of philosophy has to do with translating from one framework into another – of the basic insight of liberal (and also of Habermas' own kind of discursive) constitutionalism: that is, that the tyranny of the law and of democratic lawmaking can be avoided only if a reflexivized law subtracts some fundamental normative elements (called "rights") from the arena of interest politics and majority rule. Menke, however, connects the *liberal* form of reflexive self-limitation of the law to a pair of undesirable consequences. First, liberalism liberates the individual "from the coercion to become in its entirety a part of the legal order" only to deliver them hostage to their own private and mainly economic interest, which is tantamount to delivering them hostage to the forces of the market. Second, liberalism "leaves what it separates unaltered"

(p. 51), namely, it simply aims at insulating certain areas from the reach of the law, without ever questioning, let alone changing, "*how* the law *judges*" (p. 51, original emphasis).

For this reason Menke proposes a new understanding of the self-reflection of the law, aimed at superseding the liberal version of it. The critical point where innovation is called for is that in the liberal version the law self-limits itself in recognition of the "right" of the non-legal to remain non-regulated, but in so doing it *juridifies* it, taking back again what it purportedly offers. In Menke's words:

> The self-reflective implementation of law realizes the right of law *and* the right of the non-legal by not turning the non-legal into an element – a party, a case – in a legal proceeding, but instead bringing it to bear against its juridification. Implementing law in a self-reflective manner means meticulously executing the proceeding of impartial-egalitarian examination, consideration, and judgment *and* releasing the non-legal forces of "distraction" – of obliviousness, refusal, and incapacity. In this counteraction of the forces of distraction, the identity of self and law to which the autonomous law curses us … breaks apart. The self-reflective implementation of law … lends full expression to the contradiction, which is to say the unity of unity and contradiction, of citizen and non-citizen, of participation in and obliviousness, refusal, incapacity of law (p. 55, original emphasis).

How can this self-reflective bringing to expression the paradoxical co-presence of "unity and contradiction, of citizen and non-citizen, of participation in and obliviousness, refusal, incapacity of law" (p. 55) ever take place?

Drawing on Heiner Müller's play *Volokolamsk Highway I: Russian Opening*, Menke outlines what he calls a "utopia of equal possibility." During the Second World War, a lower officer of a Soviet battalion stationed outside Moscow to defend the city against the upcoming Nazi offensive shoots himself in the hand in order to be exempted, on account of his being injured, from fighting at the front line. The commander of the battalion orders the man to be executed and answers the question raised by the lieutenant in charge of organizing the firing squad – "Do we have the right?" – by simply saying "My order will be obeyed," and then adds "And if it was unjust let me be shot / You write the report comrade lieutenant" (p. 56). At a subsequent point in the plot, the commander will sum up the incident with the phrase, taken by Menke as exemplary of this non-regressive self-reflection of the law: "I had [him] shot and in accordance with martial law." This order exemplifies the self-reflectiveness of the law because it is "issued *in accordance with* martial law" but does not issue "*from* martial law" (p. 57, original emphasis). It is an order, argues Menke, "without knowledge of the law, and in that sense is a law-free (not a lawless) order," an order that "does not issue from law and knowledge of the law; an order counter to law: not counter to this or that law, but *counter to law as such*; counter to the right of law to make a binding determination of what will hold among us" (p. 57, emphasis added).

Underlying this interpretation is an idea of law that deserves closer inspection. Indeed, the opposition between the commander's order being "in accordance with martial law" but "not issuing from it," on which Menke rests his point, makes sense only against a dubious view of the law as capable of producing detailed directives in all relevant cases of application. That is *one* view of law, and a radically positivist one. Law is not a syllogism. To remain within the liberal camp, this view certainly does not apply to Dworkin's notion of adjudication as "making the most," nor to his idea that legal *rules* are applied under the guidance of legal *principles* that admit of no fixed a priori ranking but are rather to be balanced with each other in a context-sensitive way.[23] Furthermore, it is hard to see how the distinction between an official act, in this case an order, being "in accordance with the law" and "issuing from the law" should take us *beyond* liberalism, when the liberal understanding of the legitimacy of laws, best exemplified by Rawls' principle of liberal legitimacy, is carefully phrased by using the "in accordance with" formula: "Our exercise of political power is fully proper only when it is exercised in accordance with a constitution the essentials of which all citizens as free and equal may reasonably be expected to endorse in the light of principle and ideals acceptable to their common human reason."[24]

An important complication in the play occurs at this point, however. Once the order is issued, a film is projected on stage and the film shows a wishful, happy ending, with the commander exercising the sovereign prerogative of grace and pardoning the officer in an ensuing burst of collective and liberating laughter. The projection is then interrupted by the order of shooting and the cracking of the volley of synchronized bullets that kill the condemned officer. From this moment on, the meaning of the order is somehow transformed. Interpreting the playwright's intention, Menke claims that the utopian moment of this modality of self-reflexivization of the law consists in the equi-possibility, from a dramatic point of view, of both the pardon and the execution as outcomes of the situation. The enforcement of the law *is just one possibility alongside others*: "Law ultimately prevails over non-law, the commander orders not to pardon but to execute, yet even in doing so, he no longer maintains and enforces the right of law against non-law" (p. 60).

So far so good; but then Menke glosses over the significance of this modality of "relief of law" and praises the character of the commander for a twofold reason: he "does not disburden himself of the responsibility for his decision by passing that responsibility to the law" and therefore he "does not demand the condemned man's consent to his order as one would to a legal conviction," but assumes full responsibility for letting his order "appear exactly what it is – frank violence" (p. 61). The mythical violence of non-reflective law "eternalizes" the violence it exerts onto the extra-legal, whereas reflective law fully acknowledges the contingency of the "frank violence" it exerts. Ultimately Menke's "relief of law" relocates the conflict between law and non-law within law itself and "promises nothing more than a law that knows as much about itself," that is recognizes "to be without law," "feels *repugnance* for itself" and becomes "a law against its own will" (p. 61, original emphasis).

I find the end destination of Menke's philosophical journey through the relation of the law to violence a perfectly desirable and reasonable one, and would like to add three comments to it. Suggestive though the image of a "law against its own will" may be – a kind of late-modern alternative, like minimalist art, to the self-assured, often grandiloquent self-representation of modern law, "whispered law" as opposed to "loudly proclaimed" law – I would suggest the expression "against its own will" should be construed against the larger background of a reflection on whatever has become of the philosophical notion of reason in our philosophical horizon, after the impact of Rawls' and Habermas' work on "public" and "communicative" reason. I understand these two notions – outlined for a different purpose – as just the tip of a much more substantial iceberg, namely the differentiation of the notion of reason, prompted by the Linguistic Turn of the first half of the twentieth century. The relation of public and communicative reason to our received philosophical notion of reason is not easy to conceive unless we insert a new distinction between the general idea of reason and what we are used to calling theoretical and practical reason: namely, the distinction between "speculative" reason (of which theoretical and practical reason become two varieties) and "deliberative" reason – a kind of reason with its own distinct mode of functioning and of which public and communicative reason are two examples. Speculative reason can be said to assess arguments (a) independently of a context, (b) independently of practical constraints on action, and (c) independently of a time frame. It aims at solving a given problem in a way valid in all possible worlds. Speculative reason, in either variety, is correlated with the phenomenological experience of "epoché," namely the suspension of all commonsense or everyday assumptions concerning the question at hand. Finally, time is factored out in a dialogue that spans from Plato to the future after us.

Deliberative reason, on the contrary, assesses claims (a) with reference to a context, (b) in view of the coordination of the actions of a plurality of actors and (c) within a time frame, in order to find the best solution to the problem at hand, within the given context. Its own distinctive form of universalism consists in the power of exemplarity: the best solution to the given problem commands assent beyond its original context by virtue of its being recognized as an instance of "excellence within its own parameters," of its embedding a singular and exceptional well-formedness. From a phenomenological point of view, deliberative reason is correlated not with "epoché" but with a "sense of urgency": namely, the practical urgency of having to find an answer *before a consensus on the contested underlying principles is reached*. We have to legislate on abortion, same-sex marriage, stem cell research, and similar issues without affording the luxury of waiting for all those concerned to view the matter in light of the same principles. Temporality also affects deliberative reason in a *prospective* (and not just *genealogical*) sense, which does not apply to speculative reason.[25]

Law "against its will" or law that is "just one possibility alongside others" could then be understood as a form of law undergirded by an awareness of its resting on *deliberative* grounds. It could be conceived of as a form of law that, drawing on the idea of "democratic dualism," pioneered by Ackerman and integrated within political liberalism by Rawls, renounces the demand for the *direct* consent of all the governed (as in Müller's play, the commander renounces seeking consent to his order on the basis that it proceeds from the law) and settles for an *indirect* consent that hinges on the law's compatibility or being *in accordance with* the constitution.

Second, I find the expression "frank violence" unpalatable. The frankness of frank violence still needs a validation before some ideal tribunal – frankness can otherwise justify the most horrible acts. Again, the frankness of Menke's "frank violence" can charitably be understood as connected with the moment of "closure" that necessarily accompanies the operation of deliberative reason, the temporal constraint which is absent from more "speculative" modes of reasoning. Charity notwithstanding, the expression 'frank violence' needs rewording.

Finally, I find the idea that "relieved law" is "lawless" a bit perplexing. There is a grain of truth in such expression, in the sense that self-reflective law refuses to consider itself the mere application of a higher principle, but the phrase also conveys the potentially misleading suggestion that law is "groundless," a pure act of sovereign will. Again, drawing on Michelman's idea that even higher-law ministrations are always "under law" – in the sense of their being responsive to, and interpretive of, a kind of "proto-law," not necessarily positivized, of the political community of reference – we can reconfigure Menke's idea of the "lawlessness" of "relieved law" as the idea of its being "principle-free" but not unrelated to a prior *nomos*, which indeed could take the form of a narrative rather than that of a principle.[26]

At each of these three critical junctures on its way to overcoming the mythical relation of law to violence, Menke's argument, it seems to me, intersects the path of contemporary "political liberalism" and by no means runs counter to it or supersedes it.

Notes

1 W. Benjamin, "Critique of Violence," in *Reflections: Essays, Aphorisms, Autobiographical Writings* (New York: Schocken Books, 1978), 277–30; J. Derrida, "Force of Law: 'The Mystical Foundation of Authority,'" trans. M. Quaintance, *Cardozo Law Review*, 11 (1990), 920–1038.

2 For a more detailed account of politics along these lines, see A. Ferrara, *The Democratic Horizon: Hyperpluralism and the Renewal of Political Liberalism* (New York: Cambridge University Press, 2014), 25.

3 Plato, *The Republic*, 338c1–2, trans. D. Lee, with an introduction by M. Lane (London: Penguin, 2007), 18.

4 *Ibid.*, 352c4–7, 34.

5 See J. Rawls, "The Law of Peoples," in *The Law of Peoples, with "The Idea of Public Reason Revisited"* (Cambridge, MA: Harvard University Press, 1999), 1–128.

6 See J. Habermas, *The Postnational Constellation: Political Essays* (1998), trans., ed., and with an introduction by M. Pensky (Cambridge, MA: MIT Press, 2001), 58–112.

7 See M. Walzer, "Governing the Globe," in *Arguing About War* (New Haven and London: Yale University Press, 2004), 171–91.

8 Benjamin, "Critique of Violence," 285.

9 *Ibid.*, 296.

10 *Ibid.*, 295.

11 *Ibid.*, 295, emphasis added.

12 *Ibid.*, 295.

13 See C. Schmitt, *Political Romanticism* (1919, 1925), trans. G. Oakes (Cambridge, MA: MIT Press, 1986); *Dictatorship* (1921), trans. M. Hoelzl and G. Ward (Cambridge: Polity Press, 2014); *Political Theology: Four Chapters on the Concept of Sovereignty* (1922, 1934), trans. G. D. Schwab (Cambridge, MA: MIT Press, 1985).

14 Derrida, "Force of Law," 943, emphasis added.

15 *Ibid.*, 991, emphasis added.

16 For an interesting discussion of the relation between the two thinkers on the subject of law and violence, see J. P. McCormick, "Derrida on Law; Or, Poststructuralism Gets Serious," *Political Theory*, 29 (2001), 408–12.

17 J. Locke, *Two Treatises of Government* (1690), with an introduction and note by P. Laslett, revised edition (New York: Mentor Books, 1965), II, 16, §§ 186–87, 440, original emphasis.

18 J.-J. Rousseau, "The Social Contract" (1762), in *The Social Contract and the Discourse on the Origin of Inequality*, ed. L. G. Crocker (New York: Simon and Schuster, 1967), I, 4, 11–12, emphasis added.

19 T. Hobbes, *Leviathan* (1651), ed. with an introduction by C. B. Macpherson (London: Penguin, 1968), Ch. 27, 339–40, original emphasis.

20 See J. Rawls, *Political Liberalism* (1993), expanded edition (New York: Columbia University Press, 2005), 137; J. Habermas, *Between Facts and Norms: Contributions to a Discourse Theory of Law and Democracy* (1992), trans. W. Rehg (Cambridge: Polity Press, 1996), 121–23.

21 See F. Michelman, "Always Under Law?," *Constitutional Commentary*, 12:2 (1995), 227–47. For a more extended discussion of Michelman's thesis, see A. Ferrara, *Justice and Judgment: The Rise and the Prospect of the Judgment Model in Contemporary Political Philosophy* (London: Sage, 1999), 143–49.

22 Benjamin, "Critique of Violence," 300.

23 See R. Dworkin, *Taking Rights Seriously* (London: Duckworth, 1977), 24–26.

24 Rawls, *Political Liberalism*, 137.

25 The above comments draw on a paper on "Speculative and Deliberative Reason," discussed at the Frankfurt Colloquium of the Cluster of Excellence on Normative Orders, Frankfurt, 2011.

26 See Michelman, "Always Under Law?" and R. Cover, "The Supreme Court, 1982 Term – Foreword: Nomos and Narrative," *Faculty Scholarship Series*, Paper 2705, retrieved at http://digitalcommons.law.yale.edu/fss_papers/?utm_source=digitalcommons.law.yale.edu%2Ffss_papers%2F2705&utm_medium=PDF&utm_campaign=PDFCoverPages.

5

Law in action: Ian McEwan's *The Children Act* and the limits of the legal practices in Menke's 'Law and violence'

Ben Morgan

> We could put this less paradoxically by saying that a successful performance – as decision or practice – is made possible insofar as we no longer think of it as made possible by us (i.e., by us alone).
>
> Christoph Menke, "Ability and Faith," 609.[1]

1. Introduction: Eluding the law

I want briefly to set out one of the central issues that Christoph Menke confronts in his essay, before showing how a reading of Ian McEwan's novel *The Children Act* (2014), alongside one of the legal judgments to which the novel is indebted, can shift the grounds of analysis in a way that positively contributes to Menke's project of investigating the limits of the law.

In the lead essay, Christoph Menke posits that law is indissociable from violence: if nothing else, it imposes a set of norms to which subjects, in the process of becoming subjects, ineluctably conform. He then explores ways in which the law might reflect on this violent imposition and recognize its own lawlessness without simply abolishing itself. He calls this improved situation the "self-reflection" of the law: "the self-reflection of law leads into a paradox that does not promise a realm beyond the contention, violence, and suffering against which the law takes a stand and that it ends up reenacting within itself. The self-reflective implementation promises nothing more than a law that knows as much about itself" (p. 61) Thus, in his essay Menke doesn't move beyond the paradox he diagnoses in the law. Rather, he imagines a law that acknowledges and inhabits the apparently insoluble difficulty. Nevertheless, he does not give up all hope of maneuvering his way beyond the *aporia*. In an article on Marx's critique of the law published two years after the German edition of *Law and Violence*, he continues the project of probing the limits of legality. In the later essay, the limits of the law are always, in the last analysis, created and maintained by people: The law is a human practice, even if, in its everyday functioning, it must detach itself from the conflicts and debates of individuals and collectives that produce and change it.[2] Behind or before the law, there are the disagreements, compromises, and/or impositions from which a particular, normalizing, legal framework emerges. This might suggest that we can curb the violence of the law and escape the paradox by drawing attention to the discussions and struggles from which a normative framework arises. The law as impersonal imposition could be replaced with law as a set of negotiated standards agreed by a group of people amongst themselves, and open to renegotiation where the group sees fit. But, for Menke, this solution will not work because the people doing the negotiating are themselves already affected by the processes by which individuals are made subjects of the law. In his bleak view, legal practices "produce a form of subjectivity that underpins or causes social domination."[3] The violence of the law is always already in place in the very structure of our identities.

Menke doesn't make the case for this claim in full in the later text on Marx, but refers back to his essay on law and violence. I shall be commenting later in my essay on some aspects of the claim, particularly on its debt to Rousseau's strangely implausible account of how human life functioned before the advent of human societies. At this point in my argument, I want only to set out the conundrum with which Menke is faced as he tries to respect the law but simultaneously to elude its clutches. For if the very form of our identity is produced within the constraining framework of the law, then Menke's hope that the political arena will stand outside legal institutions to dictate their shape seems bound to be disappointed. The people trying to change things will already be shaped through and through, indeed constituted by, the normalizing social practices they hope to transform.

This is a familiar problem in twentieth-century critical theory: we find it in Horkheimer and Adorno's picture of subjects made in the image of the culture industry, and in Foucault's account of the disciplinary regimes through which modern societies reproduce forms of individual identity.[4] Indeed, Menke himself explicitly mentions the Foucauldian model in his account of the normalizing effects of social policy.[5] An antidote to this position might conceivably be found in the work of Jürgen Habermas, for whom the utopian potential of communicating in language offers an escape from the bleak vision of a constitutively violated subjectivity that we find in Horkheimer and Adorno, and in Foucault.[6] But in Menke's view, communicative competence cannot be appealed to as a universal ideal. Even if it could escape the clutches of the law, language is in practice available to people only to varying degrees.[7] An appeal to language will only reproduce, not overcome, these social inequalities.

So how might we find a way beyond the paradox of the law and of modern identity? One place to which Menke has frequently turned, inspired as he is by the legacy of Adorno, is art. From his early book on the *Sovereignty of Art* (1988) to his more recent *Force of Art* (2013), aesthetic experience is to him a phenomenon that resists incorporation into our everyday discourse. Indeed, in the later book he goes so far as to suggest that art is not a social practice at all: it is irreducible to the shared forms on which social practice depends.[8] In the closing pages of the lead essay, Menke points to Adorno's brief account in *Minima Moralia* of how aesthetic taste develops and criticizes itself as a possible model for the self-reflection of the law (p. 61). In Menke's view, art offers a space in which alternatives to the habits of the law might be developed (although it's not clear why the subjects who couldn't escape the clutches of the law to participate in political negotiations are able to leave behind their violently normalizing subjectivity to enjoy works of art – I'll be returning to this point at the very end of my argument).

In the argument that follows, I will also turn to a work of art. However, I won't follow Menke in treating art as a human practice that magically stands beyond the realm of the social. Indeed, Menke's own readings of literary texts in his essay treat texts by Sophocles, Kleist, or Heiner Müller as statements about questions in legal philosophy, and so very much as part of the conceptual discussions that are a feature of social interaction. In a similar vein, I am going to present a reading of Ian McEwan's recent novel *The Children Act* (2014), which offers a reflection on one of the questions that concerns Menke: namely, how does the law deal with groups, customs, or practices that resist the terms with which the law hopes to understand them? Rather than purporting to stand outside social practices, McEwan's novel reflects on and engages with them in a way that productively changes the terms of the debate and contributes to finding a way beyond the *aporia* articulated in Menke's essay. Art thus offers some answers, not quite in the way Menke theorizes, but in the vein in which Menke himself uses dramatic texts in his own essay: as a way of interrogating, expanding, or defamiliarizing some of our working assumptions.

2. Living the law: McEwan's *The Children Act*

McEwan answers the question of how law deals with what is beyond the law by exploring a failed encounter and investigating the human vehicles for any legal process: not abstractions, but people who act and make their decisions in the acknowledgment, imperfect as it will always be, of the needs of others. The book can thus be situated in a tradition of novels that stretches back at least as far as the 1850s, which explores the human cost of social abstraction. Indeed, the opening of Dickens' *Bleak House* (1852–53), a novel which portrays the needless misery perpetuated by the Courts of Chancery in Victorian England, is explicitly invoked in the first sentences of McEwan's text.[9] But the novelistic tradition in which McEwan's book stands also includes Dickens' treatment of economic abstraction in *Hard Times* (1854), and the study of more generally conceptual abstraction in George Eliot's *Adam Bede* (1859), with its programmatic attempt to see the difference:

> between the impression a man makes on you when you walk by his side in familiar talk, or look at him in his home, and the figure he makes when seen from a lofty historical level, or even in the eyes of a critical neighbour who thinks of him as an embodied system or opinion rather than as a man.[10]

I want to show how a return, guided by McEwan's text, to the human ground of legal systems gives us a clearer view of the resources available for a more positive understanding of the law and its limits. Having used *The Children Act* to address this question, we will have gathered some points to take back to Menke's argument and show how his reading of Benjamin in "Law and Violence" might be freed from an unhelpful debt to Derrida and recalibrated to strengthen his attempt to find relief from the law, within and alongside the law.

McEwan's novel centers on a British High Court Judge, Mrs Justice Fiona Maye, who works within the Family Division. It has been carefully researched and draws in particular on three judgments from 1993, 2001, and 2012/2013.[11] The last judgment, *Re G (Children) (Religious Upbringing: Education)* [2012] EWCA Civ 1233, [2013] 1 F.L.R. 677 by Sir James Munby, is particularly significant for the philosophical orientation of the book and we will be returning to it later.

The novel opens with Fiona's husband announcing that he wants to have an extramarital affair. But this crisis in the couple's marriage is only a stage in a wider process by which the judge's legal practice and her private life interfere with each other. As the novel progresses, we realize the problem is longstanding: Fiona is successful as a judge in part because she has not had children, having drifted "deeper into family law as the idea of her own family receded."[12] More recently, the courtroom has spilled directly into the bedroom and ruined her sex life. Fiona was involved in a case of conjoined twins, Matthew and Mark, both dependent on the functioning heart in the body of Mark. Both children would not survive together; Mark, however, could survive if separated from Matthew. Fiona ruled, against the wishes of the devoutly Catholic parents and in the interest of the child who stood to survive, to separate the twins. But after the ruling she remained haunted by photos of the two entangled children and by what she had heard from surgeons "on the cutting, splicing and folding of infant flesh they must perform to give Mark a normal life" (*Act*, 29–30). Unable to push the worries away, she "became squeamish about bodies, barely able to look at her own or Jack's without feeling repelled" (*Act*, 30). The couple's sex life disappeared. In addition to eroding the distance between the law and her private life, the case brings home to Fiona an acute sense of the violence of her judgment (*Act*, 30). Whilst we are told near the beginning of the novel that "she believed she brought reasonableness to hopeless situations" (*Act*, 4), her belief in family law is not unshakeable or unquestioning.

Like Menke, McEwan explores how the limits of the law are managed, and highlights its potentially violent effects. The cases that Fiona deals with are ones in which a secular, post-Enlightenment judiciary promotes what it understands to be the welfare of children, evaluated "by the standards of the reasonable man or woman of today" (*Act*, 16). In doing so, it must confront the customs and beliefs of groups whose standards of behavior are not the same as those of "the reasonable man or woman of today": the Catholic parents who tried to stop doctors saving one twin at the cost of the other boy's life; a divorcing couple from the North London Charedi community arguing over the extent to which their daughters should be given access to education (*Act*, 8–13); and finally a 17-year-old Jehovah's Witness refusing the blood transfusion doctors wish to give him to help him fight leukemia.

Fiona Maye operates in exactly the territory that so interests Menke, where the law acknowledges, but also differentiates itself from, the forms of life that resist it. For Menke, this process of what he calls the "self-reflection of law," is achieved, in abstract terms, "by the law's changing itself: by a law that reflects on itself in its difference from the non-legal; by a law that has become self-reflective."[13] McEwan's approach is somewhat different. He explores what it might mean for his character to face and take responsibility for the law's encounter with habits that are alien to it. The judge seeks out, and then must bear the consequences of, a direct experience of the limits of the law.

The occasion for this encounter is the case of the 17-year-old refusing a blood transfusion. Fiona decides to take the unusual step of leaving the courtroom to assess the boy herself. We then see how, having left the court, she ceases to determine the situation, which gives rise to a new dynamic. The new dynamic reinforces the impression given from the opening pages that Fiona is less in control than she hopes to be. At the start of the novel, her high-minded observation that the legal conceptions of "welfare, happiness, well-being must embrace the philosophical concept of the good life" (*Act*, 15), is formulated as she fails to respond adequately to her husband's revelations. Nor is it simply a question of the law offering inadequate protection from personal distress beyond the law. The law itself with its rhetoric and human actors demands affective engagement. Fiona can thus find herself emotionally "derailed" by a Shakespearean flourish in another judge's formulation that she quotes as she prepares her statement on welfare, for his reference to the "infinite variety of the human condition" takes her back to a performance of *Antony and Cleopatra* she acted in: "an all-female affair on a lawn in Lincoln's Inn Fields one sunny midsummer afternoon" (*Act*, 17); and further reflection on Cleopatra leads her to uncomfortable considerations of the younger woman with whom her husband is starting an affair.[14] Individuals, in McEwan's world, cannot be separated from their environment, or from the responses that other people and the world around them prompt in them. Human experience is situated, emotionally rich, fully embodied. Attempts to deny that, or run away from this situatedness, do not achieve what they hoped to, but instead run up against the situation they hope to evade.

McEwan's interest in the situated, dynamic, and embodied nature of Fiona's experience is especially clear in her visit to the hospital. The narrator observes how she "liked hospitals" (*Act*, 93) because they brought back the memories of the one time she had had to be in one herself as a teenager, passing a "glorious week without alarm or pain" (*Act*, 94). Hospitals for Fiona had "an improbable association [...] with kindness." "So now, inappropriately, as the twenty-six-storey Edith Cavell Wandsworth General rose above the misty oak trees on the far side of the common, she experienced a moment of pleasurable anticipation" (*Act*, 95). Positively primed, she is also disoriented by sensory contrasts when she enters the boy's room: patches of light and darkness; the social worker reading a magazine she cannot possibly make out in the gloom; the life-support machines seeming to emanate silence. "But there was no silence, for the boy was already talking to her as she entered, the moment was unfurling, or erupting, without her and she was left behind in a daze" (*Act*, 99).

The key development comes as she is about to leave, and asks the boy to show her his violin. He plays, in the rough manner of someone who has only been playing for four weeks, a melody she knows from performances in which she accompanies a singer and fellow lawyer on the piano: Britten's arrangement of Yeats's "Down by the Salley Gardens" (*Act*, 115). Having heard him play it once, she suggests he play it again, so she can sing the second stanza of the Yeats poem to his accompaniment. "The situation, and the room itself, sealed off from the world, in perpetual dusk, may have encouraged a mood of abandon, but above all, it was Adam's performance, his look of straining dedication, the scratchy inexpert sounds he made, so expressive of guileless longing, that moved her profoundly and prompted her impulsive suggestion" (*Act*, 116). Fiona doesn't expect to make the suggestion (*Act*, 116). In McEwan's analysis it arises partly from the physical surroundings, but more importantly in unpremeditated response to Adam's behavior.

Underpinning this scene, and indeed the novel as a whole, is a model of human identity that it is worth making explicit because it differs from that of Menke, and shapes the approach to the limits of law that the McEwan adopts in his novel. Even as it admires reasonableness, the novel puts the operations of legal reasoning in a wider context. "Stating the obvious," as she acknowledges, the judge reaffirms, in her ruling in the case of the Charedi daughters, the social aspect of well-being:

"The intricate web of a child's relationships with family and friends was the crucial ingredient" (*Act*, 16). But the novel goes deeper in its analysis of sociality. What leads an encounter between human beings is not conscious choice, or a high-level reflection on what individuals think of each other's motives. When Fiona enters Adam's hospital room, as we have seen, she has the sense that "the moment was unfurling, or erupting, without her" (*Act*, 99). A situation has its own dynamic that emerges from the interaction of the people involved and the place in which they find themselves. In the terms of a radical, embodied cognitive science, a developing experience and its insights can be explained as "the unfolding of a brain-body-environment system" that will often include a number of bodies and brains.[15] In a more phenomenological vocabulary, our focus should be on the hyphenated composite: being-with-others-in-the-world, no single element of which should be artificially separated from the other.[16] What Fiona discovers, in the course of the novel, is precisely this involvement: she hopes to protect herself by spreading legal papers on the floor around her chaise longue (*Act*, 126). But that gesture itself is an acknowledgment of her situatedness: it is done for a reason, in response to someone or something (in this case, her husband). And her own body responds as a situated body in a way Fiona's more conscious processing must sometimes catch up with. The bulk of the novel, as we shall see, traces the legal and moral consequences of this understanding of human identity.

McEwan has already explored such issues explicitly in the novel *Saturday* (2005), one of the central concerns of which is the relation between advances in neurology and ethical choices.[17] The neurosurgeon protagonist has a straightforwardly materialistic understanding of human behavior, seeing it as determined by, among other things, genetic dispositions or the effects of lipoprotein-a on the blood vessels in the brain (*Saturday*, 165). But the view taken by the narrative itself is more holistic: here, as in *The Children Act*, behavior is altered by context and interaction. The novel reflects on the resulting shades of responsibility and impotence, capturing them in a formulation that occurs early in the text as the surgeon watches a burning plane cross the London sky and wonders if he should call the emergency services. He feels: "Culpable in his helplessness. Helplessly culpable" (*Saturday*, 22). "These are contradictory terms, but not quite, and it's the degree of their overlap, their manner of expressing the same thing from different angles, which he needs to comprehend" (*Saturday*, 22). *The Children Act* could similarly be read as a reflection on the degrees of helplessness and culpability displayed by an embedded subjectivity. But the consequences of helplessness are starker, and the ethical challenge is more direct in *The Children Act* than in *Saturday*. Judge Fiona, unlike the surgeon, fails to take responsibility until it is too late, for the things that she did without planning to. Where the surgeon can make amends for the botched encounter that is the catalyst for the book's unfolding drama in the "controlled conditions" of the operating theatre (*Saturday*, 246), the judge has no such controlled arena, and that is both the promise and the terror of the law.

There is no controlled arena in the novel, "since judges are also people" (*Act*, 14): they cannot remove themselves from the insecurities of human interaction. McEwan attributes this idea to Fiona, as she formulates her judgment on the case of the disputed education of the Charedi girls in the opening chapter of the book. But the phrase has its origin in the judgment on a similar case by Sir James Munby, on which McEwan draws, and Munby is himself quoting another judgment by Lord Hoffmann.[18] McEwan thus follows senior judges in seeing legal pronouncements as embedded in the social contexts in which they are made.[19] Judgments are always part of the wider social processes through which behavior is reflected on, assessed, and regulated. The law is not the only set of behaviors involved, nor, in McEwan's view, can it be thought to be qualitatively different from other forms of behavior. Rather, there is range of humane and reasonable behaviors of which the law is only one set of practices, and the law does not have a special protected status that neutralizes human fallibility or emotion.

This view of the law differs from Menke's. If we do not accord the law any special conceptual privileges, then the idea that subjectivity is "constituted by" the law makes little sense. Identities will instead be seen to develop in a more pluralistic way, shaped by a variety of different contexts, all with their attendant expectations and habituated responses.[20] A Wittgensteinian would call these different contexts "language games": historically developing, complex forms of interaction that sometimes resemble other language games used in similar circumstances, but without being straightforwardly translatable into, or reducible to, each other.[21] The challenge that Fiona faces in *The Children Act* is to make sense of the realization that the law is not privileged or separate. Having made her judgment, and intervened in the life of the 17-year-old boy, she is uneasy when the case spills back into her day-to-day life. But she is also unable to stop or even control the dynamic process of interaction. She does not guide the situation when the boy, Adam, tracks her down to her judicial lodgings in Newcastle any more than she did when she visited him in hospital in Wandsworth. Indeed, Newcastle is again a place that has a special resonance for her that primes her responses: it is associated with love poems, "riotous fun," and a teenage romance she had with the lead singer of a rock band (*Act*, 146). The city is linked with "a hazy notion of renewal, of undiscovered potential in another life" (*Act*, 147). When Adam appears, soaking wet, having walked through the rain, his face seems "old-fashioned": "Everyone's notion of the face of Romantic poet, a cousin of Keats or Shelley" (*Act*, 157). If the encounter is shaped by resonances it awakens in Fiona, it also has a rhythm she doesn't consciously direct: she responds to his quoting her judgment by instantly quoting back to him one of the letters he wrote to her (*Act*, 164). Indeed, McEwan observes how even the charged silence that arises after Adam has finally said that he has followed her all the way to Newcastle to ask if he can come to live with her and her husband "wound itself around them and bound them together" (*Act*, 167). Being silent together is also a form of embodied interaction.

In McEwan's novel, the law does not protect the judge from the situated dynamism of human exchange, but is part of that complex process. Fiona and Adam's interaction started with a legal case, but it also resonates with previous experiences, with their one-sided correspondence, and with existing cultural models. It unfolds with a dynamic that outstrips conscious intention and which reaches its climax at the moment when Fiona comes to take leave of Adam: "Her intention was to kiss him on the cheek, but as she reached up and he stooped a little and their faces came close, he turned his head and their lips met. She could have drawn back, she could have stepped right away from him. Instead, she lingered, defenceless before the moment. The sensation of skin on skin obliterated any possibility of choice" (*Act*, 169).

Fiona is herself shocked by what she has done: "She was not prone to wild impulses and she didn't understand her own behaviour" (*Act*, 172). She is particularly worried about the effect this breach of professional ethics might have on her reputation should any of her colleagues discover it. But McEwan's narrative is less concerned with legal reputation than with the human cost of Fiona's failure to understand the concomitants of her own legal reasoning in other areas of her life: her inability to practice deliberately in interpersonal relations what she knows very clearly in theory in the regulated space of the court.

The key term in Fiona's legal reasoning is: welfare. In the first chapter of the novel, as we have seen, McEwan juxtaposes the husband's announcement of his extramarital affair with Fiona's drafting of the judgment in the dispute over the education of the Charedi girls. The judgment allows McEwan the space to elaborate on the concept, which is also central to the piece of legislation from which the novel draws its name and to which McEwan alludes in the epigraph to the text.[22] For Fiona, whose views track very closely those of Sir James Munby, welfare and well-being are inseparable, and should be thought to include "all that was relevant to a child's development as a person" (*Act*, 15). McEwan summarizes Fiona's (and Munby's thinking) further: "Well-being was *social*" (*Act*, 16). At the same time, what counts as well-being is "a mutable concept, to be evaluated by the standards of the reasonable man or woman of today" (*Act*, 16).

These legal reflections on welfare have two functions in the novel. The first is to set up the mismatch between Fiona's legal and private lives. The second is to show that the problem is not the law itself but the challenge of honestly negotiating the dynamics of a human interaction we never fully control or determine. For Menke, the law constitutes subjects in their very autonomy, and thereby hollows out their autonomy from the inside, for the subject becomes a subject by judging and imposing violence on themselves (p. 26). In McEwan's novel, the law functions alongside other social practices, and different practices demand different but related forms of integrity. The law is not the sole enabling (or disabling) framework. In the cases we see in the text, the law is invoked when other, informal forms of resolution, in the family or within and between wider groups and interests, break down. Munby, in his 2013 judgment, goes out of his way to explain that this is the proper balance. The law does not constitute and impose an idea of well-being on other areas of society. It is a special tool to be applied when other forms of negotiation and compromise don't work. Legal intervention is needed only where other ways of settling disputes over what would count as welfare have failed.[23] More importantly, when the law is deployed, it does not trump or replace the other practices. (If someone decides to drop charges and opt for informal methods of resolution, a case cannot be pursued.) The law is in constant exchange with wider social expectations and norms, and will not in every circumstance be the most salient way of dealing with an issue.[24] As Munby puts it:

> A child's welfare is to be judged today by the standards of reasonable men and women in 2012, not by the standards of their parents in 1970, and having regard to the ever changing nature of our world: changes in our understanding of the natural world, technological changes, changes in social standards and, perhaps most important of all, changes in social attitudes.[25]

In Menke's post-Foucauldian account of the law, the "standards of reasonable men and women in 2012" would count as a normalizing force. In a similar vein, Judge Ruth Herz, in her discussion of McEwan's novel, emphasizes the degree to which the normalcy presupposed by the judiciary in fact imposes the assumptions and habits of a small social group on a wider society.[26] The novel itself contains this idea in the account a colleague of Fiona's gives of the unreflective assumptions determining how his Irish client is pigeonholed by police and judge alike (*Act*, 183–90). Nevertheless, the novel also shows the wider vision of humanity that "reasonable standards" foster where they are genuinely directed towards welfare as it is most broadly conceived in a changing society. Fiona intervenes in the name of the well-being of the 17-year-old boy, arguing that his welfare is served not by the religious beliefs he has internalized as he grew up but "by the exercise of his lively intelligence and the expressions of a playful affectionate nature, and by all of life and love that lie ahead of him" (*Act*, 123). The court speaks out in the name of a human flourishing that must, in the judge's view, be the precondition of any faith, opinion, or form of behavior: a flourishing towards the future. The law does not determine or finally define this flourishing. It takes its cue from wider social debates, and is one tool, amongst many, with which a society can try to foster what its citizens take, at any particular historical juncture, to be the best vision of the good life.[27] If we don't have this sort of open-ended, undogmatic vision of human flourishing, the argument that the law is a normalizing imposition could never get off the ground in any case.[28] McEwan uses the device of legal judgments to make this positive vision explicit.

Fiona's flaw is that she finds herself, in other contexts, to be too inflexible or unimaginative to live up to the humanity of her legal judgments, despite the situations that take her beyond her own preconceptions. Having kissed Adam, she chooses again not to answer a letter he sends her, and discovers too late that, suffering a relapse of his cancer after he turned eighteen, he refused a further blood transfusion and died of his leukemia. In the final pages of the novel, Fiona understands her "transgression," as she calls it, in the following terms: through the law, she offered Adam something as "beautiful and terrifying" as a life beyond the constraints of his narrow upbringing, but she failed to support him in the new life that the intervention of the law opened up for him (*Act*, 212–13). Fiona fails to honor fully what part of her already responded to in the safe space of the legal judgment: the boy's lively intelligence, his affectionate nature, and his potential for leading a loving life.

Although insight comes too late for Fiona, McEwan's novel is optimistic about human interaction, in so far as it shows how a false understanding of the law (as a form of escape from human commitments) is overturned by the way human interaction unfolds. The law is always embedded in real situations, and so attempts to insist on separateness will fail either because judgments become distorted or because, in some more positive way, the dynamic of human interaction takes over. To return to the terms McEwan suggested in his earlier novel *Saturday*, the helplessness we see in the text is not in itself culpable. When Fiona is led beyond her plans and intentions, that is not in itself a problem. Culpability arises when she fails to take responsibility for what she has done unexpectedly, and responsibility here does not mean full conscious control of one's actions but rather the different ways available to an individual of understanding consequences, integrating them, and acknowledging how they can expand our sense of a meaningful life.[29] The law might or might not be involved in this process. *Saturday* ends with the neurosurgeon hoping he can persuade his wife not to press charges against the man who broke into their house, as he tries to make amends for a series of events to which he understands he himself contributed. In McEwan's view, legal process is one tool alongside others, which include family relations, the medical profession, and literature, among others; and all of these are subservient to the wider project of formulating and honoring what "we," pluralistically construed and in constant conversation with each other, take to be human flourishing.

3. Unlawful entry: Menke, Hart, and Derrida on problematic beginnings

McEwan's novel presents a model of the law that, first, has welfare, or a version of the Good Life, as its central concern; second, can fulfill this promise to the degree that the interconnections between legal institutions and other social practices beyond the law are acknowledged (the family resemblances between family law and family life); and third, in which the limitations of the law are positively and regularly challenged by the dynamism of human interaction. Society, in McEwan's world, is not defined or contained by the law; each legal act will in some way manage (by containing, or fostering and acknowledging it) the momentum of humanity that underlies the law as it underlies social practices.

Menke's model in his lead essay, like McEwan's, also offers a positive view of the law, and for this reason Menke never hopes to escape the law, even though he believes it to be founded on violence. Nevertheless, Menke emphasizes the paradoxical aspects of the law, where McEwan turns his attention to the ambivalent potential of situated communication. Thus, on the one hand, the law, in Menke's account, colonizes even those areas that are supposed to be beyond it, and so imposes its normalizing power on all aspects of social interaction: "Realizing and violating the right of the non-legal in law are one and the same thing" (p. 54). On the other hand, he hopes to go beyond Derrida's insistence that we simply park ourselves in the paradox, but he is wary of the claim he finds in Deleuze or Agamben that one could break with the law or open the gate to a new happiness beyond its *aporiai* (p. 55, p. 61). In the end, as we have seen, Menke's position draws on Adorno to imagine a law unhappy with the judgments it must nevertheless make, a law which makes decisions whilst simultaneously acknowledging the contingency and revocability of the decisions (p. 61).

Do we need to stay confined to the paradox in the way Menke decides to? Guided by McEwan's model of the law in its wider social context, and drawing on other theorists who help unpack the sort of assumptions that underwrite McEwan's measured optimism, I want to suggest the answer to this question is "No." To admit the historically situated, mutable, and finite nature of legal judgments does not necessarily require the conceptual apparatus that Menke employs. We have seen how McEwan draws on Sir James Munby's acknowledgment of the changing standards of welfare that inform the law. Herbert Hart's "descriptive sociology" of legal practices, inspired by a reading of Ryle, Austin, and Wittgenstein, amongst others, is a further well-known theoretical example of an approach that admits these points without making every legal act an act of violence.[30] It is not that Hart denies the element of violence the law can entail, or the possibility of miscarriages of justice, but, in his account, there is more space to consider the enabling aspects of law, as well as to imagine realms of social interaction for which law cannot always claim to be the most salient or dominant concern. This difference doesn't arise from the sort of indifference to wider social issues that has been lamented in other representatives of post-war ordinary language philosophy.[31] Rather, it stems from a differing underlying conception of human sociality, one closer to the model we see in McEwan's novels. Hart does not claim to be giving an evolutionary account of human cultural activity of the kind articulated in recent years by Michael Tomasello or Kim Sterelny.[32] Indeed, he specifically differentiates his conceptual account of the "minimum content" of a sustainable social order from empirical investigation of the psychological and biological mechanisms that might underpin it.[33] Nevertheless, what he shares with more recent evolutionary accounts, and with McEwan, is an acknowledgment of the necessarily social nature of human identity, and the recognition that this sociality is enabling every bit as much as it is constraining.

By contrast, Menke shares with Rousseau the image of human individuals naturally living in splendid isolation who are therefore transformed in some irrevocable and hurtful way by the process of joining a community. Unlike other Enlightenment thinkers such as Smith or Hume, Rousseau presupposes that "human beings are in fact radically asocial by nature."[34] Menke cites a passage from *The Social Contract* to this effect. Indeed, the way he cites Rousseau actually reemphasizes the devastating effects of joining a community. For Rousseau, the natural state of individual independence, which we leave behind when we join civil society, is also one in which human beings are enslaved to their own needs and passions. Joining a social group constrains humans, but it also changes them from being stupid and limited animals to intelligent creatures who merit the title human being.[35] When Menke quotes Rousseau, it is only the constraining aspects of the transformation that interest him (p. 64).[36] He does not share Rousseau's stark opposition between reason and animal nature, so the gains in joining the community seem lesser to him. Nevertheless, for Menke and Rousseau alike, the community imposes upon and violently transforms individuals, rather than being viewed as, amongst other things, life-giving, necessary, and even a source of happiness.

A concomitant of Menke's assumption that human beings are at root asocial is the absence from his account of a concept of enabling shared practices. For post-Heideggerian phenomenology, or for a Wittgensteinian approach to culture, we share a world because we share practices, and our identity would not be sustainable without this collective project of producing worlds. We can't separate out some core of human identity from the social activities that then, in some irrevocable way, take it away from itself. Or, to make the point in Heideggerian terms: "falling," that is to say, being involved in, caring about, and taking care of a shared world, is a deep structure of human life.[37] Nor do we need to think there is only one way of being truly human. Rather, different sets of cultural practices will disclose different ways of living as a human being, so that being political, or being legal, or being a family member, or being a musician, will be attributes that are inseparable from the particular practices through which these aspects of life are lived. Writing in the spirit of Adorno and Derrida, rather than of the early Heidegger or later Wittgenstein, Menke does not share such an upbeat and pluralistic model of human sociality. The shadow cast when we join the politico-legal collective, for Menke, leaves its trace on all other aspects of human life. He cannot endorse the view, which we saw in Munby's judgment, that informal social processes are the best place to work out questions of welfare, or that the courts will be called in only where other practices have failed. Since the very structure of identity has been shaped by the step of joining the politico-legal monolith, there is no space beyond the law in which to try things first.

Menke's assumptions affect the way he structures his argument and the sort of solutions he can imagine. Following his model, Judge Fiona in McEwan's novel ought to fail: her ideal of welfare is imposed upon a group outside the self-understanding of the law, and Fiona is herself shaped by the law, so cannot escape her own legalistic responses. Adam's self-destruction, following this line of reasoning, is the only way he can preserve a genuine autonomy in the face of the empty, because conformist, autonomy of the "reasonable man or woman." However, a reading based on these assumptions misses what is most challengingly provocative in the novel. McEwan's text focuses on those elements of interaction which take Fiona and Adam alike into new territory: both do things they wouldn't have expected to do, and in the process are transformed and brought closer to the kind of existence to which Fiona's philosophical digressions on the Good Life allude: to "all of life and love" that lies before them. McEwan, particularly in some responses to *Saturday*, has been charged with espousing an outdated and ineffectual liberalism.[38] But the social model that emerges from a reading of both that novel and *The Children Act* is not just a reinstatement of the sorts of things of which the Adorno–Derrida tradition would be rightly critical. Rather, it draws its force from the interactive dynamism of the unfolding situation, remodeling conceptions of agency in the process, and using the new model as a standpoint from which to explore the promise and limitations of law.

In an earlier essay entitled "Ability and Faith" that he wrote on the question of justice, Menke includes a formulation, which I have used as an epigraph for this article, and which, taken out of context, seems closer to the approach I have found in McEwan. In the earlier essay, Menke presents Derrida's critique, in "Force of Law," of the idea of practice. The criteria by which we could judge that a practice of any kind is successful are, for Derrida, always yet to come. We can't know for sure that we will be able to take action effectively. Menke summarizes Derrida's position, then adds: "We could put this less paradoxically by saying that a successful performance – as decision or practice – is made possible insofar as we no longer think of it as made possible by us (i.e., by us alone)."[39] A Wittgensteinian or Heideggerian would not disagree. Nor would McEwan. Individual action is shaped and supported by the cultural inheritance on which it draws. Nor is it consciously governed, but arises in response to a situation: as Fiona responds to Adam's predicament in the Wandsworth hospital. The earlier essay seems to point towards a view of embodied, shared, and situated practices in which we participate without finally controlling them. But this is not in fact the point that Menke is making. Rather, he wants to suggest that our practice is always without an ultimate grounding, and so, in some sense, is based on faith: "The certainty of the justice of a decision is a 'faith' or presumption because, contrary to its claim, it cannot be criterially grounded."[40] At this point in the essay, Menke also refers to Derrida's brief allusion to Hart's *The Concept of Law* in "Force of Law."

To tie together the different threads of my response to Menke's essay, it's worth going into the details of this citing of Hart. Doing so will clarify further the choices and assumptions that underpin Menke's argument, and thus present more clearly the room for maneuver that I'm suggesting Menke denies himself and which I aim to point out and strengthen in my reading of this essay. Derrida mentions Hart when he talks about the "mystical foundations" of authority: the fact the foundational act that establishes legitimate authority can't itself be legitimate, or only in retrospect, because the process of legitimation hasn't yet been established.[41] Not all thinkers are worried by this apparent paradox. For instance, in *How to Do Things with Words*, Austin, in his characteristically understated way, points out the problems that beset the idea of an originary social contract. He is discussing what he calls infelicities: the different ways a speech act, such as an order, can misfire. To be felicitous, an order needs to be directed at someone, who must themselves "by some previous procedure, tacit or verbal, have first constituted the person who is to do the ordering an authority, e.g. by saying 'I promise to do what you order me to do.'" Austin continues: "This is, of course, *one* of the uncertainties – and a purely general one really – which underlie the debate when we discuss in political theory whether there is or is not or should be a social contract."[42] Austin draws attention to the conventions and shared assumptions that need to be in place for social agreements, political affiliations, and legal pronouncements to be effective. We can't get a social agreement going if we don't already have enough in common to make that agreement meaningful and binding.

The main issue for Austin is that language works precisely because we generally do have enough in common. The suggestion that the foundational act is illegitimate then relies on two false premises. First, it ignores the degree to which the group involved in the act of founding something will necessarily already be doing things together: they will already share something. Second, it demands absolute standards of agreement, rather than an overlapping of habits and practices that is "good enough" to be getting on with and, in any case, revisable in the light of changing circumstances.[43]

Hart's model, like Austin's, depends on shared activity. A group of people will have customs and conventions by which they regulate how they live together. Very often, they will also generate a set of secondary rules that regulate what counts as a primary rule, and in so doing they will make the step from a custom-based to a proto-legal social process.[44] However, what finally underpins this process is the group's cultural and emotional investment in that way of doing things, and the fact that they continue to do things that way. Hart and Derrida thus agree that questions of validity are, in this context, out of place.[45] But for Hart – as for Wittgenstein, whom, as we have seen, he explicitly invokes – this only confirms that nothing can finally underwrite our customs and conventions beyond the fact that they are what we do.[46] "Explanations come to an end somewhere."[47]

Derrida, and Stanley Fish, on whose critique of Hart in his essay "Force" Derrida draws, don't see this aspect of Hart's argument. Fish attributes to Hart the idea that the violence of the law and violence of interpretation could only be contained by an irresistibly transparent language.[48] In fact, Hart, as we have seen, presents a law underpinned by social practices that do not require a mythical transparency. Fish's alternative to the desire for transparency he finds in Hart is a model of competing interpretations: "Whatever is invoked as a constraint on interpretation will turn out upon further examination to have been the product of interpretation."[49] The point of this argument is to show that nothing is beyond challenge. Stability is only ever the product of earlier negotiations. That seems uncontroversial. But what brings negotiations to a close, for Fish, is always a Nietzschean imposition of the one successful framework on others, because Fish's model lacks the idea of the shared practices that could otherwise underpin the interpretation and the process of agreement. An agreement, for him, is never an agreement in the way of life. Oddly, given his interest in interpretative communities in early work such as *Is There a Text in This Class?*, Fish relies on an atomistic model of identity, similar to the one Menke borrows from Rousseau, for which the only thing that makes people act, think, or read in the same way is force.[50]

Derrida invokes Fish's critique of Hart as a parallel to his own argument but, as we have just seen, the Derrida–Fish reading of Hart omits the historically mutable shared practices that are the only grounding Hart imagines we can give to legal conventions and our other habits. Having rescued Hart from Derrida and Fish, we can return to the moment when Menke cites this brief allusion.

Menke, like Fish, attributes to Hart the desire for "generally binding rules" that will tell us in advance if we are being just. Having set up this judgment-by-numbers version of legal theory, he concludes: "If just decision could be analyzed in this way, then [...] the realizability of justice could be guaranteed by appropriate means. Derrida's claim is to have shown why this is not the case."[51] Menke thus sets up a stark opposition between judgment as a fixed, predictable system (which would be no justice at all), and a justice which must always call itself into question: the impossible justice to come, which can never make good, but must never forget, the violence that was needed to inaugurate its rule.

At the same time, Menke isn't quite happy with Derrida's (non-) solution. In the 2005 essay, he stays with the idea of a practice that succeeds by acknowledging its impossibility – practice as a form of faith. But by the time of the German edition of *Law and Violence*, he attempts to differentiate his idea of the "self-reflection of law" from a Derridean approach to the *aporia*.[52] The path Menke *doesn't* take is that of rethinking his model of individual identity and its relation to shared practices. Or does he? To explain his alternative, self-reflexive law, he invokes Adorno's idea of self-critical taste, as we have seen, to suggest that law would ideally suffer from a sense of distaste at its own judgments. This perhaps doesn't leave much room for introducing the shared activities that underpin forms of social interaction. But there is a small opening in the Adorno passage that Menke quotes that points to the degree to which we do things always with others and in a wider context and which brings us back to something more like the model we find in McEwan's novel and in a Wittgensteinian approach to legal theory like that of Hart. Aesthetic reactions, for Adorno, are evidence for the degree to which individual identity is the product of a complex and heterogeneous cultural inheritance that leaves its traces in visceral reactions not all of which have been fully normalized or standardized by the forces of popular culture and consumer capitalism: "The individual is so thoroughly historical that he is able, with the fine filigree of his late bourgeois organization, to rebel against the fine filigree of late bourgeois organization."[53] This individual has not been fully transformed by the process of becoming a subject. He or she is a messier entity, some of whose habits and reactions can be played off against others. Hidden in the footnote, in other words, we find the traces of a more open, pluralistic, embodied version of identity, one that has the potential to give us something more than legal self-disgust to challenge the impositions of the law.

Could this aspect of Menke's arguments, and of the tradition in which he situates himself, be made stronger? In conclusion, I want briefly to turn to Menke's reading of Benjamin's "Critique of Violence" (1921) to show, in a similar fashion, how freed from the indifference to forms of social practice that he inherits from Rousseau, Derrida, and Fish, Menke has more pluralistic resources at his disposal for reconfiguring and so escaping the *aporiai* of the law.

4. Conclusions: Out of court settlements

Benjamin's argument in his 1921 early essay prepares the way for the positions we've seen developed by Derrida, Fish, and Menke, by attending to the violence that underpins normative social orders. So if we can find traces of alternative arguments in this foundational text, we will have made an important step towards realigning the way we think about the limits and the violence of the law. Writing in the aftermath of the First World War, he shares with other thinkers of the early 1920s, such as Karl Barth, a distrust of the existing human order, and imagines a paradigm shift to a different, divine order, beyond existing, fallen social practices. As Michael Jennings has argued, this shift, in "The Critique of Violence," is not yet associated with politics; the combination of a total break with the existing order and political transformation won't be worked out in Benjamin's thought until the 1930s.[54] Menke approves of Benjamin's analysis of the tangled relation between law and violence, but thinks that hope of a paradigm shift beyond violence is bought at the cost of simplifying the argument. In his view, Benjamin can only get beyond violence by artificiality separating out the violent and the nonviolent aspects of law (pp. 35–36). He rejects a violent law and, in doing so, looses the utopian promise of equality that is as important a part of legal practices as are the normalizing impositions. Menke's alternative of a "self-reflection" of the law is meant to keep both sides of law in focus: utopian promise and standardizing violence. In developing this argument, he draws on Giorgio Agamben's reading of Benjamin's idea of the "relief" (*Entsetzung*) of/from the law: escaping the law from within the law (p. 36). However, there are other elements of Benjamin's essay that neither imagine jumping into a new era of divine justice, nor stay stuck negotiating the *aporia* of eluding the law within the law, but look instead to existing social practices for an alternative.

In his essay, Benjamin notes areas of social life that do not depend on violence to resolve conflicts. At a personal level, he names open-heartedness and trust.[55] At the same time, he acknowledges that personal attitudes don't always easily translate into wider social practices. We need to find more mediated processes or cultural technologies. One example he then suggests is language. The fact that lies often go unpunished shows, in Benjamin's view, that language is a realm of human interaction beyond violence.[56] A further example is diplomacy: the delicate, casuistic approach to problem-solving that treats each case on its merits and doesn't attempt to establish laws.[57] These aspects of Benjamin's account are avenues he doesn't explore very far, and they don't play a role in Menke's reading. But, like Adorno's brief comment on the visceral reactions of a messy, historically situated individuality, they show how the lived interactions of social existence find a way into philosophy, despite deep conceptual commitments which occlude them, where thinkers are flexible in their attempt to note and analyze the details of human behavior.

Benjamin's examples share a focus on interaction: trust and openheartedness are social attitudes, ways of being available to others that Heidegger would group together under the title of "co-states-of-mind" or *Mitbefindlichkeiten*.[58] The same is true of language as a medium that arises from our shared activities. Diplomacy is a complex, social institution that nevertheless, in Benjamin's view, functions in a flexible manner, adjusting to the needs of particular situations. Adorno adds aesthetic reactions as evidence of the way we are attuned to wider social processes without necessarily being consciously aware of it. These, and similar examples from the intellectual traditions to which Menke turns, will not be visible as long as we stick to the Rousseau-esque model of the asocial individual that underpins the gloomy view of social processes as necessarily standardizing inherited from Foucault, Adorno and Horkheimer. If, instead, we give situated interaction its due place in our social analyses, then, as we see in McEwan's novel, the problems appear in a different light. The variety of interlocking practices through which conflicts can be approached will be more clearly visible, so that differences in fundamental habits can be played off against the common ground we nevertheless share. The key question is then not how law can develop an appropriate from of self-disgust, but how we can stand by and take responsibility for the forms of interaction that develop despite ourselves from the dynamics of lived situations. An immovable paradox will then give place to the careful elaboration of shades of difference in the ways we can be "helplessly culpable," some more helpful than others to the project of living "all of love and life" that lie before us.

Notes

1 C. Menke, "Ability and Faith: On the Possibility of Justice," *Cardazo Law Review*, 27:2 (2005), 595–612, here 609.

2 R. Jaeggi and D. Loick (eds), *Nach Marx: Phiosophie, Kritik, Praxis* (Frankfurt am Main: Suhrkamp, 2013), 291.

3 "Sie produziert eine Form der Subjektivität, die sozialer Herrschaft zugrunde liegt oder sie hervorbringt" (*ibid.*, 281; my translation).

4 T. W. Adorno and M. Horkheimer, *Dialectic of Enlightenment*, trans. J. Cumming (London: Verso, 1979); M. Foucault, *Discipline and Punish: The Birth of the Prison*, trans. A. Sheridan (Harmondsworth: Penguin, 1977).

5 Jaeggi and Loick, *Nach Marx*, 287.

6 J. Habermas, *The Philosophical Discourse of Modernity: Twelve Lectures*, trans. F. Lawrence (Cambridge, MA: MIT Press, 1987).

7 "Denn der Logos existiert, wie jede natürliche oder soziale Kompetenz, in Unterschieden – in Unterschieden von Graden und Auslegungen" (C. Menke, *Die Kraft der Kunst* (Frankfurt am Main: Suhrkamp, 2013), 174).

8 *Ibid.*, 14. For Menke's early account of the ineffability of art, see C. Menke-Eggers, *Die Souveranität der Kunst: Ästhetische Erfahrung nach Adorno und Derrida* (Frankfurt am Main: Athenäum, 1988).

9 "London. Michaelmas Term lately over, and the Lord Chancellor sitting in Lincoln's Inn Hall. Implacable November weather." C. Dickens, *Bleak House*, ed. S. Gill (Oxford: Oxford University Press, 1996), 11. "London. Trinity term one week old. Implacable June weather." I. McEwan, *The Children Act* (London: Jonathan Cape, 2014), 1.

10 G. Eliot, *Adam Bede*, ed. C. A. Martin (Oxford: Oxford University Press, 2008), 62.

11 For information on the cases behind the book and a (generally positive) assessment by a lawyer of McEwan's use of his source material, see B. Sloan, "'The Children Act' by Ian McEwan," *The Cambridge Law Journal*, 74:1 (2015), 168–70.

12 McEwan, *The Children Act*, 44–45. Further references will be given parenthetically in the text using the abbreviation *Act*.

13 C. Menke, *Recht und Gewalt* (Cologne: August Verlag, 2011), 68. Also see p. 39.

14 The phrase "the infinite variety of the human condition" can in fact be found in Munby's judgment. *Re G (Children) (Religious Upbringing: Education)* [2012] EWCA Civ 1233, [2013] 1 F.L.R. 677, § 40.

15 A. Chemero, *Radical Embodied Cognitive Science* (Cambridge, MA: MIT Press, 2009), 43.

16 M. Heidegger, *Sein und Zeit* (Tübingen: Max Niemeyer, 1976), 117–25 (§26). For a discussion which emphasizes the central importance of being-with-others to Heidegger's approach, see B. Morgan, *On Becoming God: Late Medieval Mysticism and the Modern Western Self* (New York: Fordham University Press, 2013), 37–45.

17 Ian McEwan, *Saturday* (London: Jonathan Cape, 2005). Further references will be given parenthetically in the text.

18 *Re G (Children) (Religious Upbringing: Education)* [2012] EWCA Civ 1233, [2013] 1 F.L.R. 677, § 13.

19 For further discussion of the wider moral context framing judicial decisions, see H. L. A. Hart, *The Concept of Law* (Oxford: Oxford University Press, 3rd edn, 2012), 204–205.

20 For developmental accounts of human identity shaped by this kind of Wittgensteinian attention to the pluralistic cultural landscape in which we grow up, see J. S. Bruner, *Child's Talk: Learning to Use Language* (Oxford: Oxford University Press, 1983). J. I. M. Carpendale and C. Lewis, *How Children Develop Social Understanding* (Oxford: Basil Blackwell, 2006).

21 On the plurality of language games and the "family resemblances" between them, see L. Wittgenstein, *Philosophische Untersuchungen: Philosophical Investigations*, eds G. E. M. Anscombe, P. M. S. Hacker, and J. Schulte (Oxford: Wiley-Blackwell, 2009), 36–38 (§§ 66–71).

22 "When a court determines any question with respect to … the upbringing of a child … the child's welfare shall be the court's paramount consideration" (*Act*, v).

23 *Re G (Children) (Religious Upbringing: Education)* [2012] EWCA Civ 1233, [2013] 1 F.L.R. 677, § 91: "The court – the State – is involved in the present case only because the parents have been unable to resolve their family difficulties themselves, whether with or without the assistance, formal or informal, of their community, and because one of the parents, in this case the mother, has therefore sought the assistance of the court."

24 Hart, *The Concept of Law*, 165–66.

25 *Re G (Children) (Religious Upbringing: Education)* [2012] EWCA Civ 1233, [2013] 1 F.L.R. 677, § 33.

26 R. Herz, "Anatomy of a Judge," *Law and Humanities*, 9:1 (2015), 123–35, here 124.

27 For a similarly situated, open-ended model of law, see J. Dewey, "Logical Method and Law," *The Cornell Law Quarterly*, 10:1 (1924), 17–27, here 26. "General legal rules and principles are working hypotheses, needing to be constantly tested by the way they work out in application to concrete situations."

28 Habermas made a similar point in relation to the ideal of "the body and its pleasures" that underpins Foucault's bleak vision without being positively articulated. Habermas, *The Philosophical Discourse of Modernity*, 284–86.

29 For a fuller discussion of this model of taking responsibility, see the analysis of Lucian's "A Slip of the Tongue in Greeting," in Morgan, *On Becoming God*, 200–207.

30 For the term "descriptive sociology," see Hart, *The Concept of Law*, vi. Hart acknowledges his debt to Austin, Ryle, and particularly Wittgenstein's *Philosophical Investigations*: *ibid.*, 279–80. For a more recent elaboration of issues explored by Hart, see J. Gardner, *Law as a Leap of Faith: Essays on Law in General* (Oxford: Oxford University Press, 2012).

31 E. Gellner, *Words and Things: An Examination of, and an Attack on, Linguistic Philosophy* (Abingdon: Routledge, 2005).

32 M. Tomasello, *Origins of Human Communication* (Cambridge, MA: MIT Press, 2008); K. Sterelny, *The Evolved Apprentice: How Evolution Made Humans Unique* (Cambridge, MA: MIT Press, 2012).

33 Hart, *The Concept of Law*, 193–94.

34 D. C. Rasmussen, *The Pragmatic Enlightenment: Recovering the Liberalism of Hume, Smith, Montesquieu, and Voltaire* (Cambridge: Cambridge University Press, 2014), 236–37.

35 J.-J. Rousseau, *Du contrat social*, ed. Bruno Bernadi (Paris: Flammarion, 2001), 57.

36 Menke is quoting Book 2, Chapter VII: *ibid.*, 75.

37 Heidegger, *Sein und Zeit*, 176 (§ 38).

38 E. Hadley, "On a Darkling Plain: Victorian Liberalism and the Fantasy of Agency," *Victorian Studies*, 48:1 (2005), 92–102.

39 Menke, "Ability and Faith," 609.

40 *Ibid.*, 610.

41 J. Derrida, *Acts of Religion*, ed. Gil Anidjar (London: Routledge, 2002), 242.

42 J. L. Austin, *How to Do Things with Words*, eds J. O. Urmson and M. Sbisà (Oxford: Clarendon Press, 2nd edn, 1975), 28–29.

43 For a similar critique of deconstruction, see M. Stone, "Wittgenstein on Deconstruction," in A. Crary and R. Read (eds), *The New Wittgenstein* (London: Routledge, 2000), 83–117. The idea that being good enough is good enough has its theoretical roots in Winnicott. D. W. Winnicott, *The Maturational Processes and the Facilitating Environment: Studies in the Theory of Emotional Development* (London: Karnac and the Institute of Psycho-Analysis, 1990), 145–46. Ellen Spolsky has powerfully redeployed the term in her cognitively-inflected response to deconstruction. E. Spolsky, "Darwin and Derrida: Cognitive Literary Theory as a Species of Post-Structuralism," *Poetics Today*, 23:1 (2002), 43–62.

44 On primary and secondary rules, see Hart, *The Concept of Law*, 79–99.

45 "No such question can arise as to the validity of the very rule of recognition which provides criteria; it can neither be valid nor invalid but is simply accepted as appropriate for use in this way" (*ibid.*, 109).

46 What underpins the process (the "rule of recognition" which underwrites legal criteria) is the fact that it is the process people use: "The rule of recognition exists only as a complex, but normally concordant, practice of the courts, officials and private persons in identifying the law by reference to certain criteria" (*ibid.*, 110).

47 Wittgenstein, *Philosophical Investigations*, 6 (§ 1).

48 S. Fish, *Doing What Comes Naturally: Change, Rhetoric, and the Practice of Theory in Literary & Legal Studies* (Durham, NC: Duke University Press, 1990), 507.

49 *Ibid.*, 512.

50 On interpretative communities, see S. Fish, *Is There a Text in This Class? The Authority of Interpretive Communities* (Cambridge, MA: Harvard University Press, 1982).

51 Menke, "Ability and Faith," 610.

52 "The following account differs from Derrida's (only) in that it understands the aporia of legal judgment as the self-reflective unfolding of the difference between the law and the non-legal within the law" (p. 74, note 76).

53 T. W. Adorno, *Minima Moralia: Reflections on a Damaged Life*, trans. E. Jephcott (London: Verso, 2005), 145. Quoted on p. 75.

54 M. Jennings, "Towards Eschatology: The Development of Walter Benjamin's Theological Politics in the early 1920s," in C. Duttlinger, B. Morgan, and A. Phelan (eds), *Walter Benjamins anthropologisches Denken* (Freiburg im Breisgau: Rombach, 2012), 41–57, here 53.

55 W. Benjamin, *Gesammelte Schriften*, ed. R. Tiedemann (Frankfurt am Main: Suhrkamp, 1974–), 2.1, 191.

56 *Ibid.*, 2.1, 192.

57 *Ibid.*, 2.1, 195.

58 Heidegger, *Sein und Zeit*, 162 (§ 34).

6

Postmodern legal theory as critical theory

Andreas Fischer-Lescano

(Translated by Gerrit Jackson)

Understanding the relationship between law and violence is one of the most urgent challenges a postmodern critical legal theory faces today. In his essay, Christoph Menke explores the thesis that violence is to be thought of not as an external quality of law but as an essential part of its constitution. While his concise analysis reveals the fundamental conflict between the autonomy and the social responsiveness of law, I will suggest that we must radicalize his conception in three ways. First, we need to reconsider Menke's belief that law requires a polity (I). Second, I will argue that the reflexivity of law needs to be conceived of as a process of fundamental democratization of law (II). Third, I will propose that the law must not just be depotentiated, as Menke writes, but transcended (III). For only transcending the law enables us to appeal to the utopian notion of a justice to come.

Although with Henryk Grossmann, Carl Grünberg, and Karl Korsch critical jurists played a considerable role in the early period of the Institut für Sozialforschung in Frankfurt, reflections on legal issues were peripheral to the social theory of the first generation of critical theory. Legal scholars such as Wolfgang Abendroth, Otto Kirchheimer, and Franz L. Neumann were never members of the Institute's inner core, and the leading authors of critical theory did not dedicate particular attention to the analysis of legal form, with the notable exception of Erich Fromm's dissertation.[1] That changed with the second generation of critical theorists. Jürgen Habermas and Ingeborg Maus, in particular, included the law among the objects of their influential analyses in social theory.[2] The third generation of critical theorists affiliated with the Frankfurt School has now established legal theory as a central field of research, also with significant contributions from scholars whose primary training is in other fields.

This trend is manifest in Axel Honneth's Hegelian philosophy of law, Rainer Forst's theorem of justification, which draws on Rawlsian liberalism, Hauke Brunkhorst's combining of systems-theoretical with discourse-theoretical perspectives on law, and Sonja Buckel's materialistically inspired legal theory.[3] Each of these approaches builds on selected intellectual tendencies from the rich tradition of critical theory, ranging from Marx to Adorno and from Kant to Hegel. What sets Christoph Menke's studies on law apart is their explicitly postmodern take; through a careful study of Walter Benjamin's "Critique of Violence,"[4] he integrates deconstructivist and systems-theoretical analyses of law into the thinking of the Frankfurt School.[5]

Habermas has remarked that Menke's project, though it presents an "interesting and independent postmodern reading of liberalism," puts an "anti-utopian spin" on the deconstruction of justice.[6] But this critique misapprehends Menke's postmodern theory of law; that becomes especially evident in Menke's essay here, in which he expounds a conception of a utopia of law that, he argues, "is not about transcending law but about depotentiating it" (p. 60). As law reflects on its relation to non-law and "recogniz[es] itself to be without law," Menke writes, the utopia of "a law that knows [...] about itself" (p. 61) comes into view.

What Menke spells out in his lead essay is the basic idea of postmodern legal theory: that law's operations are not untainted by violence.[7] Unlike legal scholars whose work is informed by Kant, Menke accepts it as a given that the differentiation of the legal sphere does not result in the nonviolent equitemporality (*Gleichursprünglichkeit*) of popular sovereignty and human rights, nor in the unity of law's authors and its addressees. He argues that the realization of the ideal of legal pacifism – the establishment of nonviolent social relations – is thwarted by a differentiated legal form that, as such, does violence to its social environment. Where the modern philosophy of law followed Kant in seeking to bring social and political violence under control by installing politics and the polity as an "applied branch of law,"[8] the postmodern theory of law discerns that element which the Kantian legal tradition wished to pacify by all legal means at the very center of the law: the positing of law is a "violence without ground."[9] Violence, as Christoph Menke puts it, "is not only part of the manifestation of law but also of its essence" (p. 21).

Menke's analytically precise distinction draws our attention to the fundamental paradoxes of law, the process of juridical decision-making in undecidable matters, and the ambivalent situation in which law is operating: justice cannot be rendered quasi-automatically, by way of a mathematical subsumption under legitimately instituted norms, but is generated in the struggle for law as the state of a just order that remains unattainable – that it is never more than justice "to come."

Menke's critique "counters the legal legitimation of violence by asserting that legal legitimation is itself violent" (p. 5). He conceives of the process in which law attains autonomy as one of expropriation: a form of conflict management mediated by the polity and implemented in legal procedures supplants the immediate social management of violence performed by the parties to the conflict.[10] Only in this process is legal subjectivity constituted. This raises the question of how the decisions rendered by the autonomous law can be adjusted to be socially responsive. To address this problem, Menke turns to Walter Benjamin's idea of an *Entsetzung des Rechts* (relief of law). Law, he writes, must be reflexive law. The self-reflection of law he sketches "leads into a paradox that," he argues, "does not promise a realm beyond the contention, violence, and suffering against which the law takes a stand and that it ends up reenacting within itself. The self-reflective implementation promises nothing more than a law that knows as much about itself" (p. 61).

This advanced deconstructive demystification of law throws the essence of the tension between its autonomy and its social responsiveness into sharp relief. Still, Menke's sketch contains the potential for a more trenchant analysis of the momentous consequences of the autonomy attained by law and the processes of juridical decision-making and a more radical normative program, a potential Menke himself does not explore any further. That is why I want to discuss Menke's central claims – I will focus on three of them – and propose a more radical version of each:

I. *Claim (Menke):* The autonomous law supplants the revenge-oriented immediate settling of conflicts by the parties and implements the rule of the polity over the partisan individuals.
Radicalization: Neither the establishment nor the preservation of autonomous law is bound up with the polity; as law of world society, it comes into being in transnational processes of coevolution between law and its social environment.

II. *Claim (Menke):* Juridical decision-makers must take the paradoxical basic constellation and the relation of the law to non-law into account in their legal decisions in order to realize a self-reflexive application of the relieved law.
Radicalization: Law is more than the sum of legal decisions; the self-reflexivity and relief of law must be realized in the procedural conjunction of decision and discussion as a democratization of the legal form.

III. *Claim (Menke):* Self-reflection of law points towards a utopian justice that consists in the depotentiation, rather than the transcendence, of law.
Radicalization: The utopian justice to come can be conceived only in transcending the law.

I

With a view to the tragedies of the Oresteia and *Oedipus Rex*, Menke portrays the establishment of law's autonomy as an evolutionary process in which the emergence of law is tied to the political community of the citizens. This nexus is not self-evident. In particular, the dynamic nature of evolving legal frameworks in the transnational constellation raises the question of how plausible it still is for a "law in global disorder."[11]

In the era of Westphalian sovereignty, the notion that legal and constitutional processes were bound up with the polity was plausible. A law outside the polity was virtually inconceivable. In Hannah Arendt's critique of the aporias of human rights, which Menke has discussed elsewhere,[12] she insisted that the declaration of universal rights remained pre-political and pre-juridical unless it was wedded to a political organization. Arendt accordingly conceived the "right to have rights" first and foremost as the right to membership of a political community.[13] The central idea is that the granting of the right to membership of polities can effectively prevent exclusion from the law. Stateless persons and refugees who fall through the cracks of this protective system can be afforded effective protection through inclusion in national entitlement schemes.

But such concepts of the community-based polity, which usually focus on its protective function, and the close conjunction they create between community and law not infrequently lead writers to presuppose a unitary constitution of that community, a highly consequential theoretical choice that appears in Menke's argument as well: "The practice of legal judgment," he writes, "executes the rule of political union over the partial individuals" (p. 16). Menke's law is constitutively tied to "the" political community: "There is no law outside the polity"; "the justice of law can exist only in a community of equal citizens" (p. 14). Both conjunctions – the unitary conception of the community and the concession of monopoly power over the law to the polity – are problematic. They tend to obscure patterns of inequality, sources of resistance within configurations of power,[14] intersectional structures of discrimination and polycentric lines of exclusion, and unequal distributions of resources.[15] Claude Lefort has accordingly substituted the conflictive character of the social for communitarian homogeneity and deconstructed concepts of political community:

> Now, it becomes apparent that the concept of "people" blankets an opposition. Or to put it differently, within a people, a visible community to which the state assigns its identity, is found the masses of those without power – "people" in the precise sense that abstracts it from the fictive unity that political language projects onto it.[16]

Not coincidentally, the theorists of community cannot reach a consensus concerning even a very basic question: what is the communality of each of the various entities in question anchored in? In the Kantian theory of democracy, the law-generating community is usually the "community under law" as the identity of the addressees and authors of the law; political conceptions of the community, by contrast, often posit the polity as its basis. When endowed with substantial content, these conceptions give rise to the adoption of homogeneity requirements and create situations of exclusion. Tying the law to homogeneous communities in this manner is the point of departure for conceptions that continue to assign a central function in the genesis of political collectivity and lawmaking to the narratives of communities of fate and homogeneous cultures and values, even if they acknowledge, in postmodernist fashion, that such communities do not strictly speaking exist. They maintain that the European Union suffers from a constitutionality deficit because the space beyond the state lacks the necessary homogeneity, and they argue that the idea of international constitutional law championed by Jürgen Habermas[17] is doomed to fail a priori. Their excessive cathexis of the community leads them to claim that only the state can be "the project of erotic love"[18] in which the civic spirit of self-sacrifice and confraternity in the law can thrive.

Menke gives a wide berth to such abusive reliance on the community. Nor does he follow Carl Schmitt in conceiving the law as growing out of a given community of fate as the self-legislating political subject. Menke's conception reverses the order of priority. The law, he argues, is constitutive of the political community. In tying the creation of law to a community, he teases out an implication of postmodern liberalism with its characteristic self-reflexive politics of equality. The concept of a politics of equality requires due consideration of the complaints of individuals "about the violence, constraint, and oppression that is implied for them by the existing practice of equality."[19] His theory thus thinks the polity with its exclusions and reflects on the emancipatory benefits that flow from granting the legal subjects subjective rights as formally free rights to equality. But having conceived the *homo iuridicus* in the form of the legal subject as a character mask, a personification of juridical relations in which the law must presuppose equality as the legal equality of abstract legal subjects, because the very contingency formula of justice commits it to equality, Menke then proceeds to bind legal equality to an entity that is extrinsic to the law: the polity. Pashukanis understood the legal subject, in structural analogy to Marx's *homo oeconomicus*, as the abstraction of the act of economic exchange instituted by a fully differentiated legal form (referred to by Marx as the commodity form;[20] Menke, by contrast, melds the legal subject to the subject of the *homo politicus*, to the political community: legal equality and the political equality of the citizens, he argues, are interdependent.

Yet this conjunction between law and political equality of the citizens is hard to reconcile with the reality of the social creation of law. If, on the one hand, what Menke conceives as citizenship or membership of a polity is a purely formal determination, any contractual relationship is necessarily at once also the perpetuation of a political community. Contracts between private persons, between transnational corporations, or between transnational corporations and states would then have to be bound in one way or another to a political community. But then this conception, to avoid losing sight of crucial legal problems of world society,[21] would have to set the bar for what constitutes a "community," a "polity," and "political lawmaking" so low that any form of social lawmaking remains bound up with a polity. This would make "community" and "polity" ubiquitous concepts that would apply even to complex structures of arbitral jurisdiction in an economic community of transnational corporations.[22]

If, on the other hand, the bond that ties law to citizenship is more than a merely formal link – if, in other words, we add substantial criteria concerning the nature and degree of political organization – we arrive at a theory that is plausible in a world defined by the Westphalian order. But this form of life has grown gray; law of world society is polycentric. As a consequence, the philosophy of law then no longer has any answers to urgent questions of global legal pluralism. This may be a species-appropriate stance for the owl of Minerva. But a philosophy of law that remains in touch with the legal-political problems of world society should query the nexus binding the law to "political communities." Both components of this conceptual conjunction are questionable: what is communal, and what is political, about the "political communities" of the transnational constellation in which the "rule of political union" over the individual is supposedly realized?

Although world society lacks political union and has neither a Weberian *Anstaltsstaat* nor a Kelsen–Merkl-style hierarchical structure of law on the transnational level, it is not without legal rules. In fact, the problem legal practice faces is usually a different one: how to correlate the different legal orders. Overlapping circles of jurisdiction and the parallel existence of widely divergent patterns of order – what Saskia Sassen has called assemblages[23] – give rise to norm collisions in the global legal pluralism and a fragmentation of international law that cannot be comprehended in the perspective of the politically organized international community: a pluralism of regimes that provokes novel conflicts of law.[24] The narrow focus on political entities is not conducive to a better understanding of these conflicts. How does it help us interpret the interplay between the legal orders of the European Court of Human Rights (which were drawn up by the Council of Europe, a political organization), the politically organized European Union (EU) and the politically organized nation states? Each of these legal systems aspires to extend the purview of its particular perspective. The relations of membership of the various institutions – the Council of Europe and the EU as well as the World Trade Organization (WTO), NATO and so on – are asymmetrical. There is no unifying entity in the system of polycentric global governance, and global law is primarily about structuring the pluriverse of legal policy by instituting obligations of mutual consideration between the various patterns of order.

Tying the law to the unified polity is not only unhelpful for an understanding of the polycentricity of political rule and political legislation, it also blinds us to the phenomena of social lawmaking. Even in the nation state, the monopoly of politics over lawmaking defines many legal issues – free collective bargaining, customary business practices as legal norms, accepted standards, and so on – in a way that shunts them off into the realm of non-law and brings them out of focus. In the transnational constellation, which is characterized by a multiplication of authors, addressees, and organizational forms of law, the theoretical fixation on the community is a doubly pernicious form of myopia.[25] The assumption of a political monopoly over lawmaking fails to appreciate the reality of national and especially of transnational legal practice.[26] For example, the *lex mercatoria*, the law of the unfettered global economy, and the *lex digitalis* of cyberspace have each evolved their own legislative dynamics. The legal questions that arise in this context can aptly be described as structurally analogous to the questions of national and European law with regard to the challenge of ensuring social responsiveness of the law.

In particular, with regard to the effort to commit private transnational corporations to human and environmental rights, the focus on the unified polity in the conception of law not only impedes a proper understanding of what law is, it also obscures the structures of the legal attribution of responsibility and the leverage points for a creation of legal responsiveness obligations. For example, Christoph Menke and Arnd Pollmann emphasize that conceptions that instate private actors as subjects of international law "overshoot the mark by declaring every single private person to be an addressee of human rights obligations. If, however, human rights […] describe entitlements vis-à-vis the public order, then […] it is primarily the institutions and representatives of states and, ultimately, the global community of states that are bound by social human rights."[27] This argument ignores the structural transformation of the public sphere and is barely in touch with contemporary legal practice. For instance, the German Federal Constitutional Court has applied the public forum theory developed by American jurisprudence to privately owned public spaces; in a decision rendered in 2011, it found that a joint stock corporation was immediately bound by constitutional law.[28] The question of how the "public order" can be conceived arises in spheres beyond the state with even greater urgency than in the national framework. The threats to human rights posed by transnational corporations highlight the fact that the dichotomy of private versus public needs to be rethought[29] in order to prepare the ground for the attribution of a horizontal binding force to human rights.[30] Shell's pollution of the Niger delta, the global trade in goods produced using child labor, private military corporations such as Blackwater: these cases call for the development of legal strategies to compel private actors to abide by human rights. The focus on the "international community of states" is of little avail in this regard. Enhancing the obligation of the states to offer protection by regulating the actions of private actors remains an important avenue of the enforcement of human rights,[31] but it is nonetheless an indirect approach that must be complemented by an expansion of the direct route of committing private actors.

In short, global law is engendered as law of world society in processes of coevolution between the law and its social environment, and not just in politically organized entities. Postmodern legal theory will have to face up to the challenges of legal practice and broaden its reflections to take into account forms of lawmaking beyond the political community conceived in unitary terms. Conflict rather than consensus, multiplicity rather than communality, engagement with polycentricity rather than the imposition of unitary templates, and social rather than political lawmaking: these are then the basic coordinates. They are also what Jacques Derrida had in mind when he argued that the "effective responsibility" of any intellectual engagement consisted in "doing everything to transform the existing state of law [...] [and] inventing new laws," a task that, he noted, is "transnational and not just cosmopolitan, because the cosmopolitan still presupposes the categories of the state and the citizen, even if the citizen is a world citizen."[32]

II

This shift towards a social conception of law also affects the creation of law and its decision-making practices. In his essay, Menke rightly severs law from the relations of civic reciprocity and describes it as one sphere of communication among others. He takes up Walter Benjamin's idea of a relief of law to stake out a position contrary to Carl Schmitt's suspension of law,[33] a decisionistic model in which the political sovereign issues legal decisions *ex nihilo* and unencumbered by any legal constraint. Using Heiner Müller's play *Volokolamsk Highway I*[34] as an example – it concludes with a military commander's decision to have a soldier executed in accordance with martial law rather than pardoning him – Menke persuasively demonstrates the duplicity of the law: that it is, as Brecht put it, "a pig in a poke."[35]

Menke paints a vivid picture of the decision-maker's anguish. Heiner Müller has been described as a purveyor of defeatist demystification,[36] and he is perhaps nowhere more so than in Menke's reading: the commander's order to execute the soldier goes unchallenged; military morale outweighs the sacredness of the person. Demystification lies in the reflection on the tension between law and non-law and the paradoxical challenge the law faces of having to acknowledge its being non-law. But Menke's analysis of this passage also throws the fact into sharp relief that, in tying law back to state authorities, he does not rigorously conceive law as a trans-subjective communicative process that is more than the sum of communicative acts performed by legal decision-makers.

The example of the 2009 Kunduz airstrike illustrates the consequences of this decisionistic reading: in the early morning of September 4, 2009, an American fighter jet responding to a call by German forces struck two fuel tankers in northern Afghanistan, killing more than seventy people, among them children and women. A number of investigations, including a committee of inquiry of the German Bundestag, subsequently sought to shed light on how the decision to order the airstrike was reached. The protocol of the hearing of Master Sergeant W. (codenamed "Red Baron," he was in charge of radio communications that night) shows how unwillingly the decision-makers reached their decision – how no one was eager to kill. In W.'s account, Colonel Klein considered the matter for an extended period of time before deciding to order the strike:

> Colonel *Klein* was very abs.orbed in thought and pondered the issue for a long time. At some point he also said he needed more time. I passed that on to the aircraft, too, if I recall correctly, that it would take a little longer in terms of making a decision. To my mind, yes, for

> heaven's sake, he wasn't, or he isn't, someone who does anything rashly or decides anything purely by gut feeling. I think he weighed the matter for himself for a very long time and really struggled with himself over whether he should make that decision or in which way he should make that decision.[37]

This example seems to corroborate Christoph Menke's position that Carl Schmitt's suspension of law in the state of war is not a correct interpretation. Indeed, all those involved that night portrayed their decision as one option "in keeping with the law of war." No one argued that the law did not apply in wartime. The decision-making situation also seems to bear out Menke's conception of unwilling legal decision-making: note the colonel's indecision and hesitation, his doubts and the drawn-out anguish that preceded his decision. And yet the question remains whether the set of instruments Menke has honed for the observation of legal decision-making processes is not still too committed to the decisionistic paradigm: does not the conception of the unwilling decision-maker in the end simply replace Schmitt's decision *ex nihilo* with a decision *ex fastidio* for which the legal norms that apply to questions of discretionary competence, procedure, and the substance of the matter are effectively so much background noise?

The "war in the commander's mind," Menke writes, "the war between law and the non-legal, between the right of law and the non-right of law, no longer ends" (p. 60). This reading narrows the self-reflection of law down to the decision-maker's anguish and interprets the trans-subjective self-reflection of law as a process of subjective reflection on the part of decision-makers instead of tapping the potential of trans-subjective reflexivity and inquiring into the relationship between the social ensemble in which law is produced.[38] This setting in which the creation of law takes place is more than the sum of executive–military decisions. The decision of the undecidable is never more than one link in a chain of communicative acts and is itself immediately subject to legal observation. It is not the individual decision-maker but law's differentiated structure with its center (courts) and periphery (public and private legal communication and lawmaking) that decides what is law and what is non-law.[39] No differentiated legal system can be said to exist until legal procedures have been evolved in which the conflict is transformed into a legal conflict and in which decisions of lawfulness or unlawfulness are rendered.[40] It is only then that the tension between law and justice becomes virulent.

Like the commander defending the Volokolamsk Highway, Colonel Klein made an executive decision in a situation of undecidability. But their cases remain to be litigated. Their decisions are merely the opening addresses in the struggle for law, a struggle in which the question of what is law and what is non-law is decided by the social communicative processes of law. In subsuming the lawmaking and the law-preserving powers under the title of mythical violence, Walter Benjamin describes two intimately interwoven components of the creation of law, which cannot be reduced to the act of the decision-maker; it is a social process. Of pivotal importance to its operativeness is the functioning reentry of the distinction (law/non-law) into what it distinguishes (law). Law must reframe the non-legal environment in the legal form. This internal reframing of the collision of incommensurable logics (*différend*), the alienating transformation of a social conflict into a legal dispute (*litige*), renders the conflict between law and non-law decidable for law – decidable as a legal conflict. Law always distorts conflicts over power, economic interests, and religious issues into legal conflicts, translating them into collisions between legal rights, interests, or spheres. Law is a King Midas machine: it cannot render the conflict between law and non-law other than as a legal conflict.

The conflict on Volokolamsk Highway is thus a collision between the military order to execute and the commander's right to pardon his subordinate; both are legal rules. The right to pardon is a legal rule that represents non-law within the law – and reframes the real social conflict as a legal collision. Dealing with such collisions is the everyday business of law. Marx had already put it in trenchant terms: "A struggle" is waged "between collective capital, i.e., the class of capitalists, and collective labour, i.e., the working-class" – "right against right [...] Between equal rights force decides."[41] Marx explicated this antagonism of law against law for the sphere of class struggle. We would have to generalize the idea of the collision of laws against laws as the struggle for law within the law and respecify it for other interfaces. Fragmented global law is rife with such collisions that pit right against right:[42]

- investment protection law (e.g., concerning the privatization of water supplies) collides with social human rights;
- WTO law (e.g., liberalization of trade in genetically modified foods) collides with the global norms on environmental protection;
- UN law (e.g., UN targeted sanctions) collides with global human rights.

It is not the war in the decision-maker's head that constitutes the undecidability of these collision situations; rather, the law is, as Jean-François Lyotard has put it, "the civil war of '"language' with itself."[43] Elsewhere in "Law and Violence," Menke acknowledges as much, writing, with a view to the social process of the creation of law rather than the decision-maker's head, that "'relieved,' both disempowered and liberated, law is at war with itself" (p. 61). The war of law supplants the law of war. This perspective on trans-subjective collisions, rather than the focus on the subjective decision-making process, captures the crucial fact of the creation of law.

The formula of the "law of the unwilling" (p. 61) must not be merely a tonic from which decision-makers draw reassurance: it must be read as a challenge to society to take possession of law.[44] This socialization of law, as Daniel Loick has recently shown with reference to Hermann Cohen and Franz Rosenzweig,[45] finds important guidance in Walter Benjamin's "Critique of Violence." Benjamin distinguished the physical violence on which law is founded from the mythical violence with its dimensions of lawmaking and law-preserving. He then introduced a third violence, which he calls revolutionary, sovereign, divine violence. To constrain Benjamin's divine violence by turning it into a relieving power in the hands of unwilling state-appointed legal decision-makers would be to misapprehend the potential of this legal theory.

Seen through the Benjaminian lens, the uprisings around the world – the protests in Greece, the Occupy movement, the indignados of the Puerta del Sol, the Arab Spring – are struggles for a new social law. The unwilling of the world are not content with the degenerate law of dictatorial regimes and global neoliberalism. They demand that global law live up to its promise of justice. The law of the unwilling is then not the law of the unwilling *comandantes y subcomandantes*, but the right of social protest. Tellingly, Benjamin invests his hopes not in the political but in the proletarian general strike, which "sets itself the sole task of destroying state power."[46] Read in the light of Benjamin's sovereign violence, the formula of the "law of the unwilling" implies a comprehensive mandate for society to take possession of the law. This appropriation must disrupt the constitutive nexus between law-making and law-preserving legal violence; it must amount to more than a reform of the existing ensemble of institutions; and it must not limit itself to merely domesticating the established and operative apparatuses of decision-making.

If the war of law against law and the clashes between global law and global law articulate real social conflicts on a global scale, we cannot cede law to the self-appointed decision-makers. Instead, as Benjamin suggests, we must get involved in the struggle over the violence of the law and champion structures that give permanent form to society's law-making power and render it independent of the statist institutions of violence: Hauke Brunkhorst has called this the democratic conjunction of decision and discussion; Gunther Teubner has described it as the coupling of domains of spontaneity and organization.[47] The core objective is to make a democratization of the form of law possible and to open up the law to protest movements. This is the point that Otto Kirchheimer and Rudolf Wiethölter aimed at with their reflections on the socialization of the law (and the heuristic formula of the evolution of a social law of justification.[48]

The perspective of democratic law requires that we shift the focus from the governmental decision-makers to the social processes of legal creation in the struggle for global law. To come back to the Kunduz case: in

February 2012 the Cologne Administrative Court heard a petition by the truck driver in Kunduz for a declaratory judgment finding that the colonel's decision was unlawful. Several actions for damages are pending, a constitutional complaint has been filed against the decision not to initiate criminal proceedings, and it is foreseeable that this military decision will also occupy international courts such as the European Court of Human Rights.[49] The victims' fight for justice will keep the law busy for years. These lawsuits, the victims' rights to participation, and the potential for the creation of law implicit in the processes of global scandalization that Niklas Luhmann, following Émile Durkheim, has described as lawmaking by *colère publique*[50] which appeals to the public's sense of injustice,[51] are surely no less decisive data for the creation of law than the anguished decision-making process in the head of a commander.

III

This expansion of the terrain on which the struggle for law is waged in turn inevitably affects the utopia of law and the realization of the ideal of emancipation. The utopia of law, Menke argues, "is not about transcending law but about depotentiating it: by seeing law and its application become *one possibility*" (p. 60, emphasis added).

But if we content ourselves with such depotentiation, we merely make ourselves a little less comfortable in the enclosures of obedience to the law – we do not call them into question as such. Benjamin thinks "decision [as] transcendent";[52] Menke, by contrast, strips legal decision-making of this transcendent dimension. But must not the sting of the call for justice be more than the demand that those who render authoritative decisions develop a sense of unwillingness? Does not the struggle of those excluded from participation command more forceful partisanship? Must not law evolve a sensitivity for their sufferings?[53] Can the 1.3 billion people living in poverty around the world rely on the unwillingness of departmental bureaucracies and the world's courts?

"Justice is the principle of all divine endmaking [*Zwecksetzung*]":[54] that is Benjamin's formula for the basis of the law's relieving violence. Menke curbs the explosive force of this proposition by following Luhmann in interpreting justice as a formula for contingency:[55] as a mandate to secure the internal consistency of the decisions rendered, to establish responsiveness vis-à-vis the non-legal, and to reframe the tension between the law and its outside.[56] Yet it is only when justice is understood as a formula not merely of the contingency, but also of the transcendence of the law, that it remains ascendant; only then can the sting of justice be an effective agent of emancipation. Law – to quote Gunther Teubner – solicits "the attempt [...] to transform the immanence of law in a non-conceivable manner [...] Justice would be realised only after actually enduring injustice."[57] The interplay between applicable consistency constraints in the law and their transcendence can give rise to a process of the transformation of law in which the "enormous gulf that," as Benjamin writes, "essentially separates law from justice"[58] may be overcome. Such transcendence is not an automatism. Injustice must be articulated and scandalized; in the juridical struggle over its interpretation, law must be forced to look into the mirror of justice.

At this point it becomes apparent that the initially purely analytical distinction Benjamin draws between divine and mythical violence may be wielded in different ways: one reading – this is Menke's – is to effectively copy divine violence into mythical violence, and thus conceive Benjamin's relief as a domestication of mythical violence. In a second variant – Derrida in "Force of Law" emphatically warns of its dangers – divine violence obliterates mythical violence; the proletarian general strike then becomes indistinguishable from the totalizing anti-legal violence of annihilation – specifically, the law-annihilating violence of the fascists. In the third reading, as Cornelia Vismann has shown in a careful reconstruction, Benjamin's Messianic-Marxist discourse intends the yearning for the other, beyond the violence of law, a new legal form that cannot be realized, as a negation of the old and instead requires a new form of violence that acknowledges the difference between divine and mythical violence, combining the two rather than subsuming one under the other.[59]

Benjamin hints at how this combination may be realized with his distinction between the political and the proletarian general strike. He is very clear that the political general strike is a token for a struggle that, in the final analysis, amounts to instrumental-strategic action, which must develop, and which inevitably becomes embroiled in political-legal forms if it hopes to succeed. The proletarian general strike, by contrast, is an expression of sovereign violence and, as such, breaks the cycle of violence, of calculation and counter-calculation, of success, concession, compromise, struggle, and so on. In its amorphousness, it is an anticipation of communism. The challenge is to develop a praxis that combines both the political and the proletarian general strike, such that Benjamin's perspective of sovereign transcendence is retained even when the proletarian strike inscribes itself in the political-legal institutions. This requires that we acknowledge the difference between the two forms, but then avoid the temptation to locate the sovereign element in the self-reflection on the part of the political decision-making bodies – on the contrary, political violence must be prevented from passing itself off as proletarian. The possibility of transcendence must not be ground to pieces in the mills of the political system. The point of Benjamin's argument is his insistence that the proletarian appropriation of the law must not obliterate it. The social appropriation of the institutions must instead keep the perspective of a transcendence of the law open in order to live up to the mandate of transcendence challenging us to transform the immanence of pervasive mythical violence through sovereign violence as the other of law. To limn this "possible use of law,"[60] which attaches to the study of the law "the promises which tradition has attached to the study of the Torah,"[61] Benjamin invokes a "culture of the heart" that provides the means of nonviolent agreement: "courtesy of the heart, sympathy, peaceableness, trust, and whatever else might here be mentioned."[62]

That implies a transcendental perspective for the law; Menke, however, negates this very perspective: "For the rule of law is the equality of citizens; beyond law, inequality rules" (p. 60).[63] Menke presses his analysis to the crucial point, but then shies away from its implications and observes of the principle of justice what Adorno demonstrated for the barter principle: the abolition of law (Menke) is no more a viable option than the abolition of barter (Adorno). Yet Adorno did not leave it at this concession to reality. If we cannot abolish the barter principle, he urged, then we must transcend it – by demanding that it make good on its promise:

> If comparability as a category of measure were simply annulled, the rationality which is inherent in the barter principle – as ideology, of course, but also as a promise – would give way to direct appropriation, to force, and nowadays to the naked privilege of monopolies and cliques. When we criticize the barter principle [...] we want to realize the ideal of free and just barter. To date, this ideal is only a pretext. Its realization alone would transcend barter.[64]

The same argument holds of the law: only the realization of the just law would transcend the law. This possibility of law as a legal force, beyond the nexus of violence that is the law, of a law "that checks and retracts itself,"[65] is what Benjamin gestures towards in his essay on Kafka, writing that "the law which is studied but no longer practiced is the gate to justice."[66] Only by integrating this possibility of transcendence will postmodern legal theory be able to carry forward the tradition of the first generation of critical theory with regard also to its demand for the realization of the ideal of emancipation and justice.

IV

In short, the constitutive conjunction between the unified polity and legal creation underestimates the degree to which the law is enmeshed in its social context. Law in world society operates independent of the polity, and so critical theories of law must go beyond a focus on the decision as an act *ex fastidio* and turn the spotlight on the institutional conditions that frame the struggle for law: they must take the social processes of legal creation into account in their reflections and engender procedural couplings between decision and discussion. Broadening the scope of legal theory in this manner is a necessity if the legal form is to be democratized, and it will release the utopian perspective of law and thus facilitate a radically critical stance[67] vis-à-vis the existing relations of justification:[68] the critique of law wants the ideal of an emancipatory and just law, which has never been more than a pretext, to be realized in the struggle of the unwilling over the appropriation of the law. This alone would transcend law.

Notes

1 E. Fromm, *Das jüdische Gesetz: Zur Soziologie des Diaspora-Judentums* [1922], ed. R. Funk (Weinheim: Beltz, 1989).

2 O. Eberl and P. Niesen, 'Demokratischer Positivismus: Habermas und Maus,' in Sonja Buckel *et al.* (eds), *Neue Theorien des Rechts*, 2nd edn (Stuttgart: Lucius & Lucius, 2006), 3–26.

3 A. Honneth, *Freedom's Right: The Social Foundations of Democratic Life*, trans. J. Ganahl (New York: Columbia University Press, 2013); R. Forst, *Justification and Critique: Towards a Critical Theory of Politics*, trans. C. Cronin (Cambridge: Polity, 2014); H. Brunkhorst, *Solidarity: From Civic Friendship to a Global Legal Community* (Cambridge, MA: MIT Press, 2005); S. Buckel, *Subjektivierung und Kohäsion: Zur Rekonstruktion einer materialistischen Theorie des Rechts* (Weilerswist: Velbrück Wissenschaft, 2007).

4 W. Benjamin, "Critique of Violence" [1921], in *Selected Writings*, vol. 1: *1913–1926*, eds M. Bullock and M. W. Jennings (Cambridge, MA: Harvard University Press, 1996), 236–52; cf. J. Butler, "Critique, Coercion, and Sacred Life in Benjamin's 'Critique of Violence,'" in H. de Vries *et al.* (eds), *Political Theologies: Public Religions in a Post-Secular World* (New York: Fordham University Press, 2006), 201–19; C. Vismann, "Two Critics of Law: Benjamin and Kraus," *Cardozo Law Review*, 26:3 (2005), 1159–74.

5 C. Menke, "Für eine Politik der Dekonstruktion: Jacques Derrida über Recht und Gerechtigkeit," in Anselm Haverkamp (ed.), *Gewalt und Gerechtigkeit: Derrida – Benjamin* (Frankfurt am Main: Suhrkamp, 1994), 279–87; C. Menke, *Reflections of Equality*, trans. H. Rouse and A. Denejkine (Stanford: Stanford University Press, 2006).

6 J. Habermas, "Kulturelle Gleichbehandlung und die Grenzen des postmodernen Liberalismus," *Deutsche Zeitschrift für Philosophie*, 51:3 (2003), 371, my translation.
7 R. M. Cover, "Violence and the Word," *Yale Law Journal*, 95:8 (July 1986), 1601–29.
8 I. Kant, *To Perpetual Peace: A Philosophical Sketch* [1795] (Indianapolis: Hackett, 2003), 116.
9 J. Derrida, "Force of Law: The 'Mystical Foundation of Authority,'" trans. M. Quaintance, in Drucilla Cornell *et al.* (eds), *Deconstruction and the Possibility of Justice* (New York and London: Routledge, 1992), 14.
10 Cf. G. Teubner, "Alienating Justice: On the Social Surplus Value of the Twelfth Camel," in David Nelken *et al.* (eds), *Law's New Boundaries: Consequences of Legal Autopoiesis* (Aldershot: Ashgate, 2001), 21–44.
11 E. Denninger, *Recht in globaler Unordnung* (Berlin: Berliner Wissenschafts-Verlag, 2005), my translation.
12 C. Menke, "Die 'Aporien der Menschenrechte' und das 'einzige Menschenrecht': Zur Einheit von Hannah Arendts Argumentation," in Eva Geulen *et al.* (eds), *Hannah Arendt und Giorgio Agamben: Parallelen, Perspektiven, Kontroversen* (Munich: Fink, 2008), 131–47.
13 H. Arendt, "'The Rights of Man': What Are They?," *Modern Review*, 3:1 (Summer 1949), 24.
14 I. Lorey, *Figuren des Immunen: Elemente einer politischen Theorie* (Zurich: Diaphanes, 2011), 293.
15 D. Loick, *Kritik der Souveränität* (Frankfurt am Main: Campus, 2011), 252.
16 C. Lefort, *Machiavelli in the Making*, trans. M. B. Smith (Evanston: Northwestern University Press, 2012), 140.
17 J. Habermas, "A Political Constitution for the Pluralist World Society?" *Journal of Chinese Philosophy*, 40 (2013), 226–38.
18 U. Haltern, 'Recht als Tabu? Was Juristen nicht wissen wollen sollten,' in Otto Depenheuer (ed.), *Recht und Tabu* (Wiesbaden: Westdeutscher Verlag, 2003), 141, my translation.
19 C. Menke, *Reflections of Equality*, trans. H. Rouse and A. Denejkine (Stanford: Stanford University Press, 2006), 31.
20 K. Marx, *Capital: A Critique of Political Economy*, vol. 1 [1867], trans. S. Moore and E. Aveling (Mineola: Dover, 2011), 96–97; in reality, of course, the category of the legal subject is abstracted from the act of exchange

taking place in the market' (E. Pashukanis, *The General Theory of Law and Marxism* [1924], with a new introduction by Dragan Milovanovic (New Brunswick: Transaction Publishers, 2002), 117).

21 On this concept see N. Luhmann, "Globalization or World Society? How to Conceive of Modern Society," *International Review of Sociology*, 7:1 (1997), 67–80.

22 But see Berman, who wants to apply the concept of the community to the *lex mercatoria* as well: P. S. Berman, "Global Legal Pluralism," *Southern California Law Review*, 80:6 (2007), 1162.

23 S. Sassen, *Territory, Authority, Rights: From Medieval to Global Assemblages* (Princeton: Princeton University Press, 2006); K. Möller, "Global Assemblages im neuen Konstitutionalismus," *ancilla iuris*, 2008:44, 44–56.

24 A. Fischer-Lescano and G. Teubner, "Regime-Collisions: The Vain Search for Legal Unity in the Fragmentation of Global Law," *Michigan Journal of International Law*, 25:4 (2004), 999–1045.

25 G. Teubner, *Constitutional Fragments: Societal Constitutionalism and Globalization* (Oxford: Oxford University Press, 2012), 13.

26 H. J. Berman, "World Law," *Fordham International Law Journal*, 18:5 (1995), 1617–22.

27 C. Menke and A. Pollmann, *Philosophie der Menschenrechte zur Einführung*, 2nd edn (Hamburg: Junius, 2009), 109, my translation.

28 See Bundesverfassungsgericht (Federal Constitutional Court), BVerfGE 128: 226 (Fraport AG).

29 G. Teubner, "Societal Constitutionalism and the Politics of the Common," *Finnish Yearbook of International Law*, 21 (2010), 2–15.

30 A. Fischer-Lescano, "Struggles for a Global Internet Constitution: Protecting Global Communication Structures Against Surveillance Measures," *Global Constitutionalism*, 5:2 (2016), 145–72.

31 J. Ruggie, *Guiding Principles on Business and Human Rights: Implementing the United Nations "Protect, Respect and Remedy" Framework*, " vol. amsker Chaussee titution. text or is it your addition?is definition of violence?March 21 (2011), A/HRC/17/31.

32 J. Derrida, "Not Utopia, the Impossible," in *Paper Machine*, trans. R. Bowlby (Stanford: Stanford University Press, 2005), 123–24.

33 C. Schmitt, *Gesetz und Urteil: Eine Untersuchung zum Problem der Rechtspraxis* (Berlin: Liebmann, 1912), 86.

34 H. Müller, "Wolokolamsker Chaussee I: Russische Eröffnung," in *Werke*, vol. 5: *Die Stücke 3* (Frankfurt am Main: Suhrkamp, 2002).

35 B. Brecht, "Kaukasischer Kreidekreis" (1949), in *Werke: Große kommentierte Berliner und Frankfurter Ausgabe*, vol. 8: *Stücke* (Frankfurt am Main: Suhrkamp, 1989), 72, my translation.

36 N. Müller-Schöll, *Das Theater des "konstruktiven Defaitismus": Lektüren zur Theorie eines Theaters der A-Identität bei Walter Benjamin, Bertolt Brecht und Heiner Müller* (Frankfurt am Main: Stroemfeld/Nexus, 2002), 411.

37 Bundestagsdrucksache (BT-Drs.) 17/7400, October 25, 2011: 64, original emphasis, my translation.

38 A. Fischer-Lescano and R. Christensen, "Auctoritatis interpositio: How Systems Theory deconstructs Decisionism," *Social & Legal Studies*, 21:1 (2012), 93–119.

39 N. Luhmann, *Law as a Social System*, trans. K. A. Ziegert (Oxford and New York: Oxford University Press, 2004), 292–93.

40 H. Kelsen, "*Hauptprobleme der Staatsrechtslehre*" [1911], in *Werke*, vol. 2, ed. Matthias Jestaedt (Tübingen: Mohr Siebeck, 2008), 352, put it bluntly: "No law without courts."

41 K. Marx, *Capital: A Critique of Political Economy*, vol. 1 [1867], trans. S. Moore and E. Aveling (Mineola: Dover, 2011), 259; C. Miéville, *Between Equal Rights: A Marxist Theory of International Law* (Leiden and Boston, MA: Brill, 2005).

42 See the contributions in K. Blome *et al.* (eds), *Contested Regime Collisions: Interdisciplinary Inquiries into Norm Fragmentation in World Society* (Cambridge: Cambridge University Press, 2016).

43 F. Lyotard, *The Differend: Phrases in Dispute*, trans. Georges Van Den Abbeele (Minneapolis: University of Minnesota Press, 1988), 141.

44 R. Wiethölter, 'Ist unserem Recht der Prozeß zu machen?', in Axel Honneth *et al.* (eds), *Zwischenbetrachtungen: Im Prozeß der Aufklärung. Jürgen Habermas zum 60. Geburtstag* (Frankfurt am Main: Suhrkamp, 1989), 794–812.

45 D. Loick, *Kritik der Souveränität* (Frankfurt am Main: Campus, 2011), 279.

46 Benjamin, "Critique of Violence," 246; H. Brunkhorst, *How Is a Critique of Violence Historically Possible?*, lecture at the 2010 Benjamin conference in Santiago de Chile and Buenos Aires (manuscript), 6.

47 H. Brunkhorst, "Das öffentliche Recht in 'Empire,'" in R. Faber (ed.), *Imperialismus in Geschichte und Gegenwart* (Würzburg: Königshausen

& Neumann, 2005), 177; G. Teubner, *Constitutional Fragments: Societal Constitutionalism and Globalization* (Oxford: Oxford University Press, 2012), 88.

48 O. Kirchheimer, "The Socialist and Bolshevik Theory of the State' [1928], in *Politics, Law, and Social Change: Selected Essays of Otto Kirchheimer*, eds F. S. Burin and K. L. Shell (New York: Columbia University Press, 1969), 3–21; R. Wiethölter, "Recht-Fertigungen eines Gesellschafts-Rechts," in Christian Joerges *et al.* (eds), *Rechtsverfassungsrecht: Recht-Fertigung zwischen Privatrechtsdogmatik und Gesellschaftstheorie* (Baden-Baden: Nomos, 2003), 13–21.

49 For the proceedings in administrative court, see Cologne Administrative Court, verdict of February 9, 2012 (Az. 26 K 5534/10) and Federal High Court of Justice, decision of October 6, 2016, III ZR 140/15, not yet final; and see the constitutional challenge before the Federal Constitutional Court (Az. 2 BvR 987/11).

50 N. Luhmann, "Das Paradox der Menschenrechte und drei Formen seiner Entfaltung," in *Soziologische Aufklärung*, vol. 6, 2nd edn (Wiesbaden: Verlag für Sozialwissenschaften, 2005), 229–36.

51 E. N. Cahn, *The Sense of Injustice: An Anthropocentric View of Law* (New York: New York University Press, 1949).

52 W. Benjamin, "Goethe's Elective Affinities" [1924/1925], in *Selected Writings*, vol. 1: *1913–1926*, eds M. Bullock and M. W. Jennings (Cambridge, MA: Harvard University Press, 1996), 346.

53 A. Fischer-Lescano, *Rechtskraft* (Berlin: August, 2013).

54 Benjamin, "Critique of Violence," 248.

55 This is the point of departure for the transformation of Luhmann's structurally descriptive systems theory into a normative theory: see A. Fischer-Lescano, "Critical Systems Theory," *Philosophy and Social Criticism*, 38:1 (2012), 3–23.

56 Menke's account of the domain of non-law remains vague. The term "non-citizen" does not distinguish between the functional rationalities (of economics, art, science, religion, etc.) as well as the human (body, consciousness) and natural environments of society. Menke instead replaces the multiplicity of social boundary relations with the difference between citizen and non-citizen or law and non-law: "Utopia is the equality of possibility between the legal equality of citizens *and* their non-legal inequality as

non-citizens. This utopian equality is not a criterion or basis for anything" (p. 60).

57 G. Teubner, "Self-subversive Justice: Contingency or Transcendence Formula of Law?," *Modern Law Review*, 72:1 (January 2009), 20; see also P. Femia, 'Infrasystemische Subversion', in Marc Amstutz *et al.* (eds), *Kritische Systemtheorie: Zur Evolution einer normativen Theorie* (Bielefeld: Transcript, 2013), 305–26.

58 W. Benjamin, "Notes toward a Work on the Category of Justice" [1916], in Peter Fenves, *The Messianic Reduction: Walter Benjamin and the Shape of Time* (Stanford: Stanford University Press, 2011), 258.

59 C. Vismann, "Das Gesetz 'DER Dekonstruktion'," *Rechtshistorisches Journal*, 11 (1992), 259–60.

60 G. Agamben, *State of Exception*, trans. K. Attell (Chicago: University of Chicago Press, 2005), 88.

61 W. Benjamin, "Franz Kafka: On the Tenth Anniversary of His Death" [1934], in *Selected Writings*, vol. 2: *1927–1934*, eds M. W. Jennings, H. Eiland, and G. Smith (Cambridge, MA: Harvard University Press, 2005), 815.

62 Benjamin, "Critique of Violence," 244.

63 Luhmann, by contrast, describes the constellation in the domain excluded from the law as one of equality in non-law. Sharelessness, to use Rancière's term, leads to equality in highly integrated unfreedom: "There is nothing to lose in the highly integrated area of exclusion, apart from control over one's own body" (N. Luhmann, *Law as a Social System*, trans. Klaus A. Ziegert (Oxford and New York: Oxford University Press, 2004), 490). On the side of inclusion, meanwhile, it is undeniable that the law is deeply implicated in the existing inequalities; it generates or at least stabilizes the differences between owner and non-owner, bourgeois and proletarian, and, by consequence, shareholder and shareless. That is why Benjamin's reflection on justice transforms the subjective right of ownership into "a claim that in no way refers back to needs but, rather, refers to justice, the ultimate direction of which probably does not tend toward an ownership right of the person but, rather, towards a good-right of the good" (Benjamin, "Notes toward a Work on the Category of Justice," 257–58; translation modified).

64 T. W. Adorno, *Negative Dialectics*, trans. E. B. Ashton (New York: Seabury Press, 1973), 146–47.

65 W. Hamacher, "Recht im Spiegel," in Georg Mein (ed.), *Die Zivilisation des Interpreten: Studien zum Werk Pierre Legendres* (Vienna: Turia + Kant, 2012), 212, my translation.

66 Benjamin, "Franz Kafka: On the Tenth Anniversary of His Death," 815; cf. A. Fischer-Lescano, "Franz Kafka's Critique of Legal Violence", *Revista Brasileira de Sociologia do Direito* 3:1 (2016), 9–51.

67 M. Foucault, 'What Is Critique?', trans. L. Hochroth, in S. Lotringer (ed.), *The Politics of Truth* (Los Angeles: Semiotext(e), 1997), 41–42.

68 M. Horkheimer, "Traditional and Critical Theory," trans. M. J. O'Connell, in *Critical Theory: Selected Essays* (New York: Herder and Herder, 1972), 188–243.

7

Self-reflection

Alexander García Düttmann

Self-reflection, the philosophical concept that plays a key role in Menke's essay on law and violence, stands opposed to all forms of spontaneity. Where – inevitably, perhaps – such reflection kicks in, or takes over, spontaneity must reveal itself to be either a form of naivety and stupidity, an immediacy that deceives itself about its own implications and mediations, or a form of ideology. The effort made to overcome thick-headedness will still seem rather improbable, at least from the perspective of the individual who lifts themselves to a level of sophistication and, once they have reached this level, once they have raised their consciousness to self-consciousness, once they have planted within themselves what Adorno calls the "ferment of intellectual or spiritual experience,"[1] will keep wondering what kind of a person they were beforehand and how such a person could have left obtuseness behind for much of the time if not once and for all. Of course a contrast needs to be introduced between self-reflection as an individual and even collective accomplishment, a subjective act that borders on objectivity the more universal it is, and self-reflection as a stage in the development of some concept, some entity that is not ready-made, that harbors the intelligibility of spirit, and that requires a specification, or further determination, to fully come into its own. Self-reflection amounts to the attainment of an awareness that deepens the understanding of whatever it is that undergoes the process, the understanding that someone has of herself or himself, or the understanding that something has of itself. Typically, such deepening is concerned with limits and limitations, with lapses, corrections, transformations, and corroborations, yet it never results in something akin to a complete abrogation. It is a critical endeavor preoccupied with the difficult distinction between an inside and an outside, a distinction it seeks to maintain, no matter how, exactly, it is drawn. The difficulty of drawing the distinction lies in that it is not always clear what belongs to the inside and what to the outside. For example, if self-reflection has an effect on action, an effect that can prove both enhancing and paralyzing, does it affect a sphere that cannot be separated from thought and should be regarded as reason's practical dimension, or does it affect a sphere that reflection, forever hesitant, cannot properly reach and that, as a consequence, constitutes a kind of exteriority in relation to thought? Would there be self-reflection in the first place without otherness, without a possibly irreducible otherness whose first manifestation is naivety, stupidity, immediacy, or ideology, or without an otherness that resides in the impossibility of deciding just how external this otherness remains to selfhood? Is the acknowledgment of an irreducible otherness marked terminologically by the difference between the words *Selbstreflexion* and *Selbstbesinnung*, self-reflection and self-examination, in philosophical German? A Hegelian author like Adorno may use both words almost as synonyms, while an author much more wary of Hegel´s influence, like Heidegger, will insist on the difference between consciousness and mindfulness as an involvement with sense and meaning, or between making something explicit and thereby becoming conscious of it, and a "releasement that discloses, and opens itself up to, what is worthy of questioning."[2]

In Menke, self-reflection as an act of the law, as an act of the law´s enlightening manifestation, has to do with unwillingness, with a peculiar reluctance to apply the law, with a repugnance inspired by such application, or execution. It is as if the law turned against itself without, however, giving itself up entirely, or as if it posited itself and at the same time refused to posit and enforce itself, placing the self of self-preservation, and the seriousness it comports, within brackets, or as if it came into its own both inside and outside of itself, exposing reflection to mindfulness, as it were. Self-reflection impinges on the will: either it uncovers an unwillingness that was buried under the willingness on which the law feeds, or it generates an unwillingness that the law did not know before. This ambiguity, especially when it is justified and exploited by dialectics, defines the idealism inherent in self-reflection, and it does so twice over, once in view of the productive energy attributed to reflection in general, and then again in view of the fact that reflection is supposed to generate a modality related not to thought but to the will. But why is this so? Why is willingness a torn willingness when considered from the point of view of the law′s self-reflection? And can the law, equipped with a selfhood capable of reflecting and directing reflection at itself, contain the otherness that such unwillingness signals? If it cannot, or if it cannot be ascertained whether it can or whether it is unable to do so, if the self is haunted from within by an other that is not another self, and if reflection is diverted from its focus by the violence a blind spot inflicts upon it, a blind spot that does not contribute to reflexivity in the manner in which negativity produces speculation, then the idea of self-reflection must be qualified. In the case of the law proving unable to contain otherness, would it still make sense to speak of self-reflection? Would the involvement with the law′s meaning not stumble over an obstacle it could not remove, precisely because this obstacle, this lack of meaning, would be constitutive of the meaning of the law, rendering it both questionable and worthy of questioning? Ultimately, the unwillingness of a self-reflective law that delays its own application for as long as possible, the unwillingness that turns the law both into a lazy, careless law and an attentive, anxious law must also be an irrepressible unwillingness to engage in self-reflection itself, since at some point an unwillingness that is more than a regenerative respite deserved and even demanded by willingness has to obscure the transparency without which self-reflection reveals itself to be fragmentary, mutilated, incomplete, delayed.

Self-reflection is the logical and genetic criterion that allows Menke to distinguish between two forms of justice: retributive justice and the justice of the law and its normative order. What is it that characterizes retribution according to Menke? Retribution consists in constantly doing the same, in repeating an act of violence as a violent counteract. It consists in an endless series of repetitions in which measure and excess are inextricably linked to each other, and installs itself in an ambivalence that makes it hover between something that merely happens, or comes to pass, and something that results from an activity, or a deed. Since acts of retribution are all the same – violent and hence disproportionate counteracts aimed at different and incompatible understandings of what it means to do justice, in a world that knows of nothing outside these competing understandings – they lack, when narrated, distinct figures of subjectivity, figures of mutual recognition, and acquire the quality of a mythic fate to which individuals, or inimical communities, are all subjected. But Menke´s argument is more radical. For in truth, the violence of the act of retribution lies in the fact of it being an act or a deed, and it is in the act itself as measureless violence that the compulsion to repeat it lies, as if the liberation from retribution were tantamount to a liberation from acting, or acting out, from the tautology of an act that already implies another act in an infinite reproduction of activity.

Retribution is a form of justice that has fallen prey to a curse. Pure or mere activity cannot but be ambivalent, something that comes to pass as much as something that is carried out. Thus retribution raises a question it cannot answer, namely how an interruption of self-reproductive activity is possible, a liberation from an unfree spontaneity, or from the activity of a spontaneity condemned to unfreedom and compulsion. But if retribution raises a question it cannot answer, then it embodies this very question and needs to abolish itself so as to find an answer. Violence, it would seem, has always something to do with a body, no matter how sublimated it may be, with a body bereft of an image in which it could reflect itself and through which it could reflect upon itself. The instant violence engages with other violence, the instant violence is perpetrated in acts of revenge or retribution, the instant violence appears as an act or an activity, the instant the body moves and is moved, it begins to turn into a question and an image begins to flicker on the horizon. Only self-reflection can therefore provide an answer to a question, to the body as a question, at least to the extent that the law which aspires to put an end to the violence of retribution can itself be reduced to a self-reproductive activity, to an operation concerned only with itself, with the violence of preserving its own normative order and establishing and imposing its own categories. By becoming self-reflective, and therefore by undergoing a crisis, or by becoming critical of itself, the law sets itself apart from retribution and generates a form of justice that no longer depends, simply, on an activity.

What is it that characterizes the law according to Menke? The law has a peculiar kinship with art since it emerges out of tragedy as the representation of proceedings, of a trial that suspends the immediacy of activity, and since art, especially drama, proves crucial to the law's effort to attain the kind of self-reflexivity that alone elevates it above the body and its violence, above immediacy, stupidity, naivety. When the law wrests itself from retribution, it creates a homogeneous sphere in which parties treated as equal follow a distancing and qualifying procedure that leads up to a decision, the settlement of the dispute. Each party recognizes the other party as a lawful subject, as a subject whose claim is worthy of consideration; and both parties acknowledge the authority of a non-partisan instance, an impartial third who is not another party involved in the case and who will judge the matter taken before the law by the parties at odds with each other.

Menke describes the sphere of the law as a sphere in which an original figure of subjectivity is produced, the figure of autonomous subjectivity. Autonomous subjectivity embodies the law in that it reflects it by virtue of a judging activity, by relating to itself, to others, and to the world, in the guise of judgments. And he also describes it as a non-tautological sphere that is essentially oriented towards an outside, given that this outside, this sphere beyond the sphere of the law, comes into existence with the constitution of the juridical sphere itself. The two descriptions are associated with one another in important ways because the autonomous subject of the law cannot avoid relating to the non-autonomous subject that resists the law and remains outside of it.

In fact, in his description of the law as productive of autonomy, Menke provides an unexpected twist that makes all the more apparent the connections between the production of autonomy and the production of an outside, of an outlaw who is not only a negative figure, or the reverse of autonomous subjectivity. The autonomous subject, the subject capable of reflecting upon themselves and judging themselves, is said to share something with the non-autonomous subject of retribution. Just as the non-autonomous subject of retribution must constantly act, must compulsively perpetrate violent acts, the autonomous subject of the law must constantly judge, and first and foremost they must judge themselves. This is why the subject of the law is a hybrid creation, a mixture of violent embodiment and liberating self-reflection. On the one hand, the law functions as a desubjectifying machine that destroys old subjects, concrete subjects, or individuals, and produces new subjects, abstract subjects, or persons, who have internalized judgment and judge themselves and others in accordance with the law, or with the form of justice instilled by the law. On the other hand, it would make no sense to state that judging is a curse, as Menke does, and that there is an aporia of the law, an antithesis, based on its violent quality and its simultaneous hostility to violence, if one did not imply that the autonomous subject is never merely an autonomous subject, that autonomy already transgresses itself and is determined by a surplus over which it has no control, and that the outside of autonomy is located within the autonomous subject. To say that the law subjugates its subjects violently as it produces autonomous subjects, to say that the law is bound to terrify its subjects, to say that the law is political and ideological, to say that autonomy is subverted by sovereignty, is to say that it has begun to loosen its reins, to renounce total internalization and self-identification, and to abandon itself to an adventure of depoliticization and non-participation, to the "non-legal forces of 'distraction' – of obliviousness, refusal, and incapacity" (p. 55), to the forces and insights of art. In short, the production of autonomy is the production of an outside of autonomy inside of autonomy. It is the production of something that confuses the limits between the inside and the outside and that is a threat to self-reflection. It is the production of something that deprives self-reflection of its ability to cognize and mediate, to judge and criticize. Only by conceiving of autonomy in this paradoxical manner can the law be distinguished from retribution. Otherwise, the law, the ubiquity of judgment, would prove as violent as retribution, the ubiquity of the deed, and self-reflection would have no means to liberate the subject from herself or himself, from the violence of its embodiment, assuming that it is self-reflection that renders freedom possible. The place of self-reflection, then, must be the place of its exposure to blindness, to the blindness of an imageless body and to the blindness of an outside that forestalls conclusions meant to achieve intelligibility, bringing about an unwillingness to execute the law. The place of self-reflection, the place that in Menke's essay is occupied by the law and configured by its instauration, is the place of a transformation of self-reflection that must protect it against turning into either a tautological activity (retribution) or an activity with a result (judging). It must distance self-reflection from itself as an activity, even if it could be adduced that this activity is already ambivalent, enmeshed in violence while critical of its entanglement, of the curse constitutive of activity as such.

The unwillingness to judge and execute the law reveals itself to be the acknowledgment of the symptom of autonomy, a recognition of the necessary manifestation of an outside, or an irreducible otherness, neither autonomous nor heteronomous, in the autonomous realm. This otherness is not opposed to autonomy but partakes of it, makes it possible and impossible at the same time, deconstructs it. It releases self-reflection from itself as it is released by self-reflection. The law cannot perform such an acknowledgment, such a recognition; it cannot relate to itself as a paradox without reflecting upon itself from the vantage point of a law of the law, and thereby conceding the right to participate in the law, to become a legal subject after all, to what is not part of the law, the non-legal subject. But how, precisely, does an unwillingness to judge and apply the law differ from a willingness to do so? Is it simply a question of reflecting upon oneself as a legal subject and of being more mindful of the intricate and intractable relationship between the inside and the outside of the law, the selfhood of autonomy and the otherness that traverses it? Can one render a judgment or reach a legally binding conclusion within quotation marks, as it were, in a sort of perpetual messianic time in which activation and deactivation cannot be told apart properly? Can a legal subject that is put to the test in a case of emergency afford a virtuousness derived from the recognition of otherness? Can it afford an unhappy consciousness, a consciousness split between, on the one hand, the universal validity of the law that establishes the truth, and, on the other hand, the contingency of an otherness that refuses to acknowledge the self-evidence of such truth? Can it afford a consciousness acutely aware of its split, a consciousness that professes to endure its diremption because of the power to resist with which self-reflection is supposed to endow it? How much time does a legal subject have to be unwilling and how does the time span of unwillingness fit into, or else outpace, the time span granted by the law in view of its proceedings? Does the legal subject's unwillingness impinge on the law and hence on herself or himself because at times it will apply the law and at times it will not, without there being any justification for the decision made, any justification backed by universally compelling reasons? Must a legal subject seek a balance between enforcements and suspensions of the law so as to do justice to the two aspects of the law's imbalance and non-identity? Is unwillingness a reminder of the law's perfectibility? Can a legal subject allow herself or himself to be a haunted subject when the law's normative order is called into question, as it is, in fact, by each suspension of the law, no matter how insignificant and innocuous it appears to be? Must the unwillingness remain largely unseen and unfelt in the realm of the public, sensed only as an inward torment, as a torment addressed, if at all, to the memory of God?

Taking his cue from literature, from a play in which an officer needs to make a decision about the behavior of a renegade soldier in a situation where the troops under the officer's command need to defend the capital against the invasion of a powerful foreign army, Menke explores the utopian potential of an alternative, or of the fact that two equally persuasive but mutually exclusive possibilities indicate ways of dealing with a situation that are no longer indebted to a logic of sovereignty, which is a logic of violence and tautological activity, a logic of self-preservation and functionality, a logic of legality devoid of self-reflection. In the play to which Menke refers, the officer, or the commander, suddenly realizes that the execution of the soldier, an execution that would set an example in a historical and political context in which the war dictates the law, is not the only option he may choose. As a consequence of this insight, the application of the law, of the military law, ceases to follow quasi-automatically from the law itself, from its prescriptive character. For it is reinscribed in a process of self-reflection and adopts the traits of a possibility distinguished from at least one other possibility: the possibility of letting the offense go unpunished. It is as if the commander had suddenly gained an awareness of the law's implication with an outside it cannot fully retain under its dominion:

> This utopian equality is not a criterion or basis for anything. It does not define a yardstick for decision-making, instead demanding that every decision – the decision in accordance with the law as much as the one counter to the law – issue from the self-reflection of law, its self-reflection in the relation that constitutes it (p. 60).

What the "utopian equality" of two possibilities, utopian inasmuch as this equality is a radical equality, not an equality determined by the constraints and violence of a legal machine, and also inasmuch as it deactivates the law from within the law and thereby marks a non-place, an impossible site in the law's midst – what the "utopian equality" discloses is the caesura of self-reflection, since the "relation" in which the law stands, the relation to an outside, must also be a non-relation, a relation interrupted. It signals the impossibility of a law of the law constituting itself and offering an anchor for self-reflection.

The commander has allowed the law – and the self-reflection it cannot suppress if it is to establish a relation between an inside and an outside and in this manner break with the immanence of retribution, with immediacy, spontaneity, activity – to carry him to its very limit, to the limit of the law. At this limit, where the law does not reign supreme and judging is withheld, he decides to have the renegade soldier executed, thereby exhibiting the violence which the law, when viewed from within, treats as a sort of fateful necessity, a violence necessary to the functionality and self-preservation of the law, and ultimately a violence necessary to self-reflection itself. In the commander´s mind, the battle, or the war, between law and non-law, between the inside and the outside of the law, continues, as Menke stresses, and it should be added that the only reason the decision triggers such a continuation is because it remains undecidable where the inside begins and where the outside ends, or because self-reflection is a victim of the war the commander fights, so to speak.

Menke observes that the commander does not ask the soldier whom he orders to be executed for his assent, as a legal conviction would require – within the sphere of the law, it is assumed that the convicted person can make sense of the conviction, make it his own. Is this the law´s truth or its infamy? The decision to execute the soldier is taken at the limit of the law and should not be considered a judgment, an outcome of the judging activity invented by the law. And yet nothing resembles a judgment and its conclusive character more closely than the decision the commander makes, his non-legal conviction, which in this case also matches a conviction "in accordance with" martial law, with the logic of sovereignty. One might even be tempted to say that the commander's decision both exposes the ideology of the law and engages in its ideological application. Why? Because the possibility of executing or killing someone, while being a possibility in formal terms and hence equal to other possibilities, is a possibility in excess of itself, as it were, a possibility chained to its actualization, a possibility that, when actualized, cannot remain a possibility for the sake of future actualization. It can be actualized only once and it is tainted by the violence of such irretrievability. To be sure, one can kill again and again, one can be a serial killer or a killing machine. Each time, however, the deed one commits is committed once and for all. One does not know what one does as one kills and kills yet again, and no self-reflection will ever remedy such stupidity. In this sense killing someone, or having someone executed, is strictly impossible, or the possibility of the impossible, even though one keeps doing it, perhaps. Inequality, violence, traverses and destabilizes the "utopian equality" of possibilities. The violence intrinsic to the possibility of killing someone, the violence of the outside of death, the violence of the blindness that pertains to the outside in general, cuts self-reflection short and reinserts the commander in the normative order of the law that he had outlived, unless it leaves him in the middle of nowhere. Therefore, Menke's appealing attempt to find an alternative to the logic of sovereignty by turning to the fiction of drama, to a play concerned with the limit case, fails on account of the inextricability of violence. The moment there is an outside, an outside created by the normative order of the law and at the same time independent of it, an outside to which one can and cannot relate from the inside, an outside that ceases to be an outside when it, too, becomes self-reflective, there is violence and one cannot escape it. The outside is a point of no return, at least when viewed from the perspective of the inside, of the law.

Of course, Menke does not claim that violence can be escaped, since the interruption of the law he discusses in terms of unwillingness is itself inseparable from the law's application, and is ultimately and paradoxically indistinguishable from legal implementation. The point is that self-reflection, this odd non-activity, presupposes violence so as to ensure and protect its own possibility. And the point is that the interruption itself, the unwillingness to apply, implement, or execute the law, involves violence, which by definition is dystopian. Or is it? Not all violence may be equal in form and in essence, but subjectively its dystopia still mimics the utopia of self-reflection in an uncanny fashion, if the task of self-reflection is to reach and ponder equal possibilities, to open up and to anticipate a radical equality beyond violence: "All violence appears the same: for the one who suffers it, it makes no difference why and how it is exercised" (p. 19).

When reflecting upon law and violence, one must either adhere to a normative order in which, and on which, the logic of sovereignty has a determining impact, or else pursue strategies of rupture that the law cannot, or must be unwilling to, accommodate.

Notes

1 T. W. Adorno, *Negative Dialektik*, in *Gesammelte Schriften*, vol. 6 (Frankfurt am Main: Suhrkamp 1970), 56, my translation.
2 M. Heidegger, "Wissenschaft und Besinnung," in *Vorträge und Aufsätze* (Pfullingen: Neske 1954), 64, my translation.

Part III

Reply

8

A reply to my critics

Christoph Menke
(Translated by Cathleen Poehler)

"Law and violence" is a short, thesis-based attempt to explore the possibility of a critique of law. At the center of this critique of law is the problem of violence, for law does not only start with violence but also leads to violence.

Law begins with the experience of violence. Law exists *because* there is violence, and because recognizing the existence of violence appears to be tantamount to saying that violence should not exist. "Pain says: 'Refrain! Away, you pain!'"[1] This is the underlying drive behind law. Its *raison d'être* is to fight against the violence which one inflicts upon another. Yet, from the very start, law can only do this by bringing violence into a form that it can deal with. Law translates the violence that one inflicts upon another into the violation of a law. The violence of one against another is always unique, always different; the violation of a law, by contrast, is a general one. This general aspect of law consists in the normative status as equals that is accorded to each person under the law. In other words, law translates a specific act of violence committed by one against another into the violation of the one and the same legal status that both parties share.

This means, first of all, that the fight against violence in law can only be selective. Law distinguishes between the violence that it is equipped to fight against and the violence that is beyond its reach, and which it thereby neutralizes and renders harmless. Law must be indifferent towards all forms of violence which it cannot conceive of as a violation of said equal legal status of the person – as defined by the law at a given time and context. This indifference of law is not a shortcoming that it can overcome. Indeed, this indifference follows from its selectiveness: It is only the type of violence that can be represented as a violation of a general law that can be addressed by law; only violations of the equal status of persons that can be punished as violence by law. This constitutes the abstractness that defines law. It follows not only that law must disregard many forms of violence, but also that, paradoxically, law must itself exercise violence. The fact that the standpoint of law is abstract means that it is external to other perspectives: Law is necessarily an *external* order. In this way, law is faced with other social practices *against* which it must likewise assert itself. Law is at once external *and* the assertion against that which is external to it. This constitutes the essential, insurmountable violence of law. In the necessarily abstract, external, yet nonetheless effective manner in which law proceeds against violence, law necessarily reproduces violence.

This is the basic idea, or intuition, that "Law and Violence" seeks to formulate. It does so in continuation of a long tradition of legal thought that has examined this dual nature of law. In modern philosophy, the most prominent model for this approach was developed by the young Hegel, and in contemporary philosophy by Jacques Derrida.[2] That said, "Law and Violence" draws less from these models directly[3] and more from the critical reflection on law in ancient tragedy (including some of its modern re-conceptions), which I read in conjunction with Walter Benjamin's "Critique of Violence." Through this double reference to literature and philosophy, I seek to identify and explore a concept of law that might be able to conceptually integrate the above-mentioned two sides – the objection of law *against* violence on the one hand, and the exercise of violence *by* law on the other. The unity of the concept of law consists of its contradiction between the fight against and the exercise of violence.

The contributions in this volume have raised a number of critical objections against this thesis and its explication, which I will address, at least in part, in this response. However, I would first like to make a remark concerning a fundamental difficulty that follows from the above-mentioned definition of law. If the unity of law involves a contradiction, then law inevitably eschews any simple conceptual determination. Thus, law is characterized by an internal antinomy that must be taken into account from the outset.

This difficulty is brought to the fore by the question of the relationship between the two fundamental determinations of law, namely, its fight against violence and its exercise of violence. On the one hand, it is a matter of showing that law can *only* be both at the same time: that there can be no concept of law that does not understand law as both one *and* the other at once. This means that both the idealistic and the realistic notions of law are to be rejected, the former seeing in law nothing other than a normative order of recognition that ensures each person the same status, and the latter restricting law to a factual arrangement of force that secures the conditions of subordination. However, at the same time, law cannot be both *simultaneously*. For when law is driven primarily by the impulse to oppose the violence of one against another, it cannot be indifferent to its own violence. The violence committed by law is a problem – indeed a scandal – for law itself. It contradicts its own claim, which it cannot renounce without betraying itself. Thus, law must, in addition, combat the violence that it commits itself.

The fact that the unity of law involves a contradiction not only means that law contains two incompatible determinations, namely, combating and exercising violence. Rather, it also points to the incompatibility of the two relationships governing these determinations: Law serves to combat violence *and* to exercise violence, yet law is also directed *against* its own exercise of violence. The meaning of law can never be captured by only one of these two relationships. Therefore, law comprises the combating of violence and the exercise of violence, *and* it turns against what it is; it turns against itself. One cannot grasp law as an entity with a specific set of qualities. Because its qualities contradict one another, law is an objection against its own existence. Thus, law constantly raises objections against itself, against the existence of law. Law itself wants to abolish law.

The same difficulty that constitutes the concept of law also determines the reflection upon the concept of law. Indeed, it is *the* fundamental difficulty faced by any attempt at a critique of law. According to the original meaning of the word "critique," critique is the act of normative, judging differentiation. To practice criticism means to say "yes" or "no" to something, and to differentiate between right and wrong. Further, it seeks to arrive at a decision that would dissolve the coexistence of these two options. Indeed, it radicalizes the contradiction of the two sides and claims that only one of the two has validity and existence. Because the difference that is constitutive of law is the difference between its opposition to violence and its exercise of violence, such a critical approach to law is at once necessary and impossible. The difference between the opposition to violence and the exercise of violence by law calls for criticism yet also makes criticism impossible. On the one hand, law needs critique, since violence is, normatively speaking, never neutral. The distinction between the opposition to violence and the exercise of violence in law requires a critical decision. It calls for the rejection of the exercise of violence by law, in other words, to decide in the name of law against the violence of law. On the other hand, the difference between the opposition to violence and the exercise of violence in law cannot be decided normatively. This is because the concept of law stands for nothing other than the insight that the one – the opposition to violence – cannot exist without the other – the exercise of violence. Because its two sides are intertwined, the distinction that characterizes law is indissoluble and hence undecidable: Law cannot be criticized. Law calls for critique, and law undermines critique. One can *only* think of law critically, and one can *not* think law critically.

Therefore, the critique of law invariably raises the question of the right to criticize, insofar as critique is drawn into its object. There can be no critique of law that does not get to the point at which the justification, indeed the possibility, of critique itself is put into question. For law and criticism are not in an external relationship. Law is itself the practice and the procedure of criticism. Indeed, the origins of the word "critique" can be traced back to law:[4] The critic, who distinguishes between the justified and the unjustified, is (like) a judge insofar as the judge is already a, if not *the*, critic par excellence. He or she criticizes the violence of the one against another. However, if it transpires that the legal act of the decision that is directed against violence turns, itself, into the exercise of violence, then this also affects the critique that is directed against law. Critique, therefore, experiences itself within law. In law, critique has the experience of being itself drawn into the cycle of judgment and violence. Just as law consists of turning against itself, so too a critique of law must turn against itself. Thus, if the critique of law seeks to do justice to its object, it must bring itself to trial.

These are the two levels at which the considerations of "Law and Violence" operate. At the first level, I introduce a notion of law that seeks to find a coherent way of conceptualizing law's opposition to violence and its own exercise of violence. At the second level, I examine the process in which the conflict between the two characteristics unfolds. This process is likewise that of a critical reflection on law as a process in law: the process of its self-criticism. The second level, therefore, examines the possibility of a different law, namely the question of how law might reflect on its aporetic constitution and thereby change itself.

The difficulties that emerge at these two levels culminate in two main questions around which the contributions in this volume revolve. The first question is: What gives rise to and what comprises the violence exercised by law itself? Is it correct that the concept of law is defined by or through the exercise of violence? And how coherent is the justification offered by "Law and Violence" with regard to this assertion? The second question is: how can law deal with the violence that it exercises? Is the concept of self-reflection proposed in "Law and Violence" a suitable one for determining this mode of interaction and thus a different form of law? In the following, I will try to reformulate and take up some of these objections.[5]

I. The violence of law

Together, the contributions to this volume have raised four different types of objections against the thesis that law and violence are structurally intertwined, hereinafter the "violence thesis." The first objection (i) views this connection in an *instrumental* sense; it rejects the claim that law necessarily uses violence as a means for enforcing its rules. The second objection (ii) questions the *adversarial* logic of law; it claims that the violence thesis defines law by an initial act of positing and hence coercive imposition. The third objection (iii) refers to the *interventionist* relation of law to its other, to society in general, which "Law and violence" ascribes to it. And the fourth objection (iv) addresses the *political* nature of law, which the violence thesis presupposes. These four objections form a sequence, insofar as the refutation of one objection leads to the next one.

In addition, these four objections elicit the following four fundamental counter-theses:

(i) Law does not necessarily depend on violent means for its enactment. In other words, it is possible to envision a kind of law that operates exclusively with *nonviolent means* of securing compliance.
(ii) Law does not have to be, indeed cannot have been, instituted by a violent act. Rather, law is grounded in the *pre-existing normativity* of the social.
(iii) Law does not stand in a relation of imposition to the other, nonlegal social practices; instead, law is just one among a *plurality of social spheres.*
(iv) Law does not depend on the legislative acts of a given political community; law rules also *beyond* the confines and the sovereign power of *the state.*

In the following, I will try to show that objections (i) and (iv) follow from a misunderstanding of the argument I developed in "Law and

Violence", which depends neither on an instrumentalist understanding of legal violence nor on a state- or nation-based concept of the legal community. Objections (ii) and (iii), in contrast, are right about the claims in "Law and Violence." However, they fail to see the exact nature of the argument I put forward for these claims and rely on highly problematic assumptions.

(i) The first objection against the *instrumental* value of violence for law stands at the beginning and center of Daniel Loick's critical reflections. He claims that, contrary to the basic assumption in "Law and Violence," "the connection between law and coercion is not a conceptual, but a historical one" (p. 100) and that "violence is not a *constitutive* part of law, but its specific historical *attribute*" (p. 102, original emphasis). Loick presents his argument against the claim of a necessary, conceptual connection between law and violence in two steps. In the first step, he identifies it with an argument that lies at the heart of the Western legal tradition – namely that law can only effectively pursue its goal to fight coercion by exercising coercion itself. According to this assumption, "the 'hindrance of a hindrance' must take the form of coercion" (p. 98). In the second step, Loick refutes this assumption by reminding us of the fact that "[the] over 200-year-long history of bourgeois society has proven that legal coercion neither prevents breaches of law, nor does it compensate for them retrospectively, nor does it work as a reliable medium for conflict resolution at all" (p. 98). The logic of Loick's argument is thus the empirical refutation of a (seemingly) conceptual necessity: The claim that the concept of law requires violent acts of coercion as the means for its enforcement can be rejected with the insight of the "empirical ineffectivity" of those means (p. 99). For means are *defined* by their instrumental effectivity; what is simply ineffective thus cannot be a means.

This argument, though convincing, fails to acknowledge the conceptual connection between law and violence, since this connection is not grounded in assumptions about the effectivity of violence for normative claims. The necessity of violence for law is not instrumental. Rather, it follows from the specifically legal *form* of its normativity: Normativity in the form of law cannot but manifest itself in acts of violence. This is because legal normativity is defined by its relation to the non-normative: Law's normativity is constitutively external; it is "the other" of the non-normative. "Law and Violence" tries to show this by reference to the experience of law in tragedy, especially the *Oresteia*, and its philosophical reflection in Benjamin's "Critique of Violence." The argument is that the specifically legal form of normativity is such that its demands are not met in a spontaneous manner on their own. Unlike the normativity of ethical habit, in other words, normativity in the form of virtue, law's normativity presupposes that its rules are usually *not* being followed, that they do *not* meet with compliance as a matter of course. Legal normativity is thus defined, in its very form, by an external relation to the non-normative (or the "natural": *nomos* in contrast to *physis*). I will come back to this argument in the context of objection (ii). At this point, however, it is important to see that with this definition of legal normativity, the claim of its essential violence also acquires an entirely different status and meaning. The violence of law is not a matter of its means but rather of its form. It hence has an ontological quality; it defines the *being* of law: the way in which it operates. With this shift from the instrumental to the ontological, the meaning of the term *violence* also changes. In an instrumental context, violence is defined according to its Latin etymology by its effects: Violence is the potential to violate, to disrupt the integrity and functioning of a body or soul. Ontologically understood, as inscribed in the legal form of normativity, however, violence means the manifestation of the normative vis-à-vis the non-normative. In this relation, the manifestation of the normative can only be non-normative itself. The violence of law in the ontological sense is the non-normative manifestation of its normative demands.

This aligns with the definition of violence which Loick, quoting Hermann Cohen, describes as: "Coercion represents, logically as well as ethically, the end of reason" (p. 102). While this seems reasonable, Loick (like Cohen) fails to see that this is precisely the place of law: Law is the form of normativity which begins with reason *and* in which reason comes to an end. Law is normativity on the edge of reason: not without reason, but not – entirely – within reason either.

(ii) The rejection of the first objection against an instrumentalist reading of the violence of law leads to the central point of the second objection against the impositional logic of law. In "Law and Violence" I claim that law is defined by its adversarial self-understanding: Law is always directed *against* some kind of violation. Thus, the assumption of a "natural" behavior that is not by itself in accordance with law is an essential part of the very meaning of law. The legal idea of normativity presupposes and hence *creates* the conceptual possibility of extra- and non-legal behavior.

According to Alessandro Ferrara, this claim is a mere repetition of a thesis that he attributes to Carl Schmitt, and that he refers to as the thesis of the "originary" or "initial violence" of law (p. 123). He equates this thesis with the "sophistic" or "radically realist" reductionist interpretation of law as an order that is maintained by nothing but threat and fear (p. 116f.). I have already indicated in my introductory remarks that such a reductionist reading fails to grasp the essentially contradictory and paradoxical nature of law and furthermore reduces the violence of law to a mere instrument of its imposition. In this way, the reductionism of which Ferrara accuses the argument in "Law and violence" seems rather to be his own. Nonetheless, his criticism deserves attention insofar as it shows that the denial of the adversary character of law results in an intellectual prize of sorts.

This becomes clear in particular in the following statement by Ferrara:

> "the factual persistence of a violent imposition of the law [...] bears no more normative significance than the persistence of car theft can be counted as counterevidence against the merit, desirability, or legitimacy of property laws. Crime, ineliminable though it is, is to the normative foundations of property laws as background noise is to communication – a nuisance to be duly taken into account and neutralized, but of no greater significance" (p. 118f.).

This remark reflects an approach to law (which Ferrara himself puts under the label of "liberalism": p. 118) that is unwilling or incapable of taking seriously the question of its form. For Ferrara, to address law as a normative order means to talk only about the "merit, desirability, or legitimacy" of its normative claims and reasons. This narrowly normativistic perspective ignores what is specific to the legal form of normativity. This form is defined by the fact that its rules had to be posited *against* attitudes of non-, even anti-normativity and thus are conceptually defined by the possibility of their ongoing persistence. A theory of law that declares crime, and hence the adversarial attitude of law against crime, to be of "no significance" for its functioning is no theory of law at all; it is (at best) a theory of morality or ethical life. If normativism (and liberalism) operates with the assumption that, Ferrara quoting Frank Michelman, "higher lawmaking, even when it amounts to an exercise of 'constituent power,' is 'always under law,'" and that hence the normativity of law is "connaturate with social life itself (according to the principle *ubi societas, ibi jus*)" (p. 126), then this shows in effect that Ferrara's normativism is just a form of naturalism. It treats the normativity of law as the second nature of the social and thereby renders invisible the fundamental relation that defines the form of law.[6] This relationship (without which there is no law) is the irreducible difference between the normativity of law and its other, the extra-, non- and even anti-legal attitudes that define the "nature" of the social (or the social as nature).

(iii) This leads directly to the main concern of the third objection, which questions whether the claim of the inherently adversarial character of law does not contradict the fact that law is just one amongst a plurality of social spheres or language games. According to Alessandro Ferrara and Ben Morgan, the argument in "Law and Violence" maintains that law violently imposes its standards on other social spheres and thereby denies their (relative) right of autonomous normative functioning. In this way, Ferrara ascribes to "Law and Violence" the view that law is "suppressing or subjugating that – be it individual, nation, or form of life – which is other, simply not reducible to law and its forms" (p. 121),[7] to which he objects: "*Law* as such is externally inert: it is entirely indifferent to what lies outside its scope, whether a natural or a social world" (p. 117, original emphasis). Ben Morgan, for his part, writes:

> The law does not constitute and impose an idea of well-being on other areas of society. It is a special tool to be applied when other forms of negotiation and compromise don't work. Legal intervention is needed only where other ways of settling disputes over what would count as welfare have failed. More importantly, when the law is deployed, it does not trump or replace the other practices (p. 149f.).

Ferrara and Morgan thus claim that there is no interventionist, and much less an impositional, dynamics in the activity of law, and that it does not have any "normalizing effects" (Morgan, p. 139f.) *because* law stands in a relationship of "indifference" (Ferrara) or even "acknowledgment" (Morgan) to the other social spheres.

Obviously this cannot be right, for it misses the normative claim of law. While Morgan at least recognizes that law plays a normative role for, and hence in, the other social spheres, Ferrara strangely adheres to an image of social systems that are sealed off from each other and that do not perform any functions for one another. It is true that law can be defined as the institution and implementation of a new, different kind of interaction between conflicting parties; this is the procedural character of law (which I describe in "Law and Violence" with reference to the *Oresteia*; LV, pp. 10–13). Therefore, law is a specific mode of social communication that is composed of its own distinct system of normative rules. Nonetheless, this does not mean that the normative force of law is confined to the spatial and temporal parameters of its procedures. This is because the material, or the content and "stuff," of the legal procedures are deeds that pertain to other social forms of communication. By subjecting this material to the requirement of its procedures, law thus establishes its own normative framework as the necessary condition for the social acceptability of all other forms of social communication. This does, of course, not advocate (as Morgan rightly states) "replac[ing] the other practices" (p. 149); however, it does mean (as Morgan, in my view, wrongly denies) that law "trumps" the other social practices. Law does not define and impose a general, all-encompassing idea of social goodness. Nonetheless, law claims to define and, if necessary, to impose the minimum conditions for the legitimacy of any deed, in any social sphere or form of communication. Law sets itself in the position of the supreme social authority.[8]

This not only shows that the role of law amidst the plurality of social spheres and practices calls for a more nuanced explanation than is provided by Ferrara's notion of law's "indifference" towards its "outside." It also brings back the question of law's "normalizing force" (whose existence Morgan doubts). For, once again, to claim that law has normalizing effects does not mean that law produces a specific type of subjectivity which it then implements as a model on the whole of society.[9] Rather, the normalizing effect of law consists of subjugating any kind of subjectivity to the confines of legal normativity. More precisely: law subjugates the subject to the demand that it subjugate *itself* to the confines of legal normativity; law *imposes* freedom as autonomy. As María Acosta writes in her concise reformulation of the argument, the "ultimate violence" of law consists in the "self-imposed ban of the subject to itself – a subject simultaneously produced and presupposed by the law – rather than the ban imposed by the sovereign's foundational act" (p. 94, note 5).

The primordial imperative of law is: "Be a person",[10] that is, be capable of law – be capable of participating in the principle of law, insofar as you can make the distinction between law and what is contrary to law. This demand by law is unconditional. And in this sense, it is the condition for anything else in society. Law thus imposes on the subject a new form: it coerces it to internalize "the law of law." Yet to internalize law means also to externalize any form of behavior that, in following its intransigent, idiosyncratic dynamic, does not remain within the confines of law. In Alexander García Düttmann's words, "the autonomous subject of the law cannot avoid relating to the non-autonomous subject that resists the law and remains outside of it" (p. 197). In the story of Oedipus, in tragedy, this relation of the autonomous subject to itself as a non-autonomous subject is the enactment of self-violation to which law condemns its subjects.

(iv) Düttmann explains the "production of an outside" to which law can only relate violently, as the result of the act of "self-reflection" by which laws emerges: Law's fundamental move consists of constituting an identity, or unity, that claims to integrate the different conflicting perspectives unfolding from the endless cycle of violence of retribution (pp. 198–199). This accords with María Acosta's analysis of the procedure of law: it is guided by the "promise [...] of being able to universally represent all the parties" (p. 86). Legal justice is the "promise of representation" (p. 88): the promise of creating a unity that consists of nothing but the equal representation and consideration of everybody (which is thereby transformed from an "individual" into a legal subject or "person"). The legal promise of offering equal representation thus unifies the conflicting parties as they become members of the *same* normative order. In "Law and Violence" I refer to this as the "political" nature of law.

This claim has been met with two objections – both arguing that the claim neglects the specific difference of the legal from the political, yet each working with opposite understandings of the political. According to the first objection, raised by Alessandro Ferrara, "Politics is contentious in a way that adjudication – the procedure of determining what the law prescribes in a given case – is not" (p. 114), since legal adjudication is grounded in principles and hence allows for a final decision by a highest authority. María Acosta's detailed reflections on the – highly problematic, even paradoxical – role of law in the process of political transitions show what is wrong with this argument: it fails to see in what way legal adjudication is itself filled with strife. This strife is due not only, and not even primarily, to the fact that in law there is always the possibility of a conflict of interpretations (as Ferrara underlines: p. 114). Rather, the political, contentious nature of law lies in the fact that the legal promise of representation "coincides in the end with its betrayal" (as Acosta puts it: p. 90). For legal representation is not neutral; it is active, transformative: it turns individuals into subjects or persons, the non-legal into something legal. The political nature of law consists in the – coercive – reenactment of this transformation which all legal procedures presuppose. As Acosta's reflections show, to politicize law thus does not mean to reduce it to "negotiated consensus" (as Ferrara defines politics: p. 114), but to bring to light the injustice of the "just" mission of creating unity through equal representation.

This is where the second objection against the definition of law having a "political" nature in "Law and Violence" becomes relevant. According to this objection, the problem with this political definition of law lies not (as Ferrara thinks) in overestimating the contentious character of law but rather, on the contrary, in overestimating its unitarian, or even communitarian drive. For Andreas Fischer-Lescano and Daniel Loick, the definition of law as a mechanism for creating political unity is merely the uncritical expression of a historically specific, and now outdated, practice that bound law and the state together. Fischer-Lescano calls it "a theory that is plausible in a world defined by the Westphalian order. But this form of life has grown gray" (p. 173). Daniel Loick agrees and confronts it with the form of Jewish law in the diaspora that functions precisely "without being represented in a state form" (p. 102). Furthermore, for both Fischer-Lescano and Loick, the different regimes of international law are paradigms that show the conceptual independence of legal procedure and political community: they are "forms of lawmaking beyond the political community conceived in unitary terms" (Fischer-Lescano, p. 176) and do not depend for their normative binding force on the representation of the community in the form of a state (pp. 174–176).

Convincing as these examples are, they also reveal the blind spot in objecting the political nature of law. This becomes clear when Fischer-Lescano equates my conception of law as political by "binding legal equality to an entity that is extrinsic to the law: the polity" (p. 173). For Fischer-Lescano, as for Loick, the unity towards which law is directed can only be external to law: a pre-given, in other words, a pre-legally constituted unity or community (e.g., a city, nation, empire). With this assumption they miss the logic of unification that is intrinsic and hence specific to law – including to its non-state forms that they describe. This unity consists in nothing but the equality that the very idea of legal procedure presupposes or implements in its promise "to universally represent all the parties" (Acosta, p. 86). There can be no equal consideration of different perspectives, positions or individuals without granting them the same status. This sameness or identity is abstract; it is engendered by law. In this way, law *creates* a community of equals[11] – it does not depend on it as something pre-given. With the institutionalization of law begins a new form of politics: wherever there is law, in other words, the attempt of "settling disputes" (Morgan) by procedures of equal consideration, already a unity or community of equals has been established.

It is easy to understand why Fischer-Lescano and Loick are looking for forms of law that are exempt from this unifying, communitarian logic, since this logic is also responsible for the exclusionary character of law. For, as Acosta has shown, the community of equals that law establishes is always, at each moment and in each instance, a specific one that necessarily excludes certain forms of life and hence necessarily betrays its own promise of equal representation. But, unlike what Fischer-Lescano and Loick seem to suggest, this predicament cannot simply be circumvented by trying to conceive of a form of law that has surrendered its political, unitarian, or communitarian characteristics while managing to retain its egalitarian promise. One invariably comes with the other; without the creation of a community of equals, which entails the violence of law, there can be no legal justice. This is the paradox, or the irony, or the tragedy, of law.

The question for the second round of discussion, then, is whether there might be an *in*direct way out of this predicament, and what this way might look like.

II. The self-reflection of law

Walter Benjamin calls the transformation of law in the face of the experience of its violence its *Entsetzung*. In most English translations of

Benjamin's works, this term is rendered as "suspension," taking up the expression used by Carl Schmitt to describe the sovereign act of declaring a state of exception. In "Law and Violence", however, *Entsetzung* is translated as "relief" (p. 5f.), since, following Agamben, I consider Benjamin's *Entsetzung* to be the opposite of Schmitt's notion of "suspension." "Suspension" in Schmitt aims at liberating the state and its powers from law; Benjamin's *Entsetzung,* by contrast, aims at the liberation *of* law *from* its own violent nature and hence its involvement with "state power." In the second part of "Law and violence", I then ask how this liberation is even conceivable if, as argued in the first part, the violence of law follows from its very essence, from its "political" origin or nature. This question also refers to the meaning of "critique" in thinking about law (see above, p. 210f). For if critique is the act of normative distinction and decision between the one and the other – the right and the wrong – then it seems that *Entsetzung*, the relief of law, can no longer serve as a critical strategy.

Schelling, who is one of the possible sources for Benjamin's use of the term, takes *Entsetzung* as the German translation of *ekstasis,* which he understands to be "the removal [of something] from a [or its] place" (my translation). Furthermore, for Schelling *ekstasis* can at times take on a more positive and at other times a more negative meaning. Thus, *ekstasis* is a "*vox anceps*," an ambiguous term:

> It just depends on whether something is removed from a place that is commensurate to or befitting [*gebührend*] it or from a place that is not befitting it. In the latter case, the *ekstasis* is beneficial and leads to reflection [*Besinnung*], while in the former case, it leads to absurdity or senselessness"[12] (my translation).

The question, then, is whether such a critical, normative distinction is possible in the case of law: can there be a good, beneficial *ekstasis* or *Entsetzung* of law that could free it from the place it currently occupies – the place of power – which is not befitting it? The criterion for this distinction is the essence of law that determines its right place; the insight into the paradoxical entwinement of law and violence, however, undermines the very possibility of identifying the essence of law and thus make such a critical distinction impossible. *Entsetzung*, the relief of law, cannot mean the removal of law from its wrong, improper place because law is always, and will always remain, at the wrong place. Thus the relief of law from power cannot consist of separating law's justice from law's violence; rather, it must aim to enact their mutual entanglement in a different way. In "Law and Violence," I describe this different form of enactment as law's "self-reflection."

This approach in "Law and Violence" has elicited three critical objections which I will discuss in the following. These objections state that the arguments in "Law and Violence"

(i) are blind towards *actual legal practice*;
(ii) ignore the actual potential for *radical transformation*;
(iii) are bound to an *idealist conception* of identity or selfhood.

According to objection (i), the violence thesis in "Law and Violence" operates with a static conception of law that abstracts from the active process of its application by a judge. "Law and Violence" thus also fails to see how law in this process, hence in its ordinary practice, already deals with its own abstractness and formalism. According to objection (ii), the insistence on the paradox of law leads to a postmodern, anti-utopian attitude of closing off any perspective of transcending the actual conditions of power and domination. Finally, objection (iii) questions the suitability of the central operational term that I propose in "Law and Violence" for conceptualizing the transformative process of the relief (or *Entsetzung*) of law, namely self-reflection. The argument of this objection is that the operation of self-reflection seems to follow an identitarian logic – it is about preserving the identity of law by folding it back onto itself – and hence fosters a conservative attitude which makes the radical transformation impossible that is needed to give an answer to the experience of law's violence. In the following, I will briefly address these three objections.

(i) Alessandro Ferrara's solution to any violent, coercive effect that law might have is to look at the actual practice of legal adjudication

– indeed, a well-known or rather well-liked solution. Ferrara describes the account of legal practice developed by the "liberal camp" as follows: "legal *rules* are applied under the guidance of legal *principles* that admit of no fixed a priori ranking but are rather to be balanced with each other in a context-sensitive way" (p. 130, original emphasis). Thus, the possible negative effects of law are to be countered with "context sensitivity" in its application. As Ferrara makes clear, this sensitivity has to meet two requirements at once: one, it cannot be governed by the same (kind of) rules that produce the distortive effects in the first place; and two, it must nevertheless be ruled by the normativity of law in the form of its "principles." The second requirement gives reason to suspect that in the end nothing is gained by the turn to context-sensitive adjudication. For in order to be legally effective, the principles of law likewise have to have the same form of normativity that – following the argument above (p. 213f) – is the source of the violence of law. It is hence not clear why the reference to principles beyond or above legal rules should make any difference in the adversarial, potentially violent logic of law. Thus, for the functioning of legal practice to count as the counter-instance to the violence of law in law, it would also have to go beyond the legal form of normativity as such.

Ben Morgan goes in his analysis a decisive step beyond the confines of liberal thinking of the actual practice of law, namely by drawing on the experience of literature. In an intriguing reading of Ian McEwan's novel *The Children Act*, whose main character is the judge Fiona Maye, Morgan characterizes the challenge that the judge is facing in her attempt at doing justice to a case as follows: "He [i.e., McEwan as the author] explores what it might mean for his character to face and take responsibility for the law's encounter with habits that are alien to it. The judge seeks out, and then must bear the consequences of, a direct experience of the limits of the law" (p. 143). The challenge, for the judge and for the novel alike, is to put "the operations of legal reasoning in a wider context" (p. 144). And the way in which law (and perhaps the novel as well) faces this challenge is to open itself up to the "dynamism of human interaction" (p. 152), which law encounters as its own other in the social practices that it tries to regulate. In its practice, law thus becomes its own other (or like its own other). Law thereby achieves a new, different normative quality: "each legal act will in some way manage (by containing, or fostering and acknowledging it) the momentum of humanity that underlies the law as it underlies social practices" (p. 152). Thus, similar to Ferrara's liberal image, in Morgan's literary experience too, law contains within it a normative claim or force that cannot be positively stated in the form of rules. However, in defiance of the liberal attempt to define this rule-transgressing normative force in terms of "principles," Morgan thinks of it as radically indeterminate; he refers to it as the (Kantian) idea of "humanity."[13] The "momentum of humanity" is thus enacted in the legal practice, but it no longer takes on the form of legal normativity; the legal practice goes beyond the legal form. Conversely, one could also say that the legal form *is* the act of going beyond itself, or of going beyond its own positive, determinate form as a set of "rules."

In Morgan's view, law is, or may become, the practice of a nonviolent human interaction that is sensitive to the distortive effects it might have on other social practices. Daniel Loick in principle agrees with this view, although he is much more critical about the present state of legal practice. Drawing on the experience of Jewish law, Loick maintains that a legal practice imaginable that would be "neither the abolition, nor the (however 'self-reflective') perpetuation of the law, but the suspension of its violent application" (p. 104). Nonetheless, both of these views raise the simple question of how these practices of "human interaction" can still be called practices *of law* at all. In other words, what is "legal" about a context-sensitive act of communication that looks to novel-writing (Morgan) or the studying of texts in the confines of rabbinic debate or the ivory tower of academia (Loick) as models? Can these forms of communication still provide an effective answer to social violence? I believe not. Morgan's and Loick's accounts drive the legal out of legal practice; their views of legal *practice* lose sight of *legal* practice. Thus, the attempt to solve the problem of the violence of law by focusing on the practice of law is condemned to failure. It amounts to dissolving law into a broad and diffuse form of sensitive human interaction. Indeed, at the very moment when the types of writing and reading, that Morgan and Loick describe, actually take on a legal form, especially when expressing a judgment – which is, by definition, an authoritative, binding judgment from a general and hence necessarily abstract perspective –, all the problems of the coercive, violent nature of the law reappear in their original, unaltered form.

(ii) It is for this reason that, according to Andreas Fischer-Lescano, it is not enough to focus only on the humanity of the legal practice when seeking to reduce law's potentiality for violence. Instead, the latter requires a truly "new form" of law, which Fischer-Lescano, using a term coined by Koskenniemi, outlines as follows: "The goal is to establish a non-violent functioning of law. Law would then no longer make any violent decisions, and instead become a 'gentle civilizer'" (my translation).[14] This is how Fischer-Lescano proposes to radicalize the program laid out in "Law and Violence" which states that the utopia of law "is not about transcending the law but about depotentiating it: by seeing the law and its application become *one possibility*" (p. 182, emphasis added), and hence not about leaving the violence of law behind but stripping it of its fateful necessity. Fischer-Lescano's answer to this claim is the following "radicalization": "The utopian justice to come can be conceived only in transcending the law" (p. 170).

Nonetheless, Fischer-Lescano does not envision that transcendence taking place by means of a simple abolition of law. Rather, he entertains the notion of a *self*-transcendence by way of which *another* law is created, in other words, the creation of another *law*. According to him, this can be accomplished if the extra-legal social processes over which the law is to decide are no longer understood merely as the substance onto which law applies its forms and norms from the outside, but as the "forces" that are internally effective in the process in which legal decisions are made. In this way, Fischer-Lescano goes a decisive step beyond Morgan, who describes legal practice as a form of human interaction that is sensitive to the consequences of the legal rules for non-legal, social practice; for according to this view, the law remains in a position that is external to social practice. With Fischer-Lescano, on the other hand, the extra-legal, the social, becomes effective within law. The transcendence of law that Fischer-Lescano proposes as the more radical alternative to the strategy of self-reflection in "Law and Violence" therefore means nothing other than "the social appropriation of the institutions" of the law (Fischer-Lescano, p. 184); "[it] implies a comprehensive mandate for society to take possession of the law" and thereby "disrupt[s] the constitutive nexus between lawmaking and law-preserving legal violence" (p. 181). The violence of law is overcome by turning the extra-legal, the social, into a force within law. And in that law, through the unfolding of the social force in law, dissolves its violence over the social, it produces no less than a just society. "This is not messianic enthusiasm but a realistic utopia of social emancipation. Society is not redeemed, it frees itself by transcending the violent order" (my translation).[15]

Yet at this precise point it becomes all too clear, yet again, why the violence of law eschews every disambiguation and thereby every critical decision between good and bad or right and wrong. For it turns out that law's violence, which law is supposed to, according to its own definition, fight with all means, is at the same time the condition for the possibility that law can develop an emancipatory, liberating force. Fischer-Lescano contends that law could contribute to the creation of a just society under the condition that it leaves its violence behind, namely by no longer controlling, normalizing and suppressing extra-legal social practices and by instead letting them act as an inner-legal force. The problem with this, however, is that an opening up of law to the social forces renders law impotent against those powers that it is targeting with its normative claim. The normative claim of law is the establishment of equality, in other words, the same normative status for each person. This normative claim leads to the violence of law. But it can also be directed in an emancipatory manner against the existing forms of societal domination. Both the emancipatory potential and the potential for violence are intertwined in law in such a way that any law aspiring to "transcend" its own violence (Fischer-Lescano) would thereby lose its power to engender societal change. Thus, when one asks, together with Fischer-Lescano, the question of how law might contribute to create a just society, one must relinquish the desire to transcend law's violence. For a law that "radicalized" its self-reflection up to a utopia of nonviolence can no longer contribute to the political struggle against social domination. Law can only have the power to intervene in the existing social conditions if it retains its power. Only a law that can exercise power can be an emancipatory law – a law that maintains the critical distance, the negativity of the normative, against the existing status quo. A law that becomes nonviolent would, in that process, become deprived of its critical force. In that case it would indeed have become social – merely a part and an instrument of existing society.

For this reason, I do not share Fischer-Lescano's "radical" conviction that the violence of law could be "transcended" rather than just "depotentiated." Through the figure of depotentiation, I tried to grasp in "Law and Violence" what Benjamin might have understood as the *Entsetzung*, or relief, of law. This operation of relief is directed against the "fateful," "mythical" violence of law. The violence is fateful because law *is forced to* continue exercising it again and again, given that the violence follows from the legal form of normativity, which stands in contrast to what happens on its own, or in nature or in society. Against this violence law must violently enforce its normativity. The violence which law exercises is thus defined by the fact that law itself is forced to assert or enforce itself. The relief of law is its liberation from this mandate, or compulsion, to enforce. This is what is meant by the "depotentiation" of law, namely, the breaking of this compulsion, in that the enforcement of law is not suspended but becomes merely *one* possibility that could be taken up *or not*. The depotentiation of law therefore means to politicize its violent enforcement, and to turn a compulsory necessity into a strategic question. This liberates the violence of law from its fate – but it does not strip law of its violence. Rather, it turns the violence of law from a fate into a weapon, or from a destiny that governs us to a means that we can employ consciously and in a controlled way.

(iii) In discussing Benjamin's program of a "relief" (*Entsetzung*) of law, we have observed a paradox on several occasions. The paradox consists of the fact that thinking a form of law that would be freed from the necessity of its violent enactment requires going beyond the legal form altogether. This is the paradox of *Entsetzung*, which mirrors and repeats the paradox of the violence of law discussed in the first part of this reply. The paradox of *Entsetzung* states that a radically transformed law can neither continue to be law nor become something other than law. In other words, the relief or transformation of law has no choice but to go beyond law, whereby it stops being a form of law. In his critical contribution, Alexander García Düttmann goes the farthest in examining this paradox. According to Düttmann, the fact that, in thinking through the liberation of law from its own violence, law itself is ultimately left behind, is not a mistake one could hope to avoid. For taking the violence of law seriously, that is, taking the Nietzschean demand which all experience of violence raises seriously, namely the demand to *go* – "Away, you pain!" (see above, p. 207) – must mean to go *beyond* law.

This is why Düttmann doubts that the concept of self-reflection is able to grasp the complexity that the concept of the relief of law is facing. Self-reflection is an, if not *the*, act of recognition: "Self-reflection amounts to the attainment of an awareness that deepens the understanding of whatever it is that undergoes the process" (p. 193). In self-reflection, a certain instance (a person, institution, system, etc.) acknowledges that it is defined by, or founded on, its relation to its other; and through this act of acknowledgement, that instance becomes an integral part of that other. In this sense, as Düttmann observes, the mere step beyond the order of retribution by which law was instituted is an act of self-reflection (p. 196f). It is the act through which each side in a conflict becomes aware of the fact that they are just one side in the conflict, no more no less. The act of self-reflection thus leads to a broader, more inclusive unity, or totality, which interiorizes the other that threatened, or appeared to threaten, to disrupt it. But if it is indeed the case that law is *constituted* of an act of self-reflection, then it cannot be relieved from its fateful violence except by a structurally identical second act of self-reflection. As Düttmann convincingly argues, the act of liberating law requires more than a mere repetition of self-reflection: It needs "a transformation of self-reflection [itself] that must protect it against turning into either a tautological activity (retribution) or an activity with a result (judging). It must distance self-reflection from itself as an activity" (p. 199). Only by transforming itself can self-reflection transform law. The challenge that Düttmann's criticism poses is to reach a precise understanding of such a transformation of self-reflection.

According to Düttmann, the problem of the concept of self-reflection is that it can only internalize law's other by simultaneously seeking to maintain "the difficult distinction between an inside and an outside, [...] no matter how, exactly, it is drawn" (p. 194). This is shown in an exemplary way in Fischer-Lescano's idea of turning the social exterior of law into a legal "force" that is operative in law, or in the words of Robert Cover, into a "jurisgenerative" force. For this to happen, the socially given drives, interests, and desires have precisely to be stripped of their otherness; they have to become, or be *made*, legally productive. These legalizing effects on the non-legal define the very functioning of law. They comprise, as María Acosta has shown (p. 89), the basic mechanism of law that is responsible for its violence and which even the act of the self-reflection of law cannot escape. Since the act of self-reflection interiorizes the other of law into law, it partakes in the same logic of legalizing the non-legal. Hence Düttmann's pivotal question:

> In the case of the law proving unable to contain otherness, would it still make sense to speak of self-reflection, would the involvement with the law's meaning not stumble over an obstacle it could not remove, precisely because this obstacle, this lack of meaning, would be constitutive of the meaning of the law, rendering it both questionable and worthy of questioning?" (p. 195).

Precisely the act of self-reflection in which law acknowledges its own other (and in which law hence also acknowledges being an other itself) must thus necessarily lead to "an irrepressible unwillingness to engage in self-reflection" (p. 195). Moreover, if "the 'relation' in which law stands, the relation to an outside, must also be a non-relation, a relation interrupted" – for only the non-relation is truly a relation to an outside, an other – then we have to break up the circle of self-reflection, then the law needs a "caesura of self-reflection" (p. 201).

I agree with this argument, and also accept Düttmann's criticism that "Law and Violence" is too hesitant in addressing this problem. I do not, however, accept the conclusion that Düttmann draws from his problematization of self-reflection. He formulates this conclusion as follows: "When reflecting upon law and violence, one must either adhere to a normative order in which, and on which, the logic of sovereignty has a determining impact, or else pursue strategies of rupture that the law cannot, or must be unwilling to, accommodate" (p. 203). But his proposed alternative is not an alternative; no choice or decision is possible between *either* the adherence to the normative order *or* the strategy of its rupture. For both sides are intertwined: The rupture of the legal order, if it is to be a liberating and not just a "dystopian" rupture (p. 203), is a violence that is directed against violence. The rupture thus, knowingly or unknowingly, operates in the name of the law against which it is directed. For the "impulse" (Adorno) or "force" (Derrida) at the ground of law is justice: the resistance to violence. For this same reason, the normative order of law always already entails the strategies of rupture which it, at the same time, according to Düttmann's formulation, cannot accommodate. This is also why, even in the face of all the problems that Düttmann rightly indicates, it remains necessary to think of the "relief" of law in terms of its self-reflection. The rupture of law comes from law itself. It is the very concept of law, its internally divided essence, which makes its rupture possible.

Notes

1 Friedrich Nietzsche, *Thus Spoke Zarathustra*, trans. Adrian Del Caro (Cambridge: Cambridge University Press, 2006), 262.

2 Some of the contributors to this volume have devoted important essays to this tradition. See María del Rosario Acosta López, "Another Kind of

Community: Hegel on Law, Love and Life in the Frankfurt Fragments," in Thomas Hanke and Thomas M. Schmidt (eds), *Der Frankfurter Hegel in seinem Kontext* (Frankfurt am Main: Vittorio Klostermann, 2015), 191–208; Alexander García Düttmann, *Derrida und ich* (Bielefeld: Transcript, 2008); Andreas Fischer-Lescano, "Radikale Rechtskritik," in *Kritische Justiz*, 2 (2014), 171–83; Daniel Loick, "Expression of Contempt: Hegel's Critique of Legal Freedom," in *Law & Critique*, 2 (2015), 189–206.

3 On Hegel and Derrida, see Christoph Menke, *Tragödie im Sittlichen: Gerechtigkeit und Freiheit nach Hegel* (Frankfurt am Main: Suhrkamp, 1996); *Reflections of Equality* (Stanford: Stanford University Press, 2006).

4 "Arguably the first terminological usage of the sub-block around krin- (krisis, kritikes, kritikos) can be found in the legal sphere" (K. Röttgers, "Kritik," in *Geschichtliche Grundbegriffe*, eds O. Brunner, W. Conze, R. Koselleck (Stuttgart: Klett-Cotta, 1982), 651; my translation).

5 This also means that I will not address all the objections that have been raised. In particular, I will disregard those criticisms which, in my view, express a misunderstanding of my project as such. An example of these is the following comment by Alessandro Ferrara: "While an assessment of Schmitt's critique of liberalism or Derrida's view of the 'force of law' exceeds the scope of my present argument, it must be noted that the crucial assumption concerning the inextricable nexus of lawmaking and naked power is reflected in Benjamin, and in Menke's adoption of Benjamin's analysis, without any acknowledgment, let alone refutation, of the objections found within the tradition of normative political philosophy" (p. 120).

6 Ben Morgan makes a similar argument when he accuses me of ignoring "the degree to which the group involved in the act of founding something will necessarily already be doing things together: they will already share something" (p. 157). See also his reference to "shared practices" against Stanley Fish's (and my) alleged reduction of judgment to force (p. 158f.).

7 In Ferrara's view, "the other" which the law (in his reading of 'Law and violence') subjugates does not only include other social spheres but other legal orders (see p.000). I did not discuss (or even mention) the second case in 'Law and violence', although I do think that it is structurally entirely different from the first one.

8 Which is not the same as ethical or spiritual authority; I agree with Ben Morgan on this point.

9 Morgan interprets me as having concluded that there is only one form of subjectivity, namely legal subjectivity, on the grounds that the law has supposedly violently suppressed all other kinds of subjectivities, namely political and aesthetic (p. 139). Yet I do not hold this view.

10 G. W. F. Hegel, *Outlines of the Philosophy of Right*, trans. T. M. Knox, revised, edited and introduced by Stephen Houlgate (Oxford: Oxford University Press, 2008), 55.

11 Following Hannah Arendt, this is the meaning of equality as "isonomy": "Isonomy guaranteed *ἰσότης*, equality, but not because all men were born or created equal, but, on the contrary, because men were by nature (*φύσει*) not equal, and needed an artificial institution, the *polis*, which by virtue of its *νόμος* would make them equal. Equality existed only in this specifically political realm, where men met one another as citizens and not as private persons" (Hannah Arendt, *On Revolution* (London: Penguin, 1990), 30f.).

12 F. W. J. Schelling, "Über die Natur der Philosophie als Wissenschaft" [On the Nature of Philosophy as Science], in *Sämmtliche Werke* (Stuttgart/Augsburg: Cotta, 1861), vol. I.9, 230.

13 For Kant, the basis of the law is the "right [Recht] of humanity in our own person"; Emmanuel Kant, *The Metaphysics of Morals*, in *Practical Philosophy*, trans. M. J. Gregor (Cambridge: Cambridge University Press, 1996), 392.

14 A. Fischer-Lescano, *Rechtskraft* (Berlin: August Verlag 2013), 65. This book is a more detailed presentation of some of the thoughts in Fischer-Lescano's contribution to this volume. For further discussion see Christoph Menke, "Die Möglichkeit eines anderen Rechts: Zur Auseinandersetzung mit Andreas Fischer-Lescano," in *Deutsche Zeitschrift für Philosophie*, 62 (2014), 136–43.

15 Fischer-Lescano, *Rechtskraft*, 66.

Index